KU-591-621

J. ANTHONY GAUGHAN

Alfred O'Rahilly

III: CONTROVERSIALIST

Part 1: Social Reformer

KINGDOM BOOKS

Printed in the Republic of Ireland
at the Leinster Leader, Naas, County Kildare,
for
KINGDOM BOOKS
79 The Rise, Mount Merrion, County Dublin.

First published 1992

BRITISH LIBRARY CATALOGUING IN PUBLICATION DATA

Gaughan, J. Anthony (John Anthony)
    Alfred O'Rahilly
        III: Controversialist
        Part 1
        I. Title
        378.41956

    ISBN 0 – 9506015 – 8 – 6

Copyright under the Berne Convention, all rights reserved. Apart from fair dealing
for study or review, no part of this publication may be reproduced, stored in a
retrieval system or transmitted, in any form or by any means, electronic,
mechanical, photocopying, recording, or otherwise, without the prior permission
of Kingdom Books.

© J. Anthony Gaughan 1992

ALFRED O'RAHILLY
III: CONTROVERSIALIST
Part 1: Social Reformer

1. Alfred O'Rahilly, chairman of the committee on article 408, International Labour Conference, Geneva, 1932

ACKNOWLEDGEMENTS

In connection with the preparation of this book I wish to thank the library staffs of the Central Catholic Library, Dublin Public Library, the library of the Jesuit House of Studies, Milltown Park, the National Library of Ireland, the Royal Irish Academy, University College, Cork, University College and Trinity College, Dublin, for their courtesy and help; the archivists, librarians and custodians of the various institutions and the private individuals mentioned on pp. 281-4 for allowing me to consult papers and records in their charge; Declan Byrne, James B. McKevitt and M. W. Ó Murchú for the use of their unpublished theses; and all who gave me information, especially those whose names appear on p. 286.

I am indebted to Professor John Coolahan, Fr Edmond Kent, S.J., Fr Michael F. McCarthy, C.S.Sp., Professor Donal McCartney, Walter McGrath, Cornelius Murphy, Fr Michael O'Carroll, C.S.Sp., Professor Kathleen O'Flaherty and Andrew Ryan for much helpful criticism.

I am grateful to Tadhg Ó Cearbhaill, who has represented the country at International Labour Conferences on a number of occasions, for valuable background information on proceedings at Geneva.

As with regard to Volumes I and II, I am particularly indebted to Pádraig Ó Snodaigh, Dr C. J. Woods and especially Maurice O'Connell for their continuing, exceptional and practical interest in the progress of this work.

I am grateful to Helen Murray for typing the manuscript and to the late Liam Miller for the design and layout of the book.

I feel honoured in having this book launched by Bishop James Kavanagh, former professor of social science at University College, Dublin, and in having the foreword to it written by Anthony Coughlan, senior lecturer in social administration and policy, Trinity College, Dublin.

Finally, I wish to acknowledge with gratitude a grant of £1,500 from the Irish Permanent Building Society towards the publication of this work.

J. ANTHONY GAUGHAN
56 Newtownpark Avenue
Blackrock
County Dublin
1 March 1992

To the social activists featured here,
persons of extraordinary generosity and vision

CONTENTS

LIST OF ILLUSTRATIONS

FOREWORD

The first two volumes of Fr J. Anthony Gaughan's monumental biography of Alfred O'Rahilly gave readers numerous insights into the educational and political life of early twentieth-century Ireland. Part 1 of this volume is a significant contribution to the labour and social history of the period. The life of O'Rahilly makes one see Ireland through the eyes of Cork, by contrast to the many Dublin-centred accounts – in itself an education of the historical sensibility!

I recall enrolling as a student at University College, Cork, in October 1953, the beginning of Alfie's last year there. We lined up in the corridor outside his office to be introduced to the president. He shook hands and said 'Be of good character, boy', putting the stress on the second syllable in Kerry fashion. Presumably it was his admonition to every student. It was the only time I met him, but he made an impression one did not forget. Here was a man who obviously had 'char-*act*-er'.

This volume shows O'Rahilly the champion of the underdog, the radical social populist and disturber of class complacency in high places. It describes his activity as an adult educationist, an indefatigable polemicist on social issues, a champion of rural development and a leading figure of the Catholic Social Movement whose deep influence on modern Ireland has been insufficiently attended to by historians to date and in relation to which this volume will be an indispensable source.

Students of labour history will be especially in Fr Gaughan's debt for his account of O'Rahilly's work at the International Labour Conferences in 1924, 1925 and 1932 and as arbitrator in Cork trade and industrial disputes over several decades. O'Rahilly was the foremost champion of St Joseph the Worker as model for the labour movement, as against secular figures such as Connolly, Larkin, Laski or Marx. Fr Gaughan's account of his anti-communist crusade in the 1940s is an important chapter of a larger story that still remains to be written. William O'Brien was happy to have Alfie on his side at the culmination of that barren feud with Larkin which split the Labour Party and Irish Trade Union Congress. It was partly O'Rahilly's exaggerated fear of the Left that led him to inaugurate social science and adult extension courses in Cork and throughout Munster and influence the founding of Dublin's Catholic Workers' College, indirectly stimulating the trade-union-sponsored People's College in response. His initiatives make him a significant pioneer of Irish adult education. This latest volume of the biography of this extraordinary man casts a flood of light on the social character of the first thirty years of the Irish State's existence.

ANTHONY COUGHLAN
Department of Social Studies,
Trinity College, Dublin (February 1992)

11

INTRODUCTION

Alfred O'Rahilly I: Academic dealt with Alfred O'Rahilly's remarkable career as an academic and scholar. *Alfred O'Rahilly II: Public Figure* treated of Alfred as a public figure and as a leader and moulder of public opinion from 1915 to 1954.

Throughout his life Alfred had an extraordinary enthusiasm for controversy. In this first part of volume III it is proposed to trace his career as a controversialist in his role as a social reformer. This arose from his commitment to the social teaching of *Rerum Novarum* and *Quadragesimo Anno* and his lifelong efforts not only to communicate it but to have it implemented.

ORIGINS OF SOCIAL AWARENESS AND EARLY YEARS AT UNIVERSITY COLLEGE, CORK

Throughout his life Alfred crusaded for social justice. By temperament he was committed to the cause of the poor, the underprivileged and the underdog. He was aware of the kindness of his O'Curry and O'Rahilly relatives and the local clergy in helping his mother to raise her large family. During his Christian formation and especially at the Jesuit novitiate he was left in no doubt of the importance of loving his neighbour in a practical way. However, it was probably during his time from 1908 to 1911 at St Mary's College, Stonyhurst, that he became convinced that the pursuit of social justice was at that time the top priority for the Catholic Church in general and the individual Catholic in particular.

St Mary's College, Stonyhurst

In the early decades of the century St Mary's College had become a centre of a newly awakened awareness of the importance of social action among the Jesuits of the English province. This was largely due to Charles Dominic Plater (1880-1922) who studied philosophy at St Mary's from 1904 to 1907 and returned after ordination to teach psychology from 1912 to 1915. It is clear from C. C. Martindale's fine biography,[1] that he was one of the most remarkable members of the English province of the Society at that time. He cast a long shadow over St Mary's College during Alfred's sojourn there. The nature and extent of his influence on his contemporaries can be gathered from the recollection of Denis Meadows who studied philosophy at St Mary's from 1911 to 1914:

1. C. C. Martindale, *Charles Dominic Plater, S.J.* (London 1922). Plater was consumed with a passion for taking Christianity out of the church into the market-place. In particular he urged a more effective presentation of the gospel to the working-class. Before he was ordained he was associated with the establishment of the Catholic Social Guild and the Catholic Medical Guild. Before and after ordination he was a well-known figure at Catholic Truth Society conferences and congresses. And he pioneered enclosed retreats for working people in Britain (ibid.).

When he joined our community he had become very keen on what, for lack of a better term, I must call social action. Perhaps applied Christianity would be more descriptive. He was not the sort of man who loves blue-books, and statistical surveys, for their own sake. He had no affinity with the bloodless statisticians who see a hungry man, or a prostitute, or a sick child, as just another case. To him they were human beings, in need of intelligent understanding, but also of food and medicine, physical or spiritual. What Fr Plater did to awaken our minds and emotions about the social implications of Christianity went far beyond whatever he gave us as a teacher of psychology.

Of course, we all knew we were our brother's keeper, and that the bitterest condemnation of *laissez-faire* at the Day of Judgment would be, 'Inasmuch as ye did it not to these . . .' Still, I imagine that to most of us it was little more than a pious formula. Charles Plater made it a live truth, something to prick our consciences.

The compilers of our Latin textbooks had not stopped with the Reformation. They gave us neat little summaries of *Socialismus* and *Communismus*, with neat refutations of them compressed into syllogisms. The trouble was that no one had ever tried to gild these scholastic pills so that the workingman would swallow them. If he were a Catholic, he might come across Pope Leo XIII's teachings on the just claims of labour, or he might have heard that in 1889 a Roman cardinal, Archbishop Manning, had succeeded in settling a major strike – to the satisfaction of the strikers – when everyone else had failed. The rank and file of the clergy, however, and devout Catholics generally, seemed hardly aware of two sides to these questions. If the underdog, who was truly an underdog in those days, let out a growl or two when you trod on his tail or kicked him, why, he was a damned Radical. If he happened to be a Catholic, he was at least suspect – what we call a fellow traveller nowadays.

Communism to us, as, I suppose, to other young Catholics of the time, was a dead heresy, buried in Highgate cemetery in North London with the body of the heresiarch, a German called Marx, who had spent most of his life in the reading room of the British Museum (and who, incidentally,

14

2. Fr Charles Dominic Plater, S.J. (1880-1922)

disliked the working-class people of the country that had given him political asylum).

Fr Plater did not talk much about capital and labour, or socialism, or the fair wage. He invited those of us who were interested in writing, or editing, or just proof reading and indexing, to be his assistants. He was at work on a yearly handbook of social action for Catholics. It was a new venture, in which he was collaborating with a secular priest, Monsignor Parkinson, who saw, as he did, that too many of us were living in an ivory tower.[2]

Society of St Vincent de Paul

Soon after taking up his appointment at U.C.C., Alfred began a lifelong commitment to the cause of the poor and the under-privileged. He joined the conference of the Society of St Vincent de Paul which was attached to St Mary's parish (the North parish), near the centre of the city. Such was his dedication that after a few months he was appointed vice-president. Each week he and a colleague visited about a score of the most destitute families resident in Bailey's Lane and Knapp's Square in the Shandon district. They helped the families with food vouchers and supplies of clothing. In addition part of their brief would have been to listen to members of those families, generally the mother, as they detailed their misfortunes and to give them friendly support and helpful advice.[3] In this way Alfred acquired a first-hand knowledge of the appalling conditions in which a substantial minority of the citizens of Cork were living. The experience deepened his conviction that the highly commendable work of bodies such as the Society of St Vincent de Paul merely dealt with the results not the causes of the problem, for which a radical solution was required urgently.

Already Alfred had given indications of his view of the social question over the pseudonym B.K.S.[4] He dismissed any attempt to find support in the New Testament for capitalism, on the one hand, or collectivism or communism, on the other. He argued that Christianity aimed not merely at the perfection of

2. D. Meadows, *Obedient men* (London 1955) 176-8.
3. O'Rahilly Papers: Scrapbook I, press cuttings; interview with Professor Kathleen O'Flaherty.
4. B.K.S., 'The social views of Christ', *Studies*, March 1914, 616-43.

individuals, but also at the improvement of institutions and society. He quoted the Lord's Prayer to refute Christians who considered that their religion was above questions of material well-being, of capital and labour, of sanitation and slums. In a commentary on the parable of the Good Samaritan he highlighted the element of personal service rendered by the Good Samaritan and concluded:

> While men do not now so commonly 'fall into the hands of robbers' in the public highway, there are thousands robbed and stripped and sweated in tenements and slum, in dock and factory. But where is the Good Samaritan?

In an exegesis of the parable of the vine-dresser who hired men at different times to work in his vineyard, he argued that Christ was proposing that an employer should deal with men not as mere machines but as brothers and that, while wages might be enforced by commutative justice, their ultimate assessment should be made by distributive justice. He added a harsh comment on 'present-day' employers who so often combined a wonderful amount of theoretic faith with an equally astonishing unconsciousness of their obligations towards their own workers.

Poverty in Cork

Soon after arriving in Cork Alfred became acquainted with Fr A. M. MacSweeney, O.P. The Dominican priest had just successfully completed an M.A. thesis on 'Poverty in Cork' and the experience had aroused in him a desire to do all he could to ease the lot of the working poor in the city. At Alfred's suggestion, MacSweeney published an abstract of his thesis.[5] This emphasised the extent of the destitution of many Cork people. He noted that a frequent explanation by better-off persons for the squalor in which so many of their fellow-citizens had to live was excessive drinking. To this he replied that, for the most part, it was poverty which led to excessive drinking rather than the reverse. One of the examples he used to illustrate, in general, the treadmill of helplessness in which many workers and their families found themselves and, in particular, want of sufficient clothing, was as follows:

5. A. M. MacSweeney, O.P., 'A Study of poverty in Cork City', *Studies*, March 1915, 93-104.

It was the case of a quay labourer. He had been working on a boat all night, it rained all the time so that in the morning he, like his fellow-workers, was drenched through. Coming home in the morning he took his paltry breakfast of bread and tea; his clothes were sodden with rain, but he had not the wherewith to change. Accordingly, in this condition he lay down for a few hours rest. He woke with a bad cold, all his bones ached, double pneumonia set in, and at the time of my visit he lay in the Incurable Hospital in a state of rapid consumption, beyond all hope of recovery, while his poor wife and three children were looking out on a darkened world with the dread phantom of starvation hovering close to their little home.

Workers' education

Alfred equated democracy with workers in general and the trade union movement in particular and considered that the future of democratic institutions depended on workers and their leaders ensuring the evolution of a more egalitarian and just society. By the spring of 1915 he had decided that an immediate start had to be made to educate workers and especially their leaders so that through their trade unions they could effect a radical change in the socio-economic system. To this end, he proposed to organise lectures at U.C.C. for trade unionists and workers. Two of his new colleagues, Sir Bertram C. A. Windle, president of the college, and Timothy A. Smiddy, professor of economics and dean of the faculty of commerce, were eager to extend the benefits of university education to the citizens at large. Smiddy successfully persuaded Alfred to revise his scheme so as to include persons other than trade unionists and workers. He was then able to obtain Windle's endorsement for the scheme and the 'University and Labour' series of lectures began in mid-December 1915 and continued until the end of March 1916.

The lectures were most successful, with an average weekly attendance of between 200 to 250. The attendances were mainly comprised of workers, but other mature students and undergraduates taking courses in commerce and economics also attended. In *New Ireland* of 12 February 1916 Alfred set out this aspect of the 'Economic Conferences' as follows:

It is expected that the intimate personal knowledge which the workers have of social and economic problems will throw light on the studies of the faculty of commerce, and will save the students from the limitations of mere book-knowledge. Perhaps, too, the association of students and workmen will render possible many systematic enquiries and social investigations which at present are largely neglected in Ireland. And in any case it will serve to foster the spirit of brotherhood and nationality between Irishmen of all classes and creeds.[6]

The success of the lecture series was largely due to Alfred. He canvassed the local leaders of the trade unions with members in Cork and so ensured their enthusiastic support. Before doing so, he had successfully appealed to James Connolly to encourage the labour and trade union leadership in Cork to support the proposed series of lectures.[7] Throughout the series the format of each lecture remained the same – a presentation by a lecturer, a general discussion and a summing-up, generally by Alfred or Smiddy. Alfred conducted half the 'Economic Conferences'. Smiddy, Fr MacSweeney and some workers and students by reading papers opened the rest. Alfred dealt with social problems and their possible solution in accordance with the principles set out in *Rerum Novarum*. Smiddy lectured on economics and MacSweeney detailed the poverty of many of the workers of Cork and pleaded for immediate and radical steps to be taken to eradicate it.[8]

In his presentations Alfred covered such topics as destitution, the poor law, trade unionism, strikes, medieval guilds, co-operation, minimum wage, the insurance act, socialism and syndicalism. He facilitated the setting up of a number of study

6. A. J. Rahilly, 'The university and the worker', *New Ireland* 12 February 1916, 220.

7. Alfred O'Rahilly, 'Conferring of the College diploma in social and economic science on twenty-four workers: address by President Alfred O'Rahilly', *U.C.C. Record*, no. 14 (1948) 28; *Standard* 15 July 1949.

8. Apart from the article cited in footnote 6, Alfred wrote extensively on these courses as follows: 'Education and citizenship', *Catholic Truth Annual* 1916; 'The education of the Irish worker', *Highway*, April 1916; 'Social study in Cork', *Catholic Social Guild Bulletin*, April 1916; and 'Social study in Cork' in the *Catholic Times* 1916. For the account of these courses I am also indebted to Canon James P. Bastible.

circles arising from the 'Conferences'. One was on the poor law, of which he was intensely critical. In 'The abuses of the poor law' in *New Ireland* of 19 June 1915 he had complained that often insufficient outdoor relief had to be supplemented by some charitable organisation of a purely voluntary kind. Thus, in any examination of the results of the poor law, this systematic exploitation of private charity should not be overlooked. He declared that he knew many cases where a widow and her family were supported from three different sources: laundry-work (at sweated rates), outdoor relief and charitable societies. In this way the operation of the poor law and private charity by supplementing the inadequate wages of workers effectively enabled employers to continue to refuse to pay a living wage to their employees. He recalled with some bitterness that when a worker who was a striking example of this anomaly drew the attention of the authorities to it, he was immediately sacked by his employer.[9]

Another of these circles dealt with co-operation among workers in Cork at that time. Basic foodstuffs, including bread, tended to be more expensive than elsewhere. Alfred was convinced that at least with regard to bread a tacit monopoly operated to ensure this. He encouraged and appealed for support for trade unionists who were running the Cork Co-operative Society. However, after a successful launch and ensuring a reduction in the price of basic food items, especially bread, this almost collapsed due to mismanagement and ultimately a lack of adequate support from workers and their families.[10]

9. A. J. Rahilly, 'The abuses of the poor law', *New Ireland* 19 June 1915, 93-4.
10. Alfred described this co-operative in 'Co-operation in Cork' in *New Ireland* 9 September 1916, 487.
He returned to the subject in 'Socialism and co-operation' in the issues of the *Irish Commonwealth* of March and April 1919. The socialist idea, he urged, meant that in some way or other workers would take business into their own hands, produce commodities without having anyone to extract surplus profit for nothing. Thus workers had to acquire business experience and practical economic knowledge. They had to train members of their own class to develop commercial and technical ability. They had to organise their demands and combine their purchasing power. This would be done not by debates on socialism nor by distributing socialist literature but by taking up co-operation. Trade unions could ensure the greatest measure of progress by insisting that every trade unionist became a co-operator. He regretted that one heard so much oratory about the Bolsheviks, but little mention of Russia's 50,000 co-operative societies and twenty million co-operators.

Most of the college staff showed no interest in the 'Economic' or as they were also referred to the 'Workers' Conferences' and they were strongly opposed to them, as they considered that U.C.C. should have nothing to do with persons, especially workers, who were not students. Members and supporters of the Irish Party regarded the 'Conferences' with the greatest suspicion, as they believed that they were Sinn Féin inspired. The local newspapers also suspected that the hand of Sinn Féin was behind them and refused to carry any reference to them.[11] Undeterred by such a lack of support and even discouragement, Alfred proposed to publish a series of booklets to complement the lecture series. For this initially he had the assistance of Smiddy. The first booklet in this 'University and Labour series' was published in 1916. Compiled by Alfred, *A guide to books for social students and workers* was ready for the 1916-17

Alfred pointed out that just as workers combined to win an increase in wages such solidarity was required to ensure that over every counter capitalism did not deprive them of that increase. He advocated that workers establish co-operative enterprises in every town and city of Ireland and thus supply themselves with bread, milk, potatoes, groceries, etc. It was sad to find a roomful of workers discussing Marx and Kautsky, talking of the possibilities of taking over the nation's industries, while not one of them bought one pennyworth from the solitary little shop controlled and managed by workers. He explained that in Cork a branch co-operative shop had recently been opened in a neighbourhood where about two hundred transport workers resided, it being understood that they would buy sixty loaves of bread a day. They did not buy even sixty loaves a week. While expositions of Marx's analysis of value, debates on socialism, waving of red flags, and cheering Bolshevism might provide an outlet for superfluous emotions, they would not bring the Workers' Republic any nearer. His disappointment at the lack of success of the Cork Co-operative was accentuated, it seems, by the fact that he had on a number of occasions appealed to meetings of trade unionists to support their own shop and bakery and had even addressed public meetings to this end, at one of which he recalled that a band had been sent to 'fetch the people and focus the emotions'.

Despite not coming up to Alfred's expectations or those of its founders, the co-operative survived until the early 1950s as the Cork Bakery Co-operative.

11. A. J. Rahilly, 'The university and the worker', *New Ireland* 12 February 1916, 220. Alfred set out the contents of his course in sociology in the *U.C.C. Official Gazette* of March 1916 as follows: (1) Social and economic study – education, study clubs, citizenship; (2) The facts of poverty – Cork, standard of living; (3) Capitalism – origin and development, position of workers, present maldistribution of wealth; (4) History of labour organisation – guilds; (5) Fabian collectivism and political socialism; (6) Problems of modern trade unionism; (7) Economic democracy and national guilds; (8) The co-operative movement; (9) Distribution and unemployment; (10) The housing problem; (11) The drink question; (12) The responsibility of the consumer; (13) Women in industry.

series of 'Economic Conferences'. On the back of this 83-page booklet he listed as follows further booklets which were planned for issue 'shortly':

> T. Smiddy, *The education of the worker*; A. M. MacSweeney, *Poverty in Cork*; R. Fleming, *The economics of co-operation*; J. Rohan, *The medieval guilds*; A. Rahilly, *Guild democracy*; T. Smiddy, *Strikes: economic and social effects*; T. Smiddy, *Minimum wage*; A. Rahilly, *The responsibility of the consumer* and *The housing problem in Cork.*

Smiddy's interest in the project, however, was waning and the only other booklet to be published was A. M. MacSweeney's *Poverty in Cork*. This was published in 1917, as was W. P. Larkin's *Marxian socialism*. In a long introductory essay to the latter, Alfred indicated his chief motivation in organising courses and providing literature on the social question for workers. If Irish workers, he warned, are not given a lead from Rome they will seek it from elsewhere.[12]

In the spring of 1916 Alfred met Fr Vincent McNabb, O.P., who was in Cork to conduct a Lenten retreat at St Mary's

12. A. O'Rahilly, 'Education of the Irish worker', *New Ireland* 13 October 1917, 362. In the *Evening Press* of 24 June 1955 Cathal O'Shannon recalled these booklets as follows: 'To those of us who were working in the labour movement, and I am sure to many others, these were most valuable and nearly forty years ago we made very effective use of them. No. 1, *A guide to books for social students and workers* was compiled and annotated by O'Rahilly himself. It did for us in Ireland what an earlier Fabian Society publication had done for people like us in Britain, and we used to give copies away to enquirers as we would propagandist pamphlets. And No. 2, *Poverty in Cork* by Rev. A. M. MacSweeney, O.P., stood me in very good stead in the south when we were building up our movement there. Harder going for some of us was *Marxian socialism* by Rev. W. Pascal Larkin, O.S.F.C., a most scholarly treatise, ranking among the most critical studies of its subject. O'Rahilly's own introductory essay to this volume has always made me think it regrettable that he has never given us a critical edition of the work of the Rosscarbery man, William Thompson, to whom he refers in this introduction'.

Others, besides those active in the labour movement, were aware at that time of Alfred's promotion of the study of the social question. Miss Anita McCarthy, secretary of the Women's National Health Association of Ireland, of which Lady Aberdeen was president, in a letter of 19 February 1920, requested his advice on (a) a suitable programme for study circles concerning themselves with Irish social and economic problems, (b) a list of books on social science, economics and Irish industrial history and (c) the outline of a course of lectures on the subjects mentioned.

3. Fr Vincent McNabb, O.P. (1868-1943)

Church. While there, he was briefed by his confrère, Fr Mac-Sweeney, on the dire poverty of most of the workers of Cork and given a tour of the most deprived areas of the city. Already well-known as an outstanding preacher and as a proponent of the Catholic faith at Hyde Park, under the auspices of the Catholic Evidence Guild, McNabb was at that time acquiring a reputation as a social activist. He was to the Dominican Order what Fr Plater was to the Jesuits. Although a mild-mannered man, there was no doubting his passion for social justice. Occasionally, conspicuous in his religious garb, he was to be seen marching with workers protesting at a lock-out or involved in a prolonged strike. At Alfred's suggestion he wrote an afterword to Fr MacSweeney's *Poverty in Cork*.[13]

On his return to England McNabb published an article in the *Catholic Times*. Using the facts made available by Fr MacSweeney's research, he described the grinding poverty of most of the working people of Cork and the deplorable conditions in which they lived. He acknowledged that Cork had no worse a tale to tell than any other city. In a letter in the following edition of the *Catholic Times* Alfred pointed out that in fairness it should be noted that a 'pioneer movement to bring the National University into touch with the working men and women of the city' had been initiated. He described the weekly series of 'Economic Conferences' and the enthusiasm with which they had been received by workers both from the point of view of attendance and participation. He recalled that at a preliminary meeting there had been a discussion on the education of the worker and his relationship to the university. Then the first topic to be discussed at the 'Economic Conferences' was the reality of poverty in Cork. One of the merits of the conference was the awakened interest of students of the economics faculty in the social problems of the city. He hoped that eventually a school of training for social service would be established at the college on a plan analogous to that which had been so successfully adopted in the universities of London, Birmingham and Liverpool. In the meantime he announced that they would be issuing the proposed University and Labour series of booklets and that arrangements were being made to carry out investigations into the housing conditions and the conditions of the

13. Bishop Daniel J. Cohalan provided the foreword.

home-workers and women workers of the city and to publish the results.[14]

Alfred, however, owing to the many calls on his time was not able to conduct these investigations. Eventually in 1944 a group of students, who attended his lectures on sociology, set out, under his direction and that of Professor John Busteed, to update Fr MacSweeney's *Poverty in Cork*. Following Seebohm Rowntree's 'human needs standard', a minimum level of need based on requirements of food, shelter, clothes, light and fuel was established, costed and adapted to local consumer habits. Those conducting the survey measured the standard of living of each family living in corporation housing in the city by comparing its income with its needs. The results of the investigation indicated that over 45% of these households were living below Rowntree's minimum standard. Mainly because of pressure of work Alfred was diverted from publishing the full report.[15]

Prior McNabb's article evoked a number of responses. Among these was a letter from 'a medical man' who was a graduate of U.C.C. This gave Alfred an opportunity to publish a further letter on the subject. He criticised 'a medical man's' request that McNabb give 'a brief sketch of a scheme which he thinks would abolish this terrible state of affairs'. No such panacea, Alfred declared, was to hand. He acknowledged that 'the writer' realised that the process of improving the social situation would be slow and educative. Sounding a little piqued, he continued: 'That is precisely what, in the face of great discouragement and difficulties, we are trying to do in Cork.' They were, he insisted, determined to ascertain the facts about poverty in Cork and to present them to an indifferent public.

Alfred recalled that during the previous week he had found 'in this Catholic city' an old woman who had just died of privation. He detailed cases known to him of adult married workers employed at 15 shillings a week[16] and of dozens of cases of

14. O'Rahilly Papers: Scrapbook I, press-cuttings.
15. L. Ryan, 'Urban poverty', *One million poor?* (ed. S. Kennedy, Dublin 1981) 38.
16. In *War and the food of the Dublin labourer* (Dublin 1916) 16, Dr W. H. Thompson, professor of physiology at Trinity College, wrote that '22 shillings and 6 pence per week for normal times' was the lowest wage-level which enabled a working-class family in Dublin 'to procure enough food to live decently and give them power to do their day's work' and he added that even at that level 'care, economy and good management are needed to make it do all that is required'.

sweated widows and girls. Mere social work or 'charity', he asserted, was not sufficient to deal with the social problem. It could be counter-productive. He expressed his oft-repeated conviction that outdoor-relief and food tickets were often in effect paid to the employer to enable him to employ widows and labourers at less than a living wage. While it was necessary to make immediate provision for the suffering and the destitute, steps should be taken to ensure that capitalism was not enabled thereby to increase its exploitation. Education was essential to social reform. The way forward was to 'help the poor – yes, and to teach them how to help themselves'. He continued: 'The worker must become educated in the best sense of the word; he must study moral principles and economic conditions; he must be taught to realise the vast unused power which lies in his hands at this moment. He is being robbed not only of the legitimate fruits of his labour, but of his share in our common spiritual inheritance. He does not know his power and his rights.' Alfred described how at a recent meeting a speaker expostulated with him on his 'socialistic' statements. The statements in question, he added, were quotations from Pope Leo XIII's *Rerum Novarum*. He recalled a similar experience with a prominent member of the Society of St Vincent de Paul who expressed the fear that if the workers were educated they would become socialists. Hence the general feeling has hitherto been to keep the unfortunate toiler in the dark, to cheat him of his claim to know his rights as well as his responsibilities. The first beginning of any real reform was to oust that obscurantist tyranny and to educate the worker. It was a curious fact that Catholic social literature was then for the first time being made accessible to the Catholic workers of Cork. He concluded: 'When the working poor realise that their lot is hard, we shall be in a better position to make that lot a better one.'[17]

At that time Alfred used every opportunity to publicise his version of the social message in Cork and elsewhere. Apart from the articles and letters referred to already, he published 'The education of the Irish worker' in *Highway* of April 1916 and in *New Ireland* of 13 October 1917, as well as 'Social study in Cork' in the *Catholic Social Guild Bulletin* of April 1916, 'Education and citizenship' in the *Catholic Truth Annual* 1916 and 'Education in Ireland' in the *Workers' Year Book* 1917. In

17. O'Rahilly Papers: Scrapbook I, press-cutting.

an article in *Studies* of June 1917[18] he made a powerful appeal for a radical change in the attitude to poverty in the city. He utilised some of the research from Fr MacSweeney's thesis to illustrate the lives of silent desperation of a high percentage of the workers of Cork. In addition, he made use of statistics collected by the city's public health department to show that the slums of Cork were as bad as those of Dublin, then incurring widespread notoriety. As a first step in dealing with that problem he called for a housing inquiry. He then declared:

> I have dwelt, at seemingly undue length, on the primary poverty of Cork, because I believe that a large percentage of the poor are poor and wretched through no fault of theirs. If this contention be true, all social effort which takes no account of these primary conditions is mere amateur tinkering. Charity, as the term is usually applied, accepts the degrading and unchristian poverty which it encounters; it does not strive to eliminate or prevent it, it just keeps it alive. A society which aims merely at providing food or clothing does not tend to reduce poverty, it simply nurses it. No doubt such material help is necessary, especially in the case of those who are temporarily dependent or disabled. But so far as primary poverty is concerned – whether due to sweating, unemployment, want of training, insanitation, bad housing – the charity of doles and tickets, however well-intentioned, merely perpetuates the system and gives it a fresh lease of life. Hence the importance of realising that the poor are largely the victims, not of individual difficulties and personal troubles, but of a social system, an organised impersonal selfishness, which betrays itself in statistics.[19]

18. Alfred J. Rahilly, 'The social problem in Cork', *Studies*, June 1917, 177-88.

19. Ibid. 184-5. Alfred provided the following example to illustrate his assertion: 'I believe that over 80% of those helped in Cork by the Society of St Vincent de Paul are widows. Yet there has been no organised investigation into the question, no constructive effort, no attempt to reform public opinion. It is calmly accepted that a widow with children has to live (1) on an obviously insufficient outdoor relief, (2) on a miserable pittance for working very long hours in laundry or factory, (3) by soliciting food tickets from a charitable society, (4) in a two-pair-back in an uninhabitable slum. While we denounce 1, 2 and 4, we keep them flourishing by No. 3' (ibid. 185).

Catholic Social League

By the early summer of 1917 Alfred's crusading for an urgent programme of social action was beginning to have results. With a number of like-minded people he organised a meeting at the Catholic Young Men's Society (C.Y.M.S.) Hall in Cork on 25 May to inaugurate a Catholic Social League. Alfred was the principal speaker and it was announced that the league was to have as its president Bishop Daniel J. Cohalan. The meeting was enthusiastic and representative, with hundreds of people not being able to find room in the large hall. Alfred told his audience that, largely for historical reasons in their overwhelmingly Catholic country, they had come to accept a condition of life and opinion which was practically uninfluenced by Catholic principles. The whole trend of public and social life was opposed to the Faith which they individually professed. Whether they realised it or not, the Catholic religion was being reduced to an affair of individual salvation or corporate worship. Giving a hint of his growing separatism at that time, he complained that the schoolboy learned his officially prescribed English history and that most of their social and political attitudes seemed to be dictated from outside their country. He emphasised their ignorance and even evasion of Catholic social principles and remedies and extraordinary apathy concerning the social conditions for which they were directly responsible.

To the objection that members of the Society of St Vincent de Paul were already helping the poor, he replied that the aim of the proposed league was to supplement not replace existing Catholic societies, increase their membership, help their efforts, co-operate with them and provide them with information and literature, and publish their work. Essentially the league would be a bureau where Catholic social students and workers could procure information and learn to co-ordinate their activities. The Society of St Vincent de Paul, as originally founded, he declared, did provide the services to be made available by the proposed league. These, however, the society no longer provided. In Cork there was no secretariat, where the poor could receive advice in their money difficulties and grievances connected with insurance, pensions, compensation, desertion, tenancy, etc. There was no centre, where people could obtain temporary employment as at the City Labour Yard in Dublin. No project was operating, such as that of the Dublin Food Supply Society which purchased at wholesale prices essential foodstuffs and sold them without profit to lowly-paid labourers. Nor was there as in Dublin a club which ensured that boys from poor families were not trapped into 'blind-alley' employment, to be dismissed again at the age of nineteen or twenty, with nothing except the ranks of the unskilled labourer open to them.

Alfred claimed that the organised charity in Cork seemed to have become an affair of food tickets and, however excellent, had not the slightest tendency to improve the lot of the working poor. He went on: 'We surely need more knowledge of Catholic principles and study of practical remedies; we need to arouse the public conscience and to publish local enquiries; we need to discuss proposals and to co-operate in devising remedies. That is the case for a Catholic Social League.' This he envisaged as consisting of (1) a small band of social workers and thinkers to act as an executive committee and (2) a large number of Catholic citizens who would contribute annually a shilling or more to expenses. At the outset a room would be provided where the poor sent by charitable societies could receive expert advice. The same room could be used as a bureau, where Catholic social students and workers could receive information and guidance. There also a lending library with the emphasis on books on social topics could be developed, Catholic social publications could be distributed and study-clubs and support groups organised. As the Catholic Social League became established there would be further tasks to be faced, such as the publication of social and economic booklets, written from an Irish and not an English standpoint. There was an urgent need for a comprehensive housing inquiry and he suggested that after the war the league might publish a monthly *Catholic Review*.[20]

At the end of the general meeting an executive committee was formed, with Alfred as a member, and it was decided that a general and public meeting would be held in mid-October to review the situation. Alfred was to be disappointed with the Catholic Social League, for it provided few significant practical results. Not many of his fellow-citizens and none of his colleagues in U.C.C. matched his commitment to the crusade for

20. Alfred J. Rahilly, 'The Catholic Social League', *Irish Monthly*, July 1917, 435-42.

social justice. At the end of 1918 he resigned from the executive and not long afterwards the league ceased to exist.[21]

Attempt to change the Society of St Vincent de Paul

Alfred continued to be an active member of the Society of St Vincent de Paul until the end of 1917.[22] Immediately after joining the local conference he had attempted to persuade his colleagues in the society in general to become more active in dealing with the social problem. He realised that the members of the society, the integrity and honesty of purpose of whom was universally recognised and who commanded respect throughout the community, would have been most valuable allies in any attempt to improve radically the lot of the working-class. From the writings of the organisation's founder, Frederick Ozanam, he argued that the society, if it was to be true to itself, should be engaged in activities leading to social justice and reform, as well as the provision of material help for the poor and the destitute. He urged that members should be involved in the education of workers by providing them with books on social and economic topics and in encouraging and assisting the development of a strong trade-union movement. Some of his colleagues in the local conference were incapable of views other than those of the *bourgeoisie*, most were opposed to social activism of any kind and nearly all regarded such activity as calculated to bring the society into confrontations with the authorities and thereby distract it from its basic purpose of materially helping the poor. Chief among those who in the local conference steadfastly opposed Alfred's campaign to make the society more socially activist was a solicitor named Charles K. Murphy.[23]

21. Interview with Professor Kathleen O'Flaherty.

22. Much of what follows on his relationship with the Society has been taken from A. J. Rahilly, 'Oznam's ideal of social work I', *Irish Monthly*, April 1918, 189-95; 'Oznam's ideal of social work II', *Irish Monthly*, May 1918, 245-51; and 'Oznam's ideal of social work III', *Irish Monthly*, June 1918, 305-18.

23. Interview with Professor Kathleen O'Flaherty. From 1920 onwards Charles K. Murphy was associated with the law faculty at U.C.C. and eventually served as professor of jurisprudence and Roman law from 1928 to 1958 and as dean of the faculty from 1930 to 1958. He was a lifelong member of the Society of St Vincent de Paul and published *The spirit of the Society of St Vincent de Paul* (Dublin 1940), *Thoughts on the lay apostolate of charity* (Cork 1941), *Humble of heart: origins of the spirituality of the Society of St Vincent de Paul*.

4. Group at U.C.C. after conferring, in July 1937, of honorary LL.D. on Finbar Ryan, O.P., co-adjutor archbishop of Port of Spain, Trinidad. *Left to right*: Alfred, Mary Ryan (professor of romance languages), the archbishop, Patrick J. Merriman (president), Charles K. Murphy (dean of the faculty of law), Joseph Downey (secretary)

Alfred O'Rahilly III: Controversialist

Besides urging a more social activist approach in his local conference Alfred plied the Council of Ireland, the society's national executive, with memoranda arguing for a change of policy. He was given a golden opportunity to present his case at the highest level when invited to prepare a discussion document for the annual meeting of the presidents of all the conferences of Ireland in the autumn of 1916. He had, however, to modify somewhat that part of his text, wherein he argued for a social activist approach.[24]

He failed to influence the conference presidents. With few exceptions, they regarded his suggestions as at best imprudent. He was not to be discouraged and remained an active member of the society for another year. His efforts to radically change the society continued and so, as the relationship with his colleagues at local and national level became more and more acrimonious, he eventually resigned.[25]

Although no longer a member, Alfred was instrumental in having a branch of the society established in U.C.C. in April 1919 and he remained a strong supporter of the society financially and otherwise for the rest of his life.[26] Typical of his support was a letter to the press, in which he appealed to the Carl

In commemoration of Frederick Ozanam (1853-1953) (Cork 1953), *The lay apostolate of charity and other essays. Foreword by Most Reverend Finbar Ryan, O.P.* (Cork 1959). He co-ordinated a number of the efforts to have Alfred released from internment in 1921 (see J. A. Gaughan, *Alfred O'Rahilly II: Public figure* (Dublin 1989) 115, 121). Although Fr James Bastible, dean of residence at U.C.C. and friend of Alfred and his wife, Agnes, was generally called upon to settle domestic disagreements between them, Murphy occasionally found himself involved in this thankless task. Alfred had a lifelong antipathy to Murphy. Apart from reasons of temperament, this probably originated from their strong and persistent disagreements in 1915-17 on the role of members of the Society of St Vincent de Paul. Notwithstanding his feelings towards Murphy, Alfred contributed a gracious review of the latter's *The spirit of the Society of St Vincent de Paul* to the *Standard* of 20 December 1940.

24. Alfred was later to recall that he had suggested that the society, with a view to adopting a more radical approach to the problems of poverty, should commission a translation of the writings of Ozanam on social topics. However, he complained, this was deleted from his text on the grounds that it was outside the scope of the society and inconsistent with its spirit. In 'Ozanam's ideal of social work' in the *Irish Monthly* of May 1918 he listed Ozanam's social writings as follows: '*The doctrine of Saint Simon*, published lectures on commercial law, works on German civilisation and Dante, articles and appeals in the *New Era* during 1848-49 and a long essay entitled "The origins of socialism"' (ibid. 246).

25. Interview with Professor Kathleen O'Flaherty.

26. Interview with Canon James P. Bastible.

Rosa opera company during its visit to Cork to organise a concert for the poor of the city. He acknowledged the efforts of the Society of St Vincent de Paul and the charitable organisations to cope with the demands made on their resources and urged the need for a generous response to their appeal for extra funds by way of a charity concert to cope with the thousands of unemployed who were not in receipt of 'the dole' and who had 'absolutely no resources'.[27]

After his resignation from the Society of St Vincent de Paul Alfred prepared an article 'Ozanam's ideal of social work'. This was published in three parts in the *Irish Monthly* of April, May and June 1918, where he set out his thesis as follows:

> The common impression that Ozanam was a man of action rather than of ideas, in matters social and economic,

---

27. See *Cork Examiner* 15 October 1925. Apart from his involvement with the Society of St Vincent de Paul there is other evidence of Alfred's practical concern for the poor even during the unsettled years of the war of independence and its aftermath. In 1920 he sat on a housing committee of Cork City Council which was attempting to provide extra working-class dwellings. On 16 January 1922 he submitted a memorandum to Dáil Éireann's department of labour on a direct labour scheme for the unemployed. In November 1922 he became involved in a controversy about the reduction in expenditure on the Cork workhouse hospital. As a result of a public intervention by Seán O'Hegarty in the autumn of 1922, it was reported that the new board of Vice-Guardians had saved £26,000 by eliminating mismanagement and consumption and that that money was to be used for 'city housing'. Some members of the Cork Workers' Council, however, suspected that the saving had been made against the interests of the poor and elderly who had to be cared for in the hospital. Encouraged by Patrick Higgins, of the Cork Workers' Council, Alfred took part in public exchanges in the press on the matter and called for a local public inquiry to clarify the situation. This caused some resentment and Seán Good, also of the Cork Workers' Council, who championed the action of the Vice-Guardians, was severely critical of Alfred's intervention, though acknowledging 'the many practical ways' he had in the past given proof 'of his sympathy with the working-classes'. Alfred concerned himself again with conditions in the Cork workhouse hospital in the autumn of 1923. In a letter, dated 22 October, to the minister for local government, he protested that the commissioners, who were then managing it, had refused to implement reforms which had been agreed by 'the late Vice-Guardians'. He also took them to task for their general tendency to reduce expenditure on the institution (O'Rahilly Papers: notification, dated 15 November 1920, from Cork City Council to O'Rahilly; letter, dated 17 January 1922, from Risteárd Mac Coitir, secretary, department of labour, to O'Rahilly; letter, dated 13 November 1922, from Patrick Higgins to O'Rahilly; *Cork Examiner* 11, 13, 14 November 1922, 22 November 1923).

is utterly false. Not only he but all the original members of the Society of St Vincent de Paul were men of study and thought, men who reflected deeply on the social problems of their time. Ozanam, in particular, in spite of his premature death, wrote on almost every topic of social importance.[28]

Alfred recalled that Ozanam in 1840, in his inaugural course of lectures on Commercial Law in the university of Lyons, enunciated views on the social question, many of which were taken up and advocated eight years later by Bishop von Ketteler of Mainz and later appeared in Leo XIII's *Rerum Novarum*. Perhaps the most important of these views was Ozanam's insistence on the right of every worker to a living wage.[29]

The priests who acted as chaplains to parish conferences of the society were almost invariably opposed to a move away from materially helping the most vulnerable members of the community to involvement in social activism. To these Alfred offered the following advice which was given on 21 April 1848 by Ozanam to his brother who was a priest serving in a parish in Lille:

> Occupy yourself always as much with servants as with masters and with workingmen as with the rich. This is henceforth the only way of salvation for the Church of France. The priests must give up their little middle-class parishes, select flocks in the midst of an immense population which they do not know. They must occupy themselves not only with the indigents but with this poor class which does not ask for alms.[30]

28. A. J. Rahilly, 'Oznam's ideal of social work II', *Irish Monthly*, May 1918, 245.

29. Ibid. 246, 251.

30. Ibid. 249. Some thirty years later Alfred had an opportunity to convey this message to the young priests of Cork diocese. At their request he conducted a seminar on the pastoral ministry every Thursday evening during the academic sessions of 1948 and 1949. Fr Christopher Walsh, presently parish priest of Monkstown, who attended these, recalled Alfred's emphasis on the importance of the pastoral care of the working-class and the young. He vividly recalled that Alfred gave his services free, as well as providing biscuits and tea, which he insisted on serving himself.

In conclusion Alfred appealed for a recognition of the need for both action and study. He acknowledged that the primary work of conferences would remain the allocation of relief, the securing of employment and the provision of advice. However, he suggested, conferences could set up study circles as special works or co-operate with some other organisation such as the Catholic Social League. In a typical sally at his opponents he declared: 'Those who deprecate study really wish to prevent further study; they are satisfied with the existing stage. Meanwhile the world is moving on.'[31] Alfred's closely reasoned and well-documented article, however, had little effect. It was no more than a final fusillade in a three-year long skirmish which he had already lost.

31. A. J. Rahilly, 'Oznam's ideal of social work III', June 1918, 310-15.

ARBITRATOR EXTRAORDINARY

From his earliest years in U.C.C., Alfred won the trust and confidence of the leaders of the labour and trade-union movement in Cork. They appreciated his support for social justice, his strong sympathy with the less fortunate members of society and his total lack of affectation. Conversely, Alfred had an extraordinary admiration and affection for the Cork trade-union leaders and, in private, frequently commented on their integrity and generosity of spirit. Throughout his years in Cork he was, in effect, an honorary and unofficial consultant to them. This was particularly the case before world war two when trade-union officers were usually popular members of their respective unions without any specific training for their posts. Trade-union branch secretaries in Cork made up for their lack of expertise by invariably seeking Alfred's advice and assistance. Consequently most of the important trade-union submissions made to employers in the period between the world wars were drafted by him.

Coincidentally Alfred was held in high esteem by the employers in Cork. They were aware of his influence with the workers in general and the trade-union movement in particular and appreciated that the settlement of an industrial dispute agreed to by him on behalf of workers would be honoured. Moreover, from discussions with him they realised that he was both independent-minded and incorruptible. As a result, in many an instance when difficulties arose which had the potential of developing into a serious industrial dispute Alfred was informally consulted by both the employer and representatives of the workers concerned and was able by his good offices to avert a strike. When strikes did occur it was usually Alfred who at the request of both sides delivered a settlement.[1]

Chairman of the Cork Arbitration Board

Alfred's position as unofficial arbitrator of industrial disputes in Cork city was formalised when he was appointed chairman of the Cork Arbitration Board towards the end of 1923.[2] The

1. Interview with Canon James P. Bastible, Cornelius Murphy and Professor Kathleen O'Flaherty, and letter, dated 7 September 1983, from Gerald Y. Goldberg.
2. Kathleen O'Flaherty, 'Dr. O'Rahilly and U.C.C. – An Appreciation', *Cork University Record*, Summer 1955, 17.

institution was established following a serious outbreak of industrial unrest in the summer and autumn of that year. After the civil war the Irish Free State government began economic and financial reconstruction. Partly because of external and partly because of internal economic conditions, the government required from employers and workers a reduction in salaries and wages. The reductions proposed were such as would have caused hardship to the lower-paid. Post-office workers went on strike, as did those in the building industry and the drapery trade. Other industrial disputes broke out all over the country. The most damaging was a national strike by dockers. Because of bitter factionalism within the Irish Transport and General Workers' Union, this was particularly intractable and continued for thirteen and a half weeks until almost the end of October 1923.[3]

Soon after his election as T.D. for Cork city in August 1923 Alfred had informal consultations with both sides in the industrial dispute at Cork docks. The gap, however, between them was so great that there was no hope of progress. By the beginning of October this national strike by the dockers, together with a considerable amount of secondary picketing, was having a serious effect on the economy. On behalf of the government, Alfred set out once more to find an acceptable formula for ending the dockers dispute in Cork, where for local reasons its effect was more acute than in other ports. To assist him in his efforts, the Cork Industrial Development Association on 4 October at a well-publicised meeting, at which many interests were represented, appointed a committee of action of six persons, to work in collaboration with him 'for a speedy settlement of the various strikes and lock-outs'.

On the following day Alfred wrote to James Hickey, spokesman for the dockers on strike in Cork, requesting that the Cork dockers agree, if acceptable terms were proposed, to an end of their industrial action independent of the solution of the dispute at the port of Dublin. The Cork employers were eager that this should happen, as the bitter factionalism among Dublin's trade unionists greatly reduced the prospects of an early settlement there. Hickey and his colleagues in the trade-union leadership in

3. For more on this factionalism, see J. A. Gaughan, *Thomas Johnson (1872-1963): first leader of the Labour Party in Dáil Éireann* (Dublin 1980) 258 and ff.

Cork were opposed to a separate settlement. At the very least, they saw it as a possible further cause of division in a movement, then under siege from without and from within. Alfred appreciated their position. The representatives of the employers sought to embarrass the dockers' representative by publishing a copy of Alfred's letter in the *Cork Examiner* of 11 October. Alfred received prior information of this and had published in the same issue a letter in which he indicated that he agreed with the attitude adopted by Hickey and his colleagues.

In the meantime the government had initiated negotiations between the two sides to the docks dispute in Dublin and eventually, on 10 October, President William T. Cosgrave publicly announced terms on which, it was hoped, a settlement could be reached. These were: (1) That on the resumption of work there should be a reduction in wages of one shilling per day, with consequential reductions in tonnage and overtime rates, and in the wages of the men who had previously followed the settlements relating to dock labour. (2) That the minister, in the exercise of his powers under Part II of the Industrial Courts Act 1919, should, as soon as possible, after the resumption of work, set up a Court of Inquiry to report on the question of dock labour. The leadership of the I.T.G.W.U. had difficulty in enabling its members to ballot on these terms, owing to the disruptive activities of James Larkin and his followers. Eventually on Tuesday night, 23 October, after a meeting of the executive committee of the I.T.G.W.U. a statement was issued that the following resolution had been unanimously adopted: 'That in view of the forcible prevention of the postponed ballot in Dublin, and the majority in favour of the terms by the branches that have been balloted, this executive committee now closes the dispute, and instructs all branches concerned to make arrangements for the resumption of work as soon as possible.'

At this time Alfred was eagerly grasping an opportunity presented to him to end the dockers' dispute in Cork. He had a letter, the contents of which had been previously communicated to both sides in the dispute, published in the *Cork Examiner* of 24 October 1923. In the letter he noted that the most recent statement and counter-statement of those in dispute made it clear that the difference between the parties had been so reduced that they could be adjusted by mutual goodwill. He continued:

Arbitrator Extraordinary

After a careful perusal of the rival manifestos, I take the liberty of suggesting to both sides the following terms of settlement, in addition to the previously agreed terms concerning the right of dismissal in the case of certain unions. These terms contain such modifications of those put forward by the employers as will, in my opinion meet the main objections published by the workers. I therefore trust that they will be immediately and favourably considered by both sides:

(1) An immediate reduction of wages amounting to one half of the employers' demand.

(2) Prior to resumption of work both sides will agree in appointing an arbitrator to decide whether and when the balance of the employers' demand is to be totally or partially put into operation, or to decide against any further reduction, in any trade or trading, for such period of stabilisation as the arbitrator or arbitrators may determine.

(3) The arbitrator or arbitrators will have power to reconsider the reduction specified in section (1) in the case of individual workers in whose trade there is no standard rate, and, if necessary, to confirm, alter or abolish this reduction as from the date of resumption of work.

(4) The decision of the arbitrator or arbitrators on the points enumerated in sections (2) and (3) and on all disputed questions concerning these terms of settlement will be binding on all parties.

Representatives of both sides found these fresh proposals to be acceptable and the strike at the port of Cork ended after a vote by the dockers in Connolly Hall on the following evening.

The termination of the dispute in the port signalled the end of the other strikes in Cork. On behalf of the Cork Employers' Federation John Rearden wrote to Alfred on 24 October 1923 as follows:

Your letter appearing in today's *Cork Examiner* has been carefully considered by my federation, and I am instructed to say that the suggestions you make are agreed to by all the employers concerned in the various disputes.

As the workers' representatives had already informally

assented to these terms, this letter, which was published in the *Cork Examiner* of 25 October, effectively ended the remaining disputes. In accordance with Alfred's proposals, a Cork Arbitration Board was established to monitor the implementation of the terms agreed. Alfred was appointed chairman and acted in this capacity until his resignation, due to pressure of work, a year later.[4]

Stresses need for a Catholic social programme

Alfred was fortunate to have been given an opportunity to effectively address workers and employers over the heads of their respective organisations while engaged in his attempt to settle the rash of industrial disputes in Cork. On 12 October 1923, in a key-note address to the annual Catholic Truth Society of Ireland (C.T.S.I.) Conference, he spoke on 'The Catholic layman in the labour movement'.[5] He appealed for the initiation of a movement which would bring employer and workers together in a spirit of Christian comradeship and to that end urged the need for the education of Catholic workers. Pointing to the current strikes, he noted that the Catholic religion of the vast majority of the Irish people was treated as irrelevant by those involved in them. In accordance with that religion he asserted the right to a living wage for honest work and that those having access to the resources of nature should act as stewards for the community. In the middle ages the guilds controlled the economic law of supply and demand. They controlled profiteering, though they called it by other names and they saw to it that every human being had, as far as possible, a chance of securing his proper share of the resources of nature. In the present harsh economic climate of depressed world markets they were bound to hold to their Christian and humane view of labour and adapt economic conditions to it rather than the reverse. Alfred queried, on the one hand, whether the lower cross-channel wage was a living wage for Irish Catholic workmen and, on the other hand, if there had been any attempt to lower the other costs of production before attempting to lower that of labour. His questioning of the fairness of making the lower cross-channel wage a norm was relevant. This wage was

4. O'Rahilly Papers: Scrapbook I, press-cuttings.
5. *Irish Independent* 13 October 1923.

the result of official British policy which was to keep the price of food low and thus contain the cost of the labour element in industry, thereby keeping British industrial goods competitive. He decried the lack of a Catholic public opinion which could be brought to bear on the provision of answers to the questions he posed. In the presence of the current impasse, they had to confess that Catholicism had no social influence or programme in the country.

Alfred referred to a pastoral letter by the Irish Catholic bishops of February 1914, which urged the establishment of conciliation boards by which issues at stake would be considered by capable men fairly representing both sides. The pastoral also expressed the view that no extreme course should be adopted except as a last resort and even then that the public should in some way be afforded an opportunity of expressing its opinion before 'war broke out'. The pastoral proposed a model scheme of industrial relations to be worked towards. This was a co-partnership system, whereby workers had an opportunity to share in the profits of an industry.

These developments could take place, Alfred declared, only if workers were educated and aware of their rights as well as their obligations. He recalled a message from Pope Pius X to the German bishops concerning their duty to provide education for Catholic workers. Elsewhere beginnings had been made to this end. In England they had a Catholic Workers' College in Oxford, where scholarships were given to workers to go through a university course. At Oxford there was also an annual summer school for workers. He pointed to a Catholic conference in Milwaukee in the U.S. in which both employers and workers participated. Referring to the collapse in 1918 of the course for workers at U.C.C., he regretted that, even after a grant was made by the corporation, a proper committee to run the course could not be found, because of apathy on the part of employer and worker alike.

Clash with Bishop Cohalan

Alfred's remark that the current rash of industrial disputes indicated that Catholicism had no social influence or programme in the country did not go unchallenged. On 12 November 1923 Bishop Cohalan addressed the men's confraternity of the North parish in St Mary's cathedral. The purpose and main thrust of his remarks was to praise workers, the trade-union movement and the Labour Party for not supporting the hunger-strike by thousands of anti-treatyites then entering a critical stage. But during his address he declared: 'We have a right to protest against the statement that the Church has lost all its influence with both employers and workers, because the Church has not determined a new adjustment of wages.'[6] In the *Cork Examiner*[7] Alfred claimed that the statement was not his, but was sufficiently close to statements by him at the recent C.T.S.I. Conference to indicate that the reference was to him and that he largely agreed with such a statement. To Cohalan's assertion that the strikes and their effects were purely economic and had no moral significance, he replied that, if that was so, then morals were apparently 'the exclusive concern of disembodied spirits'. He countered that, if the bishop had presided over as many arbitration conferences as he had, he would not be so confident about the absence of ethical arguments and considerations. He drew attention to the fact that Cohalan referred to 'unreasonable claims or practices' which 'cannot be defended on moral grounds', though he made the mistake of fancying that they were all on the side of the workers. He greeted as timely Bishop Cohalan's announcement that 'instruction on social questions' was to be provided for all the city confraternities and that the priests were to have a more direct relation to the trade unions. However, he hoped that the employers too would not be forgotten, as the deficiency was by no means all on one side.

In a typical concluding sally Alfred quoted from Pius X's address to the German bishops in 1912: 'The social question and the controversies connected with it regarding the conditions and hours of labour, wages or strikes are not of a purely economic character, and therefore are not of a kind that can be settled without reference to the authority of the Church'. He also reproduced a relevant passage from 'Ireland in transition' by Joseph Keating, S.J., in the *Month* of October 1923.[8] In the

6. *Cork Examiner* 13 November 1923.

7. Ibid. 14 November 1923.

8. Ibid. 289-99. The passage contained an unmistakable barb for Cohalan by implicitly comparing him to his disadvantage to Bishop Ketteler and Cardinal Manning. It read: 'The question naturally suggests itself – how is it that these labour troubles have arisen in a population mainly Catholic, when the moral principles which should govern the relations between labour and capital are so

light of these quotations he expressed the conviction that Cohalan would realise that the views he put forward at the C.T.S.I. Conference could not be disposed of by the bishop's remark that people would soon be blaming the Church when they 'see a drove of cattle being driven from a fair unsold'.

Urges a Christian approach to industrial relations on employers and workers

Alfred resigned as chairman of the Cork Arbitration Board at the end of 1924, but he functioned informally as Cork's arbitrator for a quarter of a century afterwards. During that period he retained the respect of the employers of Cork. Invariably he was an honoured guest at functions organised by them. Occasionally he was invited to address the annual general meeting of the Cork Employers' Federation. On such occasions he shared with them his belief in good industrial relations and emphasised the complementary and equally important role of employer and worker in every industrial enterprise.

Alfred delivered one such address on 21 January 1926. Speaking on 'The other side of business', he appealed for an appreciation by employers and workers of the good-will to be found on both sides of industry. Trade unionism had to be accepted by employers. If they or he were workingmen, they would join a trade union at once. A humane approach was essential in business. He had often seen disputes that had their origin in the wrong handling of men. Alfred acknowledged that philanthropy should not be confused with business, but in industrial relations human kindness was of real monetary value and far

---

clearly expounded in the teachings of the Church? Perhaps because there have been no prominent public men, like Ketteler or Manning, to proclaim magisterially these duties and these rights which make for just and peaceful dealings between man and man. Or, perhaps, because neither clergy nor laity, in spite of the trumpet calls of Leo XIII, have sufficiently realised in the past the profoundly ethical character of political economy, and have blindly accepted the godless system prevalent elsewhere as consistent with Christianity. The government might be well advised to ask some trusted and competent ecclesiastic to discuss the grievances between dockers and shippers in the light of Christian teaching. Meanwhile the hope of the future lies in the success achieved by the teachers of the people in prompting Christian brotherhood and abolishing class warfare, a success which will be directly proportioned to the knowledge and sympathy they display' (ibid. 296-7).

more important than the little sums involved in some disputes. He pointed out that the cost of living was an important factor in industrial unrest. Employers as much as workers should be determined to ensure that basic food items, such as bread, be kept at a reasonable cost. And, although it was not taken into account in fixing the cost of living rate, the price of stout should also be attended to.[9]

Alfred's relationship with the local leaders of the labour and trade-union movement was particularly close. He attended practically every important trade-union function. Among his lifelong friends were Dick Anthony, Jimmy Barry, Con Connolly, Con Desmond, John Good, Jim Hickey, Jeremiah Hurley and Patrick J. O'Brien. These, along with Seán Casey, who came to the fore in the 1950s and 1960s, constituted the public face and respected leadership of trade-unionism in Cork.

Alfred availed of every opportunity to emphasise to workers and their leaders his strong support for them. He impressed on them that he and everyone else who went out to work was a worker and he continually protested that he regarded himself as just another 'Pat Murphy'. Although he scarcely ever attended social functions with his colleagues at U.C.C., after meetings or conferences with Cork labour and trade-union leaders, he invariably went afterwards with them to a public house. There he would insist on buying drinks all round, would, as often as not, discover that he had no money in his pocket and would have to borrow from Professor John Busteed or someone else in the company.[10]

Just as Alfred availed of every opportunity to urge, in effect, a Christian approach to industrial relations on employers, he did likewise with less inhibitions with regard to workers. In this vein he contributed an article headed 'A Christian social policy for Ireland' to a Eucharistic Congress supplement in the *Irish Press*, but concluded in non-partisan fashion: 'In spite of the press and the talkies and textbooks, we must strive to educate ourselves in principles and in values. The family must come before the State, the community must control the individual,

9. *Cork Examiner* 22 January 1926.
10. Interviews with Canon James P. Bastible and Cornelius Murphy. To be like the rest of the company, he would order a pint of Murphy's stout. Then, to their barely concealed amusement, he would manfully dispose of it with some difficulty (ibid.).

5. Group after conferring ceremony at U.C.C. in summer of 1952. *Front, left to right:* Austin Goggin, James Hickey, T.D., Professor John Busteed, Alfred, Michael Sheehan (lord mayor), John F. Burke (chief inspector, department of education), Fr Jerome O'Leary. *Back row:* Patrick J. O'Brien, Maurice Walsh, Patrick F. Parfrey, Con Connolly, David Daly (C.E.O., City of Cork V.E.C.), Augustine Weldon (principal of Cork School of Commerce), James Barry

business must be subordinated to human welfare, and God must be over all.'[11]

Alfred indicated what that policy entailed for the worker in a lecture 'Christ, the brother of the worker', delivered to the annual Catholic Truth Society of Ireland Congress in Tuam, County Galway, on 29 June 1936.[12] He described the early Christian Church as worker spreading to workers the new message, the fishers of Galilee became the fishers of men. Christ gave a social test of religion: 'By this shall all men know that you are my disciples; that you have love one for another.' And when it was objected that ignorant workers were incapable of appreciating religious truth 'an early apologist' said that 'among us you will find unlettered people, manual workers and old women who, if they are unable in words to prove the benefit of our doctrine, yet by their deeds show the benefit arising from their persuasion of its truth'. The message of Christian brotherhood, he continued, was to be found in the gospels, the traditional teaching of the Church and the social encyclicals of the popes. He ended with a challenge and a warning:

> It is for us – citizens, voters, legislators, workers – to implement and apply it in ways suitable to our special conditions. Our power is far greater and our responsibility far heavier than in the days of the early Church. We cannot, we dare not shirk the task; for if we do, there are others who will not. There are false Christs proclaiming false brotherhood; while we sleep, the enemy is sowing tare in our wheat-field.

In addresses to trade-union gatherings Alfred indicated how he considered that the Christian ideal could be translated into practice at the work-place. One such gathering was held on the eve of the annual meeting of the Irish Trade Union Congress in Cork in the last week of July 1932. Before it opened, the Cork branch of the Irish Transport and General Workers' Union entertained delegates of the union from all over Ireland. Alfred addressed them, pointing out that the country's population was

11. *Irish Press* 20 June 1932.
12. *Cork Examiner* 30 June 1936; *Standard* 3 July 1936. He published an expanded version of the lecture as a C.T.S.I. pamphlet *Christ, the brother of the worker* in 1936.

increasing and that to cope with the increase a system other than the capitalist one should be organised. To that end, it was imperative that workers be educated, particularly their leaders. For some time workers from Cork had been attending the Catholic Workers' College at Oxford. It was the responsibility of labour leaders to see that there was such a summer school in Ireland which would be attended by labour people to be educated expressly for the movement. In the light of the economic situation throughout the world he expressed his conviction that the only solution to the crisis was to be found in guilds composed of employers and employees. At every level both socialism and nationalism were less than satisfactory. They meant no more than one or other set of politicians attempting to run things. For them the ideal to be sought was communal control, whereby a real Christian family spirit would be introduced into industry.[13]

At a subsequent reception at U.C.C. for all the congress delegates, organised and chaired by Alfred, he declared that it was Labour's first duty 'to look after their own people'. He pleaded for the adoption of a policy establishing guilds in the primary industries, whereby workers and employers would come together on a council and jointly control the working of an industry, with a judge at the head to represent the community. The government had adopted this scheme partially with regard to the flour-milling industry. He feared, however, that this experiment would not be successful because it was only a partial implementation of the scheme. It was important that the trade-union movement ensured that this pilot scheme was a success so that the guild system could thereafter be applied to boot and shoe, woollen, cement and other industries.[14]

Apart from occasionally sharing his Christian blue-print for industrial organisation with labour and trade-union leaders from other parts of the country, Alfred regularly urged it on members of the Cork Workers' Council. His enthusiasm in so doing was exceptional. Presumably on the assumption that a picture is worth a thousand words, during his address at the annual reunion of members of the Council in February 1936 he

13. *Cork Examiner* 26 July 1932.
14. *Cork Evening Echo* 30 July 1932. See also *Cork Examiner* 26 July 1932. For more on the milling guild proposed by Alfred, see J. A. Gaughan, *Alfred O'Rahilly II: Public figure*, 320, 482.

promised to present to them a picture of 'Christ and the workers' for their Council Chamber. The promise was fulfilled at the same function on 30 January 1937. Alfred's influence was clear in the opening address of the Council's chairman, Jeremiah Hurley, on that occasion. Alfred was unable to be present and Professor John Busteed made the presentation on his behalf. The picture, together with one of James Connolly, was displayed in the Council Chamber for many years afterwards.[15]

In the meantime Alfred continued to be involved in the ending of strikes. A bitter dispute between the National Federation of Building Trade Operatives (N.F.B.T.O.) and the Irish Transport and General Workers' Union (I.T.G.W.U.) concerning the recognition of members of the former union led to a ten-week strike in the Cork building industry. Alfred was requested by Councillor F. J. Daly, the lord mayor, to assist him in his efforts to settle it. The negotiations proved difficult and protracted, but eventually a settlement was reached, on 8 August 1930. In announcing it to the public Daly singled out Alfred for fulsome praise for his role.[16]

15. *Cork Examiner* 1 February 1937.

16. *Cork Examiner* 11 August 1930. The terms drafted by Alfred were:

'(1) The Builders' Association hereby recognise the N.F.B.T.O., its constituent union, all legitimate unions of building trades at present in Cork, and the Builders' Labourers' section of the I.T.G.W.U.

'(2) When a class of workers belong to two different recognised unions, all negotiations and arrangements concerning the wages and hours of this class shall be made with both unions jointly.

'(3) All disputes, including inter-union disputes affecting building operations, but excluding disputes concerning alterations in wages and hours, shall be referred for immediate decision to an arbitrator, who shall act with the following consulters: two from each union or body affected and four from the employers. For one year from this date, and thereafter until all the recognised unions and Builders' Association decide upon a successor, the arbitrator shall be the present lord mayor of Cork (F. J. Daly, H.C.), and in case of his absence, his nominee. On receiving notice from any of the interested parties, the arbitrator is to summon the tribunal within forty-eight hours, a decision is to be reached within a further forty-eight hours, and this will be valid, even if one of the interested parties fails to attend. Pending a decision, the work in dispute is to stop.

'(4) Work to be resumed immediately and the ban to be removed from all black jobs. At the request of the lord mayor, no question of wages arises at this juncture.

'(5) The N.F.B.T.O. and the I.T.G.W.U. to agree to an investigation by the national executive of the Irish Trade Union Congress, if such an investigation be called for in accordance with the machinery provided above' (ibid.).

Just over a year and a half later, in the first week of April 1932, there was a critical dispute in the Fordson factory in Cork. The management announced that the wages of about 400 men would be cut by ten per cent. The workers downed tools. Henry Ford and his senior colleagues sent word that in the event of a continuation of the strike the plant would be transferred to another location. To avoid such a major economic setback to the city, Lord Mayor Daly, T. P. Dowdall, T.D., and Alfred intervened. Alfred had to exercise all his influence with the labour and trade-union leadership in Cork to have them persuade the Fordson workers to resume work, after a stoppage of only one day, while negotiations proceeded. Eventually he persuaded the workers, in effect, that in the circumstances then prevailing there was no choice other than to accept for the most part the original terms imposed by the management.[17]

Champion of the ex-tramwaymen

Probably the group of workers most indebted to Alfred for championing their cause were the ex-tramwaymen. The unfortunate predicament in which they found themselves began with the establishment of the Electricity Supply Board (E.S.B.) Under the Electricity (Supply) Act, which became law in August 1927, the E.S.B. assumed responsibility for providing lighting for Cork city. In so doing, it acquired the Cork Lighting Company, which had provided the city with lighting and a tram service. Some of the company's power workers were to be employed by the E.S.B., the rest were to be compensated for the loss of their jobs. The company's tramwaymen proposed the running of trackless trolley buses, but vested interests and legal disabilities led to this being rejected.

Under the Electricity (Supply) Act the E.S.B. was not obliged to pay compensation to the ex-tramwaymen and did not do so. Their plight became a live local issue. Cork Corporation proposed that those who supplied buses for hire in the city, in lieu of the trams, should pay an annual amount towards compensating the disemployed tramwaymen, but this was rejected by the government. Representatives of the ex-tramwaymen then proposed that compensation should be levied on the Cork area of charge by the E.S.B. This was approved by Cork Corporation

17. *Cork Examiner* 8 April 1932.

and by the government. However, the city's chamber of commerce had expressed strong opposition to the proposal and it was subsequently rejected by the government.

In the campaigning during the general election held on 16 February 1932 representatives of all parties promised to deal with the problem. The new minister for industry and commerce, Seán Lemass, met a deputation of ex-tramwaymen and declared that he intended to do something before the men died of slow starvation. He intimated that he had a scheme and asked for information on how much Cork Corporation might be willing to contribute from the rates, conditional on the scheme meeting with approval. The corporation agreed provisionally to contribute an amount not exceeding the addition to the rates of 3d in the pound for twenty years.

The decision of the corporation was communicated to Lemass but no acknowledgement or any other correspondence was received from him or his department for some months. Then the anxious tramwaymen heard unofficially that consideration of their case had been postponed indefinitely. In desperation they turned to Alfred. At the urgent request of Jeremiah Hurley, N.T., chairman of the Cork Workers' Council, and a member of Cork Corporation, he took up their case. On behalf of the ex-tramwaymen, he insisted on having a formal reply from Lemass. This came in the form of a new offer by the minister which Alfred rejected.

Accompanied by T. P. Dowdall, T.D., Jeremiah Hurley, N.T., and a deputation of ex-tramwaymen, Alfred addressed a meeting of the corporation on 16 August 1932. Showing a mastery of his brief, he gave a detailed account of all aspects of the case up to that time. He set out the reasons why he was convinced of the justice of the ex-tramwaymen's claim to compensation.[18]

18. *Cork Examiner* 17 August 1932. He claimed that the Cork Lighting Company had been under a contractual obligation to provide, even at a loss, a tram service for the city, the lighting of which was entrusted to it only under those express conditions. When the Oireachtas passed the Electricity (Supply) Act 1927 no cognisance was taken of such conditions. The Act made void the contract of the Cork Lighting Company and enabled the E.S.B. to take over responsibility for lighting the city and to drop the company's liability to provide transport. Thereby, without consultation or compensation, the citizens were deprived of rights they had acquired and the tramwaymen were deprived of their livelihood. This, he argued, was particularly unjust. The tram service was

He criticised the new scheme proposed by Lemass, whereby a lump sum was to be paid to each employee with not less than twenty years service, as 'exceedingly mathematical and inhuman'. Under it a man with 19.9 years of service would get nothing. He recalled that in a former resolution the corporation had, in effect, agreed to grant an annual sum of between £2,000 and £3,000. He now proposed that it should provide £1,500 a year, at an extra rate of 2d. in the pound, for twenty years and that the government should contribute another £1,500 a year over the same period. This would ensure the distribution of £40,000 among the employees who had five years service and upwards. He claimed that this was a relatively small sum in the circumstances and a lot less than the minister had initially indicated would be available. In a typical riposte he regretted that with regard to his first tentative proposal it would appear that 'Mr Lemass has had one of those attacks of loss of memory which close contact with highly-paid civil servants in Dublin seems to induce at times in ministers'.

A motion drafted by Alfred and setting out his proposal was passed by Cork Corporation.[19] Lemass, however, improved his scheme only marginally and had it incorporated in a proposed Compensation Bill. This prompted Alfred to bring his campaign for the ex-tramwaymen before practically every public and political body in Cork, where he had resolutions demanding

a necessary and integral part of the concern which generated electricity. The company's right to generate electricity depended on their employing tramwaymen to supply transport. When it ceased to generate electricity, the tramwaymen lost their employment in the same way as the generating men. Therefore the tramwaymen had the same right to compensation as had been admitted in the case of men in the generating stations (ibid.).

19. The motion read as follows:

'(1) We reiterate our view that, owing to the special contractual relationship existing in Cork between lighting and transport, the disemployed tramwaymen are as entitled to compensation as the men in generating stations; (2) our previous proposals having failed, we now accept the principle laid down by the minister for industry and commerce that compensation should be provided by the government and by the corporation conjointly; (3) we propose that the corporation should be empowered to levy a special rate of 2d in the pound for twenty years, producing approximately £1,500 per annum. We propose that the government out of general revenue should provide an equal amount; (4) we propose that the distribution of this fund, whether capitalised or not, should be administered by a small Advisory Committee under the authority of the minister, and that the distribution be guided by considerations of equity and humanity after investigation of the individual case' (ibid.).

fair-play passed. He drafted a formal petition to de Valera, the president of the executive council, to this end and had it signed by twenty of the twenty-one members of Cork Corporation, the four deputies from the Cork city constituency and scores of leading business people. However, Lemass and his department were unmoved. At that stage, prompted by Alfred, seven of the ex-tramwaymen set out on a Jarrow-style hunger march to Dublin. The seven represented seventy ex-tramwaymen excluded from benefit under the proposed bill. They set out for Dublin on 4 June 1933 to appeal personally to the leaders of all the political parties. During press interviews they stressed that, while they and their colleagues were struggling to live on Home Assistance, the share-holders of the Cork Lighting Company had been generously compensated to the extent of 30 shillings for every pound share. At the same time Alfred was privately urging the ex-tramwaymen's case on de Valera and Frank Gallagher, editor of the *Irish Press*, both of whom had good reason to feel indebted to him.

Eventually Lemass and his department had no choice but to concede in good grace the compensation fair-minded observers considered to be long overdue.[20] On 25 January 1934 at a euphoric meeting in the chamber of the Cork Workers' Council Alfred was presented with a silver cup. The thrust of all the speeches was that it was his intervention and assistance which ensured that the ex-tramwaymen's struggle for justice ended in success. References were made to the honour Alfred had won for his country at the International Labour Organisation Conference in Geneva. He savoured the occasion and made a characteristic reply, insisting that, while he was grateful for the compliments and presentation, he had simply done his duty, was a working man himself and was always going to be a Pat Murphy.[21]

20. Ibid.; *Cork Examiner* 5 June 1933; O'Rahilly Papers: Scrapbook I, press-cuttings.

21. *Cork Evening Echo* 26 January 1934. On the same occasion presentations were made to Jeremiah Hurley and Eoin O'Mahony, B.L., both of whom had also been active in the ex-tramwaymens' cause. A friend received O'Mahony's, as he was 'unavoidably absent' (ibid.). It is likely that O'Mahony did not attend the meeting as he did not wish to be present at the 'crowning of Alfred'. The two did not have much regard for each other. Alfred regarded O'Mahony was an Anglophile, a notorious snob and a trifler, and the two clashed in public on a number of occasions. Alfred's first public shaft at O'Mahony was contained in the following letter in the *Cork Examiner* of 24 October 1930:

6. Group at Cork Workers' Council annual dinner on 20 February 1950. *Front, left to right:* Seán McCarthy (lord mayor), Senator Richard S. Anthony, Alfred, Con Connolly (trades council), Professor John Busteed. *Back row:* T. Healy (4th from left), W. O'Neill (6th from left), J. Delaney (8th from left)

Ends many strikes

At the end of the same year Alfred was requested by a priest friend to help end a strike in the Cork victualling firm of John O'Flynn. Initially both parties agreed to his mediation. Soon after Alfred had begun examination of the case the proprietor indicated that he no longer wished him to mediate in the matter. Alfred, however, completed his report and sent a copy to the proprietor and a copy to the secretary of the Cork Trades' Council. In the columns of the *Cork Examiner* Mr O'Flynn complained about this action and alleged that Alfred was attempting to exert unfair pressure on him. Probably because the *Cork Examiner* was also a family business, the editor refused to publish Alfred's version of events or a summary of his report on the case. Eventually in a letter published in the *Irish Press* Alfred criticised the conduct of the *Cork Examiner* and gave a summary of the conclusion of his report.[22] In the *Irish Press* John O'Flynn rejected Alfred's 'wail' and claimed that, in the event, he was wise to have rejected Alfred's mediation, as it was 'obvious that he had pre-judged the case'.[23]

'It is a pleasure to note in your issue of today that, notwithstanding the obscurantist efforts of the Catholic bishops and others, clever boys of this city are not hampered by having to come to University College, Cork. In your news item you announce that "C. J. Pelly, of Clongowes Wood College and Trinity College, Dublin", has entered the Indian civil service, and that Mr Eoin O'Mahony, also of Clongowes Wood College, is auditor of Trinity College Historical Society. There are several other Cork Catholics who have found T.C.D. more congenial for their sons than U.C.C. A complete list might be helpful to other parents, whose ambition is dissatisfied with our local institution.'

One of O'Mahony's endearing qualities was a capacity for telling memorable and irreverent anecdotes about 'the great and the good' which often caused considerable offence. Throughout his life O'Mahony particularly enjoyed debunking Alfred. After attending the funeral of Alfred's wife, he described to a mutual friend how Alfred was 'howling with grief' during much of the proceedings. He added: 'Of course that is always the case when a husband or wife lose a partner with whom they have been fighting all their lives' (interview with Thomas J. McElligott). Alfred's assessment of Eoin O'Mahony was somewhat unfair. While the latter was generally regarded as an erratic, at times exasperating and an amusing individual, he was, above all, a kindly eccentric. Known as the Pope O'Mahony, because he was 'infallible', knowing all the answers in his class in school, he was the butt of many practical jokes. Selected to contest an election, a colleague had him canvassing in an area outside his constituency! In political circles he was seen as 'a patron of lost causes'.

22. *Irish Press* 20 September 1933.
23. *Irish Press* 23 September 1933.

Alfred's inevitable reply included the following:

> ... I have been connected with the settlement of
> industrial disputes in Cork for twenty years, and never
> before has my impartiality been impugned ... The plain
> issue is the following. I hold that Messrs O'Flynn are bound
> in justice (1) to recognise the men's union as entitled to con-
> duct collective negotiations; (2) to observe the conditions
> accepted by all their competitors. Messrs O'Flynn refuse to
> recognise the Butchers' Society and have tried to smash it;
> they claim the arbitrary, unrestricted right to order their
> men to disobey the registered rules of their union. They
> refuse to agree to the six days' holiday granted by every
> other victualler in Cork. And when I asked them for their
> reasons they replied: 'We refuse to be bullied'.[24]

After this exchange, a settlement along the lines proposed by
Alfred was reached between Mr O'Flynn and his employees.

In the fourth week of August 1934 Alfred intervened to help
end a strike in Waterford. He did so at the joint request of Monsignor William Byrne, parish priest of Ballybricken in the city,
and the mayor, Alderman William Jones. The strike initially was
by builders' labourers, but eventually all building workers,
including plumbers and painters, became involved.[25] Towards
the end of April and at the beginning of May 1935 Alfred chaired
meetings between the Cork city manager and representatives of
eight trade-unions, to whom the municipal workers, then
threatening to strike, belonged. He facilitated an amiable settlement of the matter at issue.[26] At a meeting of the Cork Workers'
Council a week later the secretaries of the various unions, which
had been involved in the threatened strike, vied with each other
in lauding Alfred for his part in bringing about an agreement.[27]

24. *Irish Press* 25 September 1933.
25. *Cork Examiner* 22 August 1934.
26. *Cork Examiner* 3 May 1935.
27. *Cork Examiner* 11 May 1935. (See also *Cork Examiner* 27 Janaury 1936.)
This occasioned the following fanfare from Alfred in the *Cork Examiner*:
'Sir, I am sorry my friends in the Workers' Council gave my name a prominence it did not deserve. Any credit for the friendly settlement is due to the city
manager and to the workers. With one unfortunate exception, we in Cork have
of recent years succeeded in settling our disputes without causing unnecessary
suffering or dislocation of business. I hope that we shall continue to give this
good example to the rest of the country' (*Cork Examiner* 13 May 1935).

Shop-assistants were among the poorest paid workers in Cork. True to character Alfred was particularly supportive of them and their union, the Cork branch of the Distributive Workers. In August 1935 he facilitated a settlement of a strike of assistants in the retail boot and shoe shops in the city. Alfred, it seems, had during the year also helped in other less-publicised disputes involving members of the union. The thirty-fourth annual report of the Cork branch of the union for the year ended 31 December 1935 concluded: 'We wish to pay a tribute to Professor O'Rahilly for the interest he has taken and the precious time he has donated to the settlement of disputes. The best tribute that could be paid to him is to say that he has always been accepted as an arbitrator both by the employers and the workers.' In a reply to the report Alfred, who was guest speaker at the branch's annual general meeting, stated that the union had always stood by the weaker class of the community, the exploited worker. He hoped that the members of the union would not for one moment turn their backs on that principle. The real shopkeeper was the person who treated his employees as Christians. They had not voted for tariffs nor had they voted to protect their frontiers to put profits into the pockets of pro-fiteers or to raise sweat shops for young girls who should be at home. He hoped that they would continue the spirit for which Cork had been justly praised and ensure that they never became so respectable as to cease to belong to a trade union.[28]

In May 1936 Alfred, at the request of both parties, was appointed arbitrator in a dispute between Sunbeam Wolsey & Co. Ltd and three of the company's travellers. His adjudication was accepted in writing by both sides. Then on 11 June Cork Trades' Council and the Travellers' Federation complained that his award was being evaded and requested him to investigate the matter. On the same day he asked the proprietor of the company, William Dwyer, to submit the matter to him and to suspend a lock-out of the travellers in the meantime. Dwyer refused but on the following day wrote promising the assistance of the company secretary in the investigation. He continued: 'If you examine our side of the case and having done so, if you consider that we have been unjust, I presume that you will say so.' This was a safe presumption on Dwyer's part. After due consideration Alfred informed Dwyer, the Cork Trades' Council

28. *Cork Evening Echo* 8 February 1936; *Cork Examiner* 10 February 1936.

and the Travellers' Federation that the initial award was being evaded, indicating that two clauses which the company were insisting on adding to a new contract conflicted substantially with it. He also had his adjudication published in the *Evening Echo* of 13 June 1936. He prefaced it by giving an account of the background to it and stated that it was the duty of an arbitrator to protest against any violation or evasion of his award. Some months earlier he recalled, the employer in a certain trade complained to him that the workers were 'boggling' at a decision he had given and he had taken effective steps to ensure acceptance of it. In the *Cork Examiner* of 20 June 1936 Dwyer formally accepted Alfred's decision and announced generous terms to his travellers on points not covered by it. Before concluding, however, he had a side-thrust at Alfred which the latter duly replied to in that same day's issue of the *Evening Echo*.[29]

Rejects compulsory arbitration

There were numerous and some very protracted strikes throughout the country as well as in Cork in 1933, 1934, 1935 and into 1936. Many people, apart from the government and its supporters, considered that the industrial situation was becoming so serious as to require a radical approach to the question of strikes. In one of the Cork University-Extension lectures at U.C.C. for 1935-36 the Reverend Professor Cornelius Lucey of St Patrick's College, Maynooth, proposed the introduction of compulsory arbitration. The lecture was published.[30] Lucey described compulsory arbitration as the system wherein the government compels all disputes in industry to be submitted to a special tribunal when the parties themselves have reached deadlock. The judicial award of this tribunal, he pointed out, is automatically binding on the management and employees concerned, just like the judicial award of a civil or criminal court. Strikes and lock-outs are illegal; to organise or take part in one would, therefore, be a punishable offence. He acknowledged that all fascist and communist States – Italy, Germany and the Soviet Union – had adopted that system, but, he argued, there was nothing distinctively fascist, communist, or totalitarian in

29. *Cork Evening Echo* 13, 20 June 1936; *Cork Examiner* 20 June 1936.
30. Cornelius Lucey, 'Strikes and compulsory arbitration', *Studies*, June 1936, 177-90.

compulsory arbitration. He pointed to its use in Australia, New Zealand, Norway and in Britain during world war one. He urged the introduction of such a system because of the Irish Free State's appalling record in industrial relations. He illustrated statistically the fact that strikes in the Free State invariably tended to be more frequent and about twice the length in duration than those in Britain. Another strong argument, he suggested, for compulsory arbitration was to cater for the lowest paid, such as farm labourers and others who had not the industrial muscle of more skilled workers.

Fr Patrick J. Connolly, S.J., appended to Lucey's article the comments of six persons, (1) Archdeacon John Kelleher, P.P., V.F.; (2) Alfred; (3) John O'Neill, president of the Dublin Chamber of Commerce; (4) Eamon Lynch, secretary of the Trade Union Congress; (5) Peter McCarthy, secretary of the Federation of Saorstát Industries; and (6) Bernard F. Shields, professor of commerce, U.C.D.[31] Next to Lynch, Alfred was the most adamant in his opposition to compulsory arbitration. He recalled that during the previous twenty years he had often acted as arbitrator and that, since Dr Lucey seven months earlier had read his article as a paper in U.C.C., he had acted in that capacity on no fewer than four occasions. He claimed that his views were shared by all the representatives of employers and employees with whom he had discussed the matter. His opposition to compulsory arbitration he then summarised as follows:

(1) I am not convinced that the system has been a success in other countries. I believe that its introduction here would be regarded by the vast majority of the workers as a piece of 'fascism' and would actually increase the influence of those subversive elements whose activities Dr Lucey deplores.

(2) Consideration of the plight of the unorganised rural workers seems to me to be quite irrelevant to the issue. The remedy for this is for the State to come to the rescue of these unfortunate workers, at present totally bereft of any collective bargaining power, much less of the capacity to strike.

(3) I see no analogy between the functions of the ordinary judicial courts and those of arbitration proceedings. In the

31. Ibid. 190-203.

former case we have a definite code with accepted principles of justice, which legal men can interpret and apply.
Whereas, according to my extensive experience, the worst
arbitrations are those in which lawyers intervene! There are
no fixed accepted principles – for example, concerning
fair rates of profit, the position of the employees in a business, the right and amount of a living wage, and so on –
and the arbitrator cannot indulge in the exegetic activities
of the legal mind. A broad humanity, wide experience of
actual business relations, knowledge of the real difficulties
and of the character of the men involved, the ability to
secure a working compromise which is compatible with
existing capitalism – to which I would like to add a good
supply of pachydermatous tissue – these are some of the
qualifications required in an arbitrator.

(4) Hence I would not anticipate much success from a
system of compulsory arbitration administered either by
bureaucrats or by lawyers. It would, in my opinion, merely
increase the discontent of the workers, and often would
irritate and shackle the employers. It is, I admit, deplorable
that we have not more of the clergy and laity, competent
and acceptable to both sides, who could and would intervene in industrial disputes. What we need is not to supersede voluntary arbitration or mediation – and the threat of
compulsion would have this effect – but to increase the
number of those willing and able to act as mediators and
arbitrators.

(5) As to inter-union disputes – the most difficult and bitter of all – the time has come to call upon organised Labour
to provide a systematic remedy. As a matter of fact, the
Trade Union Congress has just set up a special committee
for this purpose.

(6) I admit that strikes are no more an ideal method of
adjustment than is war. If we had a guild structure in our
economic life, in which the workers were recognised as
human beings and not merely as 'hands', in which they
were regarded as co-functionaries with employers in producing for the community, then indeed there would be
little reason for strikes. But, in my opinion, it would be
unjust and disastrous to inject the element of compulsion
into the present system (capitalism plus bureaucracy). It

would be tantamount to taking away from the workers their last vestige of liberty – a spiritual loss in distinction from the material damages on which the author dwells – without having *first* guaranteed, protected and organised their natural rights. A trade union is certainly not an ideal organisation of society. But I am not prepared to support any diminution whatever of its powers until not only I but trade unionists themselves proclaim their conviction that they have secured something better.[32]

In early July 1937 Alfred was requested to attempt a settlement of a bitter three-month long strike in the building industry in Cork. After protracted negotiations he succeeded in facilitating a settlement.

A year later Alfred was again involved as arbitrator in an equally bitter dispute, this time in the plastering trade in Cork city. The dispute originated when members of the Operative Plasterers' Trades Society, an Irish body, refused to work with members of the National Society of Operative Plasterers, an English union, the former asserting that according to the terms of their union they were forbidden to work with anybody but their own members. The Joint Industrial Council for the Building Trades, which was established following the six-months' strike in the building industry in 1937, supported the National Society of Operative Plasterers and the result was a lock-out of members of the rival union. After an arbitration, presided over by Alfred in Cork City Hall, the seventeen-week-old strike ended on 7 December 1938.[33]

Stand against abuse of industrial power by workers

By the 1940s the trade-union movement was well organised and adequately equipped to ensure justice for its members. At this time also the thrust of Alfred's adjudications began to change. Until then they included an unmistakeable bias in favour of workers. This Alfred was always able to justify to employers and the public at large by the unequal strength of

32. Ibid. 192-4. It is of interest to note that these views of Alfred proved acceptable to both trade unions and employers, and have had a significant influence on Irish industrial relations' practice ever since.
33. *Cork Examiner* 8 December 1938; *Cork Evening Echo* 9 December 1938.

employers *vis-à-vis* workers in industrial disputes. He always confronted any attempt by employers to exploit their position of strength whether by virtue of their monopoly position or by a successful lock-out. When in the 1940s sections of the work-force began to exploit their own new position of strength, to the detriment of social justice, they found him equally prepared to condemn this unjustifiable conduct with characteristic courage and integrity. In addition, despite life-long friendships, he used the most unequivocal language in laying the onus for dealing with such groups of workers on the trade-union leader-ship at local and national level.

The first strike in Cork in which Alfred took a strong public stand against workers began in early October 1942. Workers in the confectionery firm of Messrs F. H. Thompson and Sons Ltd. went on strike and were promptly locked out. After a stalemate lasting a month, both sides at the request of the president of the Cork Chamber of Commerce, C. F. Murphy, agreed to the case being submitted to arbitration by Alfred. When the confec-tioners had returned to work, Alfred, on 5 November, heard both sides arguing at length before him. His award was in the hands of both parties on 10 November and was to come into operation on 1 February.[34]

The sequel Alfred described as follows:

> I received no further communication from the workers until Monday, 25 January, when I received a note (dated 21st) from Mr Harrington, curtly repudiating my award and attributing to me the nefarious design of dissolving their Union. I at once demanded reasons for this high-handed action and challenged the union to a public debate. My offer still stands; and if and when the members of the union condescend to give reasons to their fellow workers and to the public to excuse the dishonouring of their written pledge and to substantiate the attack on my impartiality, I am prepared to justify myself to the citizens of Cork. Mean-while, the onus of explaining and justifying their conduct lies upon the Confectioners' Union.
>
> So far, except for the disedification caused by this immoral repudiation and its consequent effect on all future trade disputes in the city, the people of Cork would not be

34. *Cork Examiner* 28, 31 October, 6 November 1942; 28, 30 January 1943.

seriously inconvenienced. For after all, the confectionery business is really a luxury trade which the government might conceivably suppress altogether in wartime. The really serious issue, especially for the poor with limited fuel and gas supplies, arises out of the super-added threat conveyed in Mr Harrington's letter dated 21 January (and delivered on 23rd) to the Master Bakers. This is a declaration signed by Mr Christopher Fitzgerald, secretary of the Cork Bakers' Union, that, if the employers dare to put the award into operation on 1 February, or at any subsequent date, they will cease all production of bread in Cork city. These operative bakers took no part in the confectioners' strike, they did not appear at the arbitration, they have had no communication whatever with me. Moreover, they are bound by an entirely separate agreement with the Master Bakers, dated 18 October 1938, in which they agreed – Mr Christopher Fitzgerald being one of the signatories – that "all matters arising out of these conditions, or generally in the industry" should be dealt with by a joint standing committee. Repudiating this solemn printed agreement, terminating their neutrality concerning the strike and the negotiations, professing no grievance of their own, the men who produce our bread have now suddenly joined in declaring war on the people.

The workers in this luxury trade of confectionery, having failed in their arguments before an independent arbitrator, voluntarily chosen by themselves, decided to bully the employers into acceptance of conditions described by me as grossly unjust.

But fearing that they could not thus intimidate the public, they entered into an alliance with the operative bakers, whom they persuaded to butt in on a dispute with which they had nothing whatever to do. The public, especially the working class, would not feel the loss of cakes and buns so the confectioners decided to force their unjust demands by threatening to deprive us all of our daily bread. So determined were they that, before learning of the week's postponement granted by the Master Bakers at my request, officials of the Cork Operative Bakers' Trade Union ordered the foremen of several of our largest bakeries to refuse to bake any extra bread on Friday and Saturday.

They wanted to make quite sure that the pinch of hunger would really be felt by their fellow workers on next Monday.

Alfred publicly addressed the labour and trade-union leadership:

> We have another week in which labour has to decide whether it intends to keep its own house in order, in which the government has to determine whether this gigantic hold-up is to be permitted, in which we, the citizens of Cork, have to make our voice plainly heard as to whether we are going to submit to the truculent dictatorship of a small group of workers in a sheltered luxury trade which they even refuse to organise.
>
> I have stood all my life for the just demands of the workers, for the implementation of Catholic social principles. For over twenty years I have been gratuitously arbitrating in industrial disputes in this city. Never before has my integrity or impartiality been questioned. I owe it to the social principles for which I stand, to protest publicly against this attempt to sabotage all honourable and friendly settlements of trade disputes and to impose upon us a dictatorship which may have dire consequences in the future, if we now supinely acquiesce.[35]

There followed a flurry of activity. At Alfred's request, in the interests of the public and to obviate a stoppage of the city's bread supply, the Cork Master Bakers' Association, which represented the sixteen bakeries in the city, consented to defer for a week the operation of the award. In a letter to James Harrington, Alfred accused the Confectioners' Union of using its trade union status 'to bring anarchy and disorder into the workers' movement'. He protested to the Cork Trades' Council at 'this immoral and unjustifiable threat of a small sheltered section of labour in what is practically a luxury trade, abetted by the Operative Bakers in repudiating their pledged word'. He added: 'I hope the government, local labour leaders, the executive of the trade union concerned and the public finally will make it quite clear to this misguided section of labour that

35. *Cork Examiner* 30 January 1943.

it is not entitled to hold the public or the employers to ransom by intimidation in defiance of its plighted word'. He made all this correspondence available to the *Cork Examiner* which kept the public informed.[36]

In the meantime the Cork Chamber of Commerce and the Federated Union of Employers appealed to Seán Lemass, minister for industry and commerce, to intervene. He despatched the department's chief conciliation officer, Donal O'Sullivan, to deal with the urgent situation. Denis Cullen, general secretary of the Bakers' and Confectioners' Union, and local trade-union leaders, aware of the harm which could be done to the movement by a prolongation of the dispute, exerted considerable pressure on the strikers. A conference of all the parties involved was arranged for 4 February at the premises of the Cork Chamber of Commerce. The lord mayor, Richard S. Anthony, presided, flanked by Alfred and O'Sullivan. The strikers agreed to abide by Alfred's arbitration. To save face they requested that the award be deferred until 1 October 1943. The Cork Master Bakers' Association readily agreed to this.[37] Cork's business community heaved a collective sigh of relief and soon afterwards Alfred was honoured with life membership of the city's Chamber of Commerce.

At the beginning of September 1944, Alfred succeeded in

36. *Cork Examiner* 28, 30 January, 1 February 1943; *Irish Independent* 1 February 1943.

37. *Irish Independent* 1 February 1943; *Cork Examiner* 1, 5 February 1943. Alfred anonymously provided the following report on the satisfactory resolution of the matter for the *Standard* of 12 February 1943:

'The chief conciliation officer, Mr D. Sullivan – a Corkman with a fine record in Cork – went down from Dublin last week and managed to secure a settlement of what was likely to prove a nasty business and to do untold damage to Labour. The public – including trade unionists – was overwhelmingly in favour of the confectioners' acceptance of the arbitration award; public morality simply had to be vindicated. Luckily the men gave in; and the employers, by reliable report a very decent set of men, agreed to postpone the operation of the award until October 1 so as to give the union time to organise the confectionery establishments now employing non-union female labour at unknown wages.

'Denis Cullen, general secretary of the Bakers and Confectioners' Union, was very keen on observance of the award. He told a *Standard* correspondent that he was in Geneva when the arbitrator (Prof. A. O'Rahilly) was chairman of the Committee on the Abolition of Night Work in Bakeries and that Mr Curtin, the present premier of Australia, was a member of the Commission and a great backer of the Professor.'

settling a bitter dispute at Ballyclough Creamery, near Mallow. The strike was in its fifth week when a curate in the neighbouring parish of Glanworth, Father John O'Brien, persuaded the workers, management and creamery committee to accept Alfred as arbitrator. Before considering the case Alfred insisted on the strikers returning to work and a week later both sides accepted the settlement terms he proposed.[38]

In the first week of June 1945 Alfred was involved in ending two strikes. Cork's municipal workers had stopped work because the corporation employed two labourers who were not members of their union, namely, the I.T.G.W.U. At the request of Alfred and Fr James Bastible, the men resumed work and in accordance with an agreement of November 1935 submitted the issue to arbitration by Alfred. At the same time, again after an initiative by him and Fr Bastible, he was acting as arbitrator in a 'Cork Vanmen's dispute'. This arose from a claim by bread-van drivers and their indoor colleagues for a fortnight's holiday with pay. For his convenience it was agreed that Alfred conduct the arbitration in the Staff House of U.C.C. Representatives of the City of Cork Master Bakers' Association, the I.T.G.W.U., the Irish Master Bakers' Association and the Federation of Employers presented submissions and soon afterwards his adjudication, favourable to the workers, was accepted.[39]

Labour Court

With the ending of the war and the impending lifting of the emergency control of wages which had obtained since 1941, the government feared that there would be widespread industrial conflict as the trade unions sought to recover the ground lost during the period of wartime control. To avert such a conflict or at least diminish it, Seán Lemass, minister for industry and commerce, had the Industrial Relations Act 1946 passed. It was largely an agreed measure, accepted by both the congresses into which the trade-union movement had then divided and by the Federated Union of Employers. It provided for the establishment of a Labour Court as an independent body on which workers and employers had equal representation and whose recommendations could be accepted or rejected by the parties

38. *Cork Examiner* 26 August 1944.
39. *Cork Examiner* 25, 28 May, 9 June 1945; *Cork Evening Echo* 7 June 1945.

to the dispute. The court consisted of two employer-members and two employee-members, with R. J. P. Mortished as chairman and Francis Vaughan Buckley, S.C., as deputy chairman. It reached its decisions by majority vote and differences of opinion among members were not revealed. While the decisions reflected the court's concern with constraints imposed by the public interest, Mortished, a life-long labour and trade-union activist, ensured that the worker's viewpoint was not neglected.

The first meeting of the Labour Court was held on 23 September 1946. During the following five months all but a few of its recommendations were accepted.[40] During those early months of the operation of the court, however, members of the Irish Transport and General Workers' Union in the countrywide sugar-beet industry, in the Cork Gas Consumers' Company, in the Cork Yeast Company and in the Cork Distilleries Company rejected the recommendations of the court.[41]

Settlement of disputes at Cork Distilleries Company, Cork Gas Company and Cork Yeast Company

The industrial situation in Cork in the third week of February 1947 was dire. Two hundred and fifty employees of the Cork Gas Consumers' Company decided to go on strike on 22 February. Employees of the Cork Yeast Company and of the Cork Distilleries Company were already on strike. The action of the workers in the Cork Yeast Company had the potential of causing extraordinary hardship to the people of the city and the country at large. The company supplied the yeast used in all the bakeries in the country. To compound the situation a pending strike at Liverpool docks made it unlikely that the supply required countrywide could be imported from elsewhere. Political representatives of all parties and even the trade-union

40. Charles McCarthy, *Trade unions in Ireland 1894-1960* (Dublin 1977) 375 and ff. See also J. A. Gaughan, *Thomas Johnson (1872-1963): first leader of the Labour Party in Dáil Éireann* (Dublin 1980) 387-9.

41. After the failure of the Labour Court to settle the dispute in the sugar-beet industry, on 6 December 1946 Eamon O'Neill, T.D. for the constituency of Cork West, sought the help of Alfred, who agreed to go to Mallow at once and start trying to effect a basis of agreement between the parties involved. Although this offer was published in the *Cork Examiner* on the following day, it was not availed of (*Cork Examiner* 7 December 1946).

leadership in Cork failed to persuade those involved to make any move towards a settlement.[42]

In a letter in the *Cork Examiner* Alfred appealed to the workers and employers involved in the industrial disputes. To the workers he declared:

> I have never wavered in my support for the right to strike; I have used against Communism the argument that it does not and cannot admit this right. But this right is not unlimited or absolute. It should be used with due consideration for the interests of the public; and only in the last extremity should it be exercised when it involves widespread and serious hardship, especially on the poor. A continuance of the stoppage of yeast will mean the cessation of commercial baking throughout Ireland.
>
> The cutting-off of gas in the city will deprive most people of the chance of baking or cooking at home. And the crisis will come upon us when there is already general suffering due to the severe weather and the fuel shortage.
>
> Surely, there can be no comparison between the grievances, however real, of the small number of workers directly involved and the widespread distress which these two strikes involve.
>
> Therefore, I feel justified in appealing to the men to defer action and to give an opportunity for further discussion and consideration. Such a decision will redound to the credit and to the sense of responsibility of labour; I feel sure that the gesture will not be misinterpreted as a sign of weakness or as a withdrawal of their claims.

He appealed to the employers to agree to further conferences, under the chairmanship of himself or of someone else acceptable to both sides. The editorial in the same issue of the *Cork Examiner* incorporated Alfred's appeal. It highlighted his assertion that a continuation of the attitude of those concerned would result in 'an unnecessary infliction of widespread suffering on those who are least able to bear it and most deserve our sympathy'.[43]

At the request of the leaders of trade-union branches in Cork,

42. *Cork Examiner* 21, 25 February 1947.
43. *Cork Examiner* 21 February 1947.

I.T.G.W.U. employees of the Cork Yeast Company and the Cork Distilleries Company agreed to come to a meeting in Connolly Hall to hear a proposal by Alfred for a way out of the impasse. There was general dismay when, at that meeting, Alfred's offer of mediation was rejected. To increase public pressure on the trade-union movement in general and the striking yeast company and distillery workers in particular, he then issued the following statement to the press.

> This afternoon, accompanied by Rev. Dr Bastible, and with his support and concurrence, I attended a meeting in Connolly Hall of the yeast and distillery workers. I am interested not in the supply of gin but in the country's bread. Both categories of workers, however, form one section and vote as a unit.
>
> I proposed that the men and girls on strike should, without withdrawing their claim, go back to work for the present, in order to avoid inflicting on the entire country, especially on working-class families, the hardship of a deprivation of bread during the present severe weather and fuel shortage. I promised that, if they did so, I would impartially investigate their claim and take up the issue with their employers. On a ballot vote, my proposal was rejected by 94 votes to 37.
>
> This decision relieves me of an offer which I made with considerable qualms, as it was tantamount to reconsidering, and, perhaps, revising, the decision of the Labour Court. This court was established by parliament, with the full approval of the Labour Parties and of the trade unions; and no one can say that its constitution is biased against the workers. It is not claimed that its awards are binding; also, being a human institution, it does not pretend to be infallible. But it is universally admitted that, after the removal of the wages ceiling, such a court was indispensable, if the country were to avoid runaway inflation and irresponsible stoppages, if the conditions of labour were to be improved with orderly progression and without anarchic pressure-campaigns by privileged sections of workers.
>
> We expect the employers to accept the decisions of the court, even if they loudly proclaim their dissatisfaction; and there would be an angry outburst if they did not give effect

to disagreeable awards, at least for a fair period of trial. I cannot see why action which would be reprehensible in employers should not be equally condemned in the case of workers.

But the main argument I used against the strike was much more fundamental. Having on many previous occasions taken the side of labour, I feel it to be my duty on this occasion to give public expression to my considered conviction that the present exercise of the right to strike by the yeast workers is unjustified. It accidentally happens that about sixty workers – apparently including a number of young girls – in Cork have temporarily the power to deprive three million people of bakers' bread, which for the vast majority means a complete deprivation of bread. About thirty tons of yeast per week were being supplied to the country from Cork. In the absence of this supply, about ten tons were procurable from the United Yeast Co., but, if the Liverpool strike comes off, this import will be cut off and no more bakers' bread can be made. It is conceivable that if the yeast operatives were in extreme necessity they would be justified, after due notice to the public, to cease work and to shut down this essential service. But in actual fact the workers' grievance, which remains after the substantial increase awarded to them, is concerned with only 10% of their monetary wages.

I am passing no judgment on this grievance, for I have been given no opportunity of investigating it. But I do emphatically say this grievance, alleged in spite of the verdict of the Labour Court, is utterly trivial in comparison with the hardship now being deliberately inflicted on the entire working class. I say 'deliberately', for my proposal was not to renounce the strike but only to defer action which, if still considered necessary, could be taken later on when the present severe crisis has passed.

In spite of my appeal backed by Rev. Dr Bastible and approved by responsible trade union leaders, a handful of workers in Cork have decided to assert their monopoly of power, to avail of the national crisis to inflict great hardship, which is shortly to be accentuated in Cork by the action of their fellow workers in the gas industry. If in similar circumstances a few employers had decided to shut down an essential industry, what protests and denunciations we should hear from labour.

Why should a small section of workers assume that, without even submitting their claims to impartial inquiry, they are entitled to hold the country up to ransom by the accidental fact that they have a stranglehold on our yeast and that the suffering they can inflict will be intensified by the severe weather and the shortage of fuel and gas? They are actually looking forward to the country being without bread in a week's time, so that they may obtain ten shillings extra per week.

In the interests of the community, of responsible labour, even of this Cork industry, I publicly protest against this unjustifiable action, as a reckless and anti-social misuse of a national monopoly, which is, unfortunately, in the hands of a handful of workers who failed to produce a single argument against the proposal I put to them.

Alfred's statement was carried in whole or in part in most newspapers ranging in time from the *Cork Examiner* of 25 February to the *Standard* of 7 March 1947.

In an unsigned editorial also in the *Standard* of 7 March, headed 'Labour Court and Strikes', Alfred gave an admirable summary of the working of the Labour Court, stated that the crucial difficulty in industrial relations was the exercise of the right to strike in industries which were national or municipal monopolies and emphasised the need for a sense of responsibility on the part of such workers. He urged an educational campaign to impress on workers the principle that not every exercise of the right to strike was morally justifiable. In his illustration of the need for this, he obviously had the current situation in Cork in mind. He called on labour and trade-union leaders to exercise greater responsibility and authority and warned that, if they did not, the hard-pressed consuming public could take restrictive measures against those small sections of workers who had power to inflict grave injury on the community.[44]

By mid-March the proprietors of the Cork Yeast Company were taking steps to transfer the industry from Cork. This prompted Alfred and Fr James Bastible to write to Patrick J.

44. For the full text of the editorial, see Appendix 1.

O'Brien, a local leader of the I.T.G.W.U., proposing that both sides should make a determined effort to settle the dispute and rehabilitate the yeast industry which was in serious danger of extinction in Cork. The letter quoted section 70 of the Industrial Relations Act 1946, which envisaged a trade dispute being submitted to the arbitration of one or more persons. Alfred and Bastible proposed that both sides should request the Labour Court to ask them to act as arbitrators in the dispute. On 20 March O'Brien, who was a life-long friend of Alfred, urged acceptance of the proposal at a meeting of the strikers and they did so unanimously. The employers also agreed to it. Within ten days of the resumption of work, Alfred and Bastible delivered the result of their arbitration and it was accepted by both sides.[45]

The gas workers subsequently agreed to refer their outstanding claims and grievances to Alfred. He delivered his report on 29 March and it was accepted at a meeting of the workers on the following day. It proposed (1) A modification of the Labour Court recommendations by an investigating committee acting as arbitrators and (2) A registered agreement eliminating all strikes for a minimum period of two years. After some prevarication the directors of the Cork Gas Consumers' Company declared that they would not accept the new settlement terms worked out by Alfred and would insist on abiding by the recommendations of the Labour Court. They explained their stand by stating that if the company was to concede the workers' present demands, or to agree to any compromise, or even to the intervention of third parties with this object in view, this would amount to a repudiation of the Labour Court.

With characteristic impartiality Alfred publicly criticised both parties to the dispute. He reminded the workers of the hardship being caused to the community, particularly to the families of fellow workers. He regretted their rejection of his appeal not to call out the men heating the retorts. This meant that even after a settlement was reached it would not be possible to supply gas to the public for three weeks. By such conduct they merely alienated public opinion still further. He called on the employers to recognise the paramount rights of consumers and the public at large and regretted that they were unable to accept his proposals, as within the previous week they had offered the

45. *Standard* 21 March 1947.

71

workers a wage increase exceeding that which would have satisfied both sides in early March. Soon afterwards under the pressure of public opinion both sides compromised and reached a settlement on virtually the terms proposed by Alfred.[46]

Assists the farm labourers

Because of considerable aggravation which he suffered during the gas and yeast workers' strikes, Alfred confided to his close friends that he would never again become involved in an industrial dispute.[47] This, however, was not to be the case. With the lifting of the wartime freeze on salaries and wages, farm labourers, like other workers, sought an improvement in their wages and working conditions. They were among the lowest paid and had little industrial bargaining strength. In County Cork their demands were ignored by farmers. After a number of threats of industrial action the committee of the Cork County branch of the Federation of Rural Workers (F.R.W.) decided on 8 April 1947 to organise a strike, beginning a week later.[48] The representatives of the union considered it unlikely that they could conduct an effective strike. Daniel (Dan) Desmond, secretary of the Cork branch of the F.R.W., appealed to Alfred for help. After an initial perfunctory refusal, Alfred agreed. Desmond was a long-standing friend and Alfred, aware of the lack of industrial muscle of the farm labourers, considered that it would be shameful if they did not succeed in bettering their lowly wages and difficult working conditions.[49]

The F.R.W. issued notice of a strike by its members in County Cork in pursuit of a claim for a substantial increase of twelve shillings and six pence a week in their wages. Alfred, on the following day, 10 April, intervened by inviting the secretary of the Cork County Farmers' Association and a representative of the F.R.W. to a meeting to discuss the matter at issue. The F.R.W. accepted and withdrew the strike notice. However, the secretary of the Cork County Farmers' Association declined the invitation and explained that farm workers' wages were under

46. *Cork Examiner* 8 July 1947; O'Rahilly Papers: Scrapbook 5, press-cuttings.

47. Interview with Canon James P. Bastible.

48. *Cork Evening Echo* 9 April 1947; *Cork Examiner* 10, 23 april 1947.

49. Interview with Canon James P. Bastible.

the control of the Agricultural Wages Board which had the matter under consideration and added that 'in these circumstances we think it would be unwise for us to take any action that may anticipate or embarrass this Board'.[50]

A meeting of the Cork branch of the F.R.W. on 17 April considered this to be mere temporising and the strike was refixed to begin on 23 April.[51] On 19 April Alfred wrote to the secretary of the Agricultural Wages Board in Dublin. He informed him of the pending strike of the rural workers of County Cork and of his correspondence with the secretary of the Cork Farmers' Union. The latter had replied that there had recently been a meeting of the regional committee in Limerick and the question of adjusting minimum wages was to be settled by the board. Alfred continued: 'The workers' representative, however, has informed me that no decision will be given for several months and that his men are getting restive. I have, therefore, taken the liberty of writing to you to ask you to be good enough to hasten the new decision.' On 21 April the secretary of the Agricultural Wages Board replied that it was likely that a meeting of the board would be held within the next few weeks to consider the recommendations of the five Agricultural Wages Area Committees on the question of new minimum rates for agricultural workers.[52] This was not regarded as satisfactory by Dan Desmond nor, indeed, by Alfred. Once again Alfred intervened. At his request the F.R.W. strike was suspended, while he and Fr Jerome O'Leary, his assistant in the lectureship of sociology, went to Dublin and made direct representations to the minister for agriculture, with the object of ensuring that the Agricultural Wages Board would come to a speedy decision.

On 24 April Alfred wrote two letters to Patrick Smith, the minister for agriculture. In strong and emotive language he urged him to see that a speedy and equitable increase in wages was given to farm workers and asked that the minister should see him and Fr O'Leary on the matter by the following Monday, 29 April. Smith replied next day that the Agricultural Wages Board was to meet during the following week. He pointed out that this body possessed the statutory authority by an act of the Oireachtas to fix minimum rates of agricultural wages and that

50. *Cork Examiner* 12, 19, 23 April 1947.
51. *Cork Examiner* 19, 23 April 1947.
52. *Cork Examiner* 23 April 1947.

he, as minister for agriculture, had no function in the determination of such questions. Consequently, he suggested, there was
no reason why Alfred and Fr O'Leary should travel from Cork
to meet him. In any case, he declared, the Wages Board had
obtained recommendations from its five area committees and
should be able to arrive at a decision within a few days. With
Alfred as much as anyone else in mind, he concluded: 'Surely all
the interests concerned can muster sufficient patience to wait
that length of time.'[53]

The Cork Farmers' Association, the various boards involved
and Smith resented Alfred's collusion with Desmond and his
F.R.W. colleagues in urging that the increase in wages
demanded by farm workers be given. Nor did they appreciate
the fact that Alfred exerted pressure on them throughout by
having his correspondence on the matter published. Conversely, Desmond and the F.R.W. were very pleased. From a
vague promise to have their wages demand considered within
months, they had their demand effectively conceded and not
merely for their members in County Cork but, as they had
hoped, countrywide.

The last strike which Alfred attempted to settle was a long
drawn-out dispute in the butchers' trade. He was at Mungret
College, outside Limerick, in August 1949 for the annual rural
week organised by Muintir na Tíre, at which he was to deliver
one of the major addresses. His friend, Canon John Hayes,
founder of Muintir na Tíre, appealed to him to see both sides in
the dispute. He agreed. However, it seems he no longer had the
patience or sensitivity[54] necessary for delicate industrial
negotiations and it was left to Canon Hayes to persuade both
sides to make the concessions which facilitated a settlement.
Stephen Rynne, biographer of Canon John Hayes, gave an
unsympathetic, although probably accurate, account of Alfred's

53. *Cork Examiner* 24, 26, 29 April 1947.
54. These were not the only qualities which Alfred had brought to industrial
negotiations. Two years earlier a columnist had written: 'Dr. O'Rahilly . . . has
a wonderful reputation in Cork and elsewhere for his sterling work in settling
industrial disputes. He is a prodigious worker. I am told that his capacity to concentrate, despite surrounding distractions, is something beyond belief. This
report comes to me from a man who saw him sit down in a corner of a crowded
room, in which people were talking loudly, and produce a detailed report of
one of Cork's more famous strikes. Not one correction of that report was
required' (*Times Pictorial* 15 November 1947).

final involvement in industrial arbitration. He recalled that representatives of the employers and of the butchers were accommodated in separate rooms. Alfred went to one group, Canon Hayes to another. Rynne continued: 'Sunk in Thomism and learned in Catholic social principles, the professor confused his hearers with extracts from the encyclicals of Popes Leo XIII and Pius IX. No one listened. He was outraged. "There is no use talking to them," he said. But Fr Hayes fixed the dispute.'[55]

55. Stephen Rynne, *Father John Hayes, founder of Muintir na Tíre; people of the land* (Dublin 1960) 219-20. The fact that this was the last dispute in which Alfred became involved was due only partially to his having become tired of such interventions. In the years after the establishment of the Labour Court, its officials became more and more skilful at settling disputes. They were also seen as having responsibility for continuing good relations between employers and workers not only in the enterprise in which a strike occurred but in every enterprise throughout the country. Both employers and trade-union leaders were acutely aware that the settlement of a strike by Alfred or some such individual often caused problems elsewhere and so were no longer eager for such initiatives. Thus, by 1949, when Alfred was persuaded to become involved in the butchers' strike, the role of the unattached independent mediator, which he had filled with such distinction for so long, had been superseded by the bipartite industrial relations service of the Labour Court.

IMPACT AT THE INTERNATIONAL LABOUR CONFERENCES OF 1924, 1925 AND 1932

Apart from his involvement in settling industrial disputes in Cork, Alfred won credit for his country and for himself when acting as the senior government delegate of the Irish Free State at the International Labour Organisation (I.L.O.) annual conferences at Geneva in 1924, 1925 and 1932. The I.L.O. had its roots in world war one. As the war increased demands on workers for effort in the factories and for sacrifice on the battlefields, labour and trade-union leaders asserted claims for representation at the peace conference and for a peace settlement which would not neglect the issues of social and economic justice. The Russian revolution made the need for world statesmen to accommodate the demands of labour more acute. An international trade union conference in Berne, Switzerland, early in 1919 demanded an international labour parliament, with law-making powers, in which labour would have half the votes. The peace conference set up a commission for international labour legislation, headed by Samuel Gompers, president of the American Federation of Labour. The commission put aside the more ambitious claims for an organisation with legislative authority and proposed a body with powers of recommendation to national governments for action by them. In this body half the representation would be by governments and one-fourth each by labour and by employers. The peace conference adopted these proposals and, by inserting them in the treaty of Versailles, set up the I.L.O.

Edward J. Phelan

Part XIII of the treaty was the charter of the I.L.O. Much of it was drafted by Edward J. Phelan,[1] a member of the British delegation to the peace conference. He served in the British board of trade and in the ministry of labour during the war and was highly regarded by Lloyd George. Both were convinced of

1. For more on this remarkable Irishman, see J. A. Gaughan, *Alfred O'Rahilly II: Public figure* (Dublin 1989) 226-7; Brian Hillery and Patrick Lynch, *Ireland in the International Labour Organisation* (Dublin 1969) 10-14; and *Standard* 21 July 1944 for Alfred's formal presentation of Phelan who, on the former's initiative, was conferred with an honorary doctorate by the National University of Ireland.

the merits of representatives of the working-class having a significant influence on the ordering of world affairs. While Phelan shared with the British prime minister a revulsion at the cavalier attitude, whereby industrialists, high-ranking officers and patrician politicians had acquiesced in the slaughter of hundreds of thousands of members of the working-class in the recent war, he had besides an abiding commitment to social justice. This is reflected in nine guiding principles set out in article 427, the key-note of the charter of the I.L.O. Three of these principles read: 'Labour shall not be regarded merely as a commodity or article of commerce; the right of association for all lawful purposes by the employed as well as by the employers; the payment to the employed of a wage adequate to maintain a reasonable standard of life.' For the origin of these one need look no further than the social teaching of *Rerum Novarum*, of which they are an admirable abstract.

Irish Free State becomes a member of the International Labour Organisation 1923

From the outset the I.L.O. has ensured that these principles have not remained mere academic platitudes. Its chief organs to that end have been its annual conference, at which all members are represented; its governing body of forty members and a permanent secretariat, known as the International Labour Office, under a director-general. The I.L.O.'s chief forms of activity are proposing international treaties, known as conventions; recommendations; technical assistance; investigations; and research and publicity. This activity has meant that, in effect, it has concerned itself with all forms of labour and social legislation and labour law administration, with hours of work, wages, the health and safety of workers, social security, welfare facilities, social services and every other aspect of industrial relations.[2]

2. For a general account of the International Labour Organisation, see J. T. Shotwell (ed.), *The origins of the International Labour Organisation I-II* (New York 1934); E. J. Phelan, *Yes and Albert Thomas* (London 1936); Austin Van der Slice, *International labour, diplomacy and peace 1914-1919* (Philadelphia 1941); and Harold Butler, *The lost peace* (London 1941). The Republic of Ireland's involvement in the Organisation is described in Brian Hillery and Patrick Lynch, *Ireland in the International Labour Organisation* (Dublin 1969). For an account of Edward J. Phelan's contribution to the Organisation, see the general accounts of the I.L.O. and the sources referred to in footnotes 1 and 21. For much information about Phelan I am also indebted to his friend, Tadhg O'Carroll.

Alfred O'Rahilly III: Controversialist

When Alfred's attention was first drawn to the I.L.O. in 1922 he publicly urged that the Irish Free State become a member. He argued that it was distinct from the League of Nations and that a country could join without first being a member of the League. In this he was later vindicated, when the United States of America, although not a member of the League of Nations, joined in 1934 and when subsequently Brazil, Hungary and other nations remained members of the I.L.O. after withdrawing from the League.[3]

On 10 September 1923 the Irish Free State was elected a member of the League of Nations, thereby becoming a member of the I.L.O. Composition of the Irish delegation to the annual conference of the I.L.O. six weeks later was:

> *Government delegates:* Professor Joseph B. Whelehan, former assistant minister in the ministry of industry and commerce, and Robert Campbell Ferguson, chief administrative officer in the industrial branch of the ministry of industry and commerce.
> *Adviser:* Miss Brighid Stafford, of the ministry of industry and commerce, inspector of factories and workshops.
> *Employers' delegate:* William Hewat, T.D., chairman of the Dublin Coal Merchants' Association and of the Shipping Federation.
> *Workers' delegate:* Thomas Johnson, secretary of the Irish Labour Party and Trade Union Congress.
> *Adviser:* Thomas MacPartlin, member of the Amalgamated Wood Workers' Trade Union.
> *Substitute for adviser:* Ronald James Patrick Mortished, assistant to Thomas Johnson.[4]

Government delegate to I.L.O. conference 1924

The Irish delegation to the annual conference held in 1924 from 16 to 30 June was:

> *Government delegates:* Professor Alfred O'Rahilly, T.D., University College, Cork, and Robert Campbell Ferguson,

3. *Standard* 21 July 1944.
4. Brian Hillery and Patrick Lynch, *Ireland in the International Labour Organisation*, 16, 29. See also J. A. Gaughan, *Thomas Johnson (1872-1963): first leader of the Labour Party in Dáil Éireann* (Dublin 1980) 249-51, 253.

7. The Irish delegation to the International Labour Conference in Geneva, 1924, with Edward J. Phelan. *Left to right*: Senator Thomas Farren, Miss Brighid Stafford, Ronald J. P. Mortished, Alfred, Senator Thomas Foran, Robert C. Ferguson, Andrew O'Shaughnessy, Edward J. Phelan

director of industries department of the ministry of industry and commerce.

Adviser: Miss Brighid Stafford.

Employers' delegate: Andrew O'Shaughnessy, T.D., managing director, Dripsey Woollen Mills Ltd.

Workers' delegate: Senator Thomas Foran, member of the National Executive of the Irish Labour Party and Trade Union Congress and president of the I.T.G.W.U.

Advisers: Senator Thomas Farren, member of National Executive I.L.P. and T.U.C. and secretary of the Dublin Workers' Council, and Ronald James Patrick Mortished.[5]

Alfred in his subsequent report on the conference stated that he set out for Geneva 'at exceedingly short notice, utterly ignorant of the agenda and almost equally unaware of the political and social importance of the work conducted there'.[6] At Geneva he met Edward J. Phelan who had become chief of the diplomatic division of the I.L.O. in 1920. Alfred was later to recall that it was 'in that capacity that I myself and many other Irish delegates to Geneva experienced the unrivalled competence and inexhaustible kindness of Mr Phelan, who never regarded his steadfast Irish nationalism as incompatible with his strenuous international idealism'.[7] Phelan introduced Alfred to Albert Thomas, first director-general of the I.L.O. From the outset Alfred and Thomas became very good friends. They were alike in many ways, mercurial in temperament, possessing seemingly boundless energy, gifted with extraordinary ability and, above all, with an unqualified commitment to social justice.[8]

Alfred threw himself into the work of the conference with characteristic enthusiasm. He was elected chairman of a committee on night work in bakeries. In sessions of the full conference he made important contributions on workmen's compensation and allied matters. He strongly supported a new procedure whereby the text of a proposed convention was read and discussed at two consecutive annual conferences before being

5. Brian Hillery and Patrick Lynch, *Ireland in the International Labour Organisation*, 29.

6. O'Rahilly Papers: International Labour Conference 1924: report to President Cosgrave.

7. *Standard* 21 July 1944.

8. *Irish Press* 14 May 1932.

passed.[9] On his own initiative he had the Irish Free State delegation photographed and the picture sent to Dublin. A grateful
Seán Lester, the government's director of publicity, wrote to
him on 2 July that it was published in the daily press.[10] Before
the various delegations headed for home Alfred, again on his
own initiative and at his own expense, until this was subsequently recouped, gave what he described as a dinner
generally agreed to have been one of the most enjoyable and
informal during the conference.[11]

Alfred revelled in the atmosphere at Geneva. When he so
wished he could be very good company. During his attendances
at I.L.O. conferences he was popular with labour and trade-
union representatives. They found him to be a kindred spirit in
his uncomplicated concern for the victims of social injustice. He
became particularly friendly with Ben Tillett[12] of Great Britain

9. E. J. Phelan, 'Ireland and the International Labour Organisation', *Studies*,
March 1926, 5-17; *Irish Independent* 25 June 1924; Brian Hillery and Patrick
Lynch, *Ireland in the International Labour Organisation*, 27. This procedure
is but the beginning of the ratification process. When a draft convention is
passed in two consecutive years by a two-thirds majority at the general assembly
of the annual conference, each member state is obliged to bring it before its
parliament within a maximum period of eighteen months. Parliaments then
decide whether or not the convention is to be ratified. If ratified, it becomes a
binding treaty and the ratifying government binds itself to ensure that effect is
given to the provisions of the convention in national law and regulations and
that these legal provisions are fully enforced and observed (Brian Hillery and
Patrick Lynch, *Ireland in the International Labour Organisation*, 15).

10. O'Rahilly Papers: International Labour Conference 1924, report to President Cosgrave; letter, dated 2 July 1924, Lester to O'Rahilly; *Irish Independent*
1 July 1924; *Cork Examiner* 3 July 1924.

11. O'Rahilly Papers: International Labour Conference 1924: report to President Cosgrave.

12. In a letter to Alfred, dated 20 December 1961, Phelan reminisced as
follows about the 1924 conference: 'The bar at the Club International I remember well. I have a vivid recollection of going in with you one evening. We sat
at a table against the wainscotted wall. Someone sitting on one of the high stools
against the bar turned round and recognised you. He raised his glass and burst
into song

> Are you the O'Rahilly
> They talk of so highly?
> Are you the O'Rahilly
> That Kapes this hotel?

'The singer of this greeting was Ben Tillett – already a legendary figure. That
your name should have come so readily to his lips was proof of how well-known
a figure you had become at the conference' (O'Rahilly Papers: letter, dated 20
December 1961, Phelan to O'Rahilly).

and John Curtin of Australia (see p. 64, n. 37). From the outset he was convinced of the significant tangible and intangible advantages to be gained by the Irish Free State from active participation in the annual I.L.O. conferences. In his report to President William T. Cosgrave on the I.L.O. conference of 1924 he wrote:

> The political implications, though not easy to describe briefly on paper, are quite obvious to us. The expenses incurred by poor countries like Poland and Czechoslovakia in maintaining permanent representation in Geneva and in sending their ablest men; the interest taken by great states such as Great Britain (with a delegation of thirty) and Japan (which sent nearly sixty delegates); the keen rivalry for places on commissions; the pamphlet-propaganda of states like Romania and Finland; above all, the unique position of Ireland, with its connection with the United States, with the leadership of the small nations within its grasp, and on the other hand with its power to secure the votes of Great Britain and of the Dominions in preference to an outsider; all these considerations have convinced us that these annual conferences deserve the heartiest support from our government. These international gatherings give us a unique chance of making Ireland known in the world, of laying the foundations for friendly relations and commercial agreements, of demonstrating that Ireland possesses political ability and a desire for social progress, of increasing our political and economic credit, of taking a prominent part in shaping the social legislation of practically the entire civilised world, of asserting our international independence.[13]

In his report Alfred proposed that certain improvements be made in the approach of the Irish Free State to the conference. He asserted that there should be continuity in the government delegation. Geneva was at first very bewildering to one who had no previous experience and was not acquainted with many of the delegates nor understood the various groupings and interests. The great majority of states, especially those which had attained an influence disproportionate with their commercial

13. O'Rahilly Papers: International Labour Conference 1924: report to President Cosgrave.

8. Alfred (*Second from left*) socialising between sessions of the 1924 International Labour Conference in Geneva

importance, such as Cuba, Sweden, Finland, Poland, sent the same delegates or delegate year after year. Moreover, he pointed out, the influence acquired by a country, especially a small country, was almost entirely dependent on the personality of its chief delegate. He expressed his conviction that if it became the policy of the Free State to send experienced and trained representatives it would in a few years assume a 'preponderating' position, including the chairmanship of the conference. There were other reasons in favour of continuity of representation, such as the new procedure involving two readings on consecutive years of proposed conventions. Besides, he noted, that in 1925 there was to be an election for the governing body, to which he considered that the Free State representative had a good chance of being elected. He disingenuously protested that he did not wish to be seen as recommending himself and asserted that he would not agree to travel to Geneva again unless the ministry of industry and commerce kept him fully informed of its I.L.O.-related investigations, answers to questionnaires, agenda and any other proceedings preliminary to the annual conference. He urged the inauguration of a policy of regarding the delegates to the I.L.O. conference as non-political experts or experienced advisers, the chief delegate to concentrate on raising Ireland's international status, the other delegate to concern himself chiefly with the technical details of proposed social legislation, it being understood that these functions overlapped.

Alfred suggested other steps which should be taken to ensure that the Irish Free State reaped to the full advantages accruing from participation in I.L.O. conferences. He noted that no arrangements had been made for propaganda or news in connection with the conference. He recalled that, on learning of that, he had one of his speeches cabled to the U.S.A., as well as having photographs of the delegation sent to Dublin.[14] He recommended that the Irish Free State's representative in Geneva, Michael MacWhite, be appointed as an adviser. This sort of thing was done by other nations, it would strengthen an inevitably small delegation, and make readily available to it that person's knowledge and experience and probably enhance his status. On the question of the employers' delegate, he pointed

14. R. J. P. Mortished also showed initiative in this matter. He published an interim report on the conference in the *Irish Independent* of 25 June 1924.

out that such a person should be chosen in good time and as far as possible be engaged in a business which was the subject of the most important proposed convention and/or recommendation on the conference agenda. He urged that the government should seriously accept all its international contractual obligations in connection with adopted conventions. It should also see that arrangements were made in England, France and Switzerland for granting full diplomatic privileges to the delegates. He stressed the importance of providing hospitality for other delegations and, as an aside, he suggested that there was an obvious opening for selling Irish bacon, whiskey and biscuits in Geneva.[15]

From the time of his arrival at Geneva and after conferring with Phelan, Alfred became acutely aware of the use which could be made of the Irish Free State's membership of the League of Nations and participation in the work of the I.L.O. to enhance its international status and independence from Britain. As has been noted elsewhere,[16] he was instrumental in having the Anglo-Irish treaty eventually registered with the League of Nations on 11 July 1924. He considered that the Irish Free State's membership of the I.L.O. provided it with even better opportunities for asserting its international position. When the Irish Free State became a member in 1923 the British government had already ratified certain conventions of the I.L.O. 'in respect of the United Kingdom of Great Britain and Ireland'. Alfred considered it to be of the first importance from the point of view of constitutional and international law that the Irish Free State should not consider itself bound by such pre-Anglo-Irish-treaty ratifications. The issue arose in the annual report of the director-general. Alfred stated: 'Being completely in the dark concerning the view of the government, if it has any, I did not feel free to speak. Therefore I dissuaded a certain other delegation from saying anything. This is a very unsatisfactory state of affairs and I think the government is bound to come to a definite decision on this matter.'[17] This it did soon afterwards.

15. O'Rahilly Papers: International Labour Conference 1924: report to President Cosgrave.

16. J. A. Gaughan, *Alfred O'Rahilly II: Public figure*, 224-31.

17. Brian Hillery and Patrick Lynch, *Ireland in the International Labour Organisation*, 19; O'Rahilly Papers: International Labour Conference 1924: report to President Cosgrave.

When copies of all conventions were sent to the Irish Free State government by the I.L.O. it had the Oireachtas approve two which had not been the subject of previous British ratification. In regard to conventions which had been ratified on Ireland's behalf before the Anglo-Irish treaty the government re-ratified six of them and thus asserted the independence of the Irish Free State in international law.[18]

Alfred was still under the spell of Geneva when he wrote to Edward J. Phelan on 8 August 1924. He told Phelan that he had volunteered for membership of the delegation to the pending general assembly of the League of Nations, on learning that Eoin MacNeill was not likely to be able to act on it. Phelan replied that he had read in the *Freeman's Journal* that Alfred had resigned from Dáil Éireann, but hoped that he would be at the next I.L.O. conference and continued:

> We look to you to get the bakery convention finally afloat.[19] After you left Geneva I heard a large number of exceedingly flattering opinions on your work on the commission and in the full conference. I should think that you stand quite clearly at the top of the panel of presidents of commissions, and I heard it on the best possible authority that you may be regarded as being in the running for the presidency of the conference at some later date. That is certainly too much to throw away, not for your personal advantage but for the Free State.

18. Brian Hillery and Patrick Lynch, *Ireland in the International Labour Organisation*, 20. Alfred and the proponents for this course of action argued that under the terms of the Anglo-Irish treaty the constitutional position of the Irish Free State in the British Commonwealth was equal, for example, to that of Canada. But when Canada ratified treaties the instrument of ratification was signed by the British king. It was not clear, however, whether the king in signing was advised by Canadian or British ministers. It was urged that the equality and independence of the Irish Free State as a member of the League of Nations, on the same footing as all other members, would be in question if, before adhering to a covenant of the League of Nations, a preliminary confirmation by another member state was necessary. So it was imperative that the Irish Free State, by ratifying I.L.O. conventions and registering them directly with the secretary-general of the League without any intervention by British ministers, assert its diplomatic independence from the British government and thus signal its entry into international affairs (ibid.).

19. It is hardly surprising that Phelan should express himself in this way. His father and grandfather were master mariners and his life-long and chief recreation was yachting on Lake Geneva (interview with Tadhg O'Carroll).

9. Meeting of the Bakery Commission on 18 June 1924. Alfred, the chairman, is in the centre foreground

Phelan also reminded Alfred of a proposal he had made while in Geneva to have some articles on the I.L.O. published in *Studies*. The first was to be by Alfred, the second, a sequel, by himself.[20] By the time of the 1925 conference Alfred had not prepared his promised article; instead he urged Phelan to write the articles and this Phelan did.[21]

Following his attendance at the I.L.O. conference in 1924, Alfred conducted a regular correspondence with Edward J. Phelan. In this way he kept abreast of developments at Geneva. Conversely Phelan availed of the correspondence to keep himself informed of attitudes in the Irish Free State to the I.L.O. It seems he kept a close eye on the English language press. In a letter, dated 12 February 1925, he informed Alfred that he had noticed in the *Irish Independent* of 7 February the following: 'The South African employers' representative on the governing body of the International Labour Bureau of Geneva, Mr Gemmell, told a Reuter's representative yesterday that the organisation cost £300,000 per annum and had done very little to justify its existence.' Phelan expressed his anxiety that this might be quoted by a member of Dáil Éireann when the next vote for the Irish Free State's financial payment to the I.L.O. was to be taken.

20. O'Rahilly Papers: letter, dated 18 August 1924, Phelan to O'Rahilly.

21. They were published as follows: 'The International Labour Organisation: its ideals and results' in *Studies*, December 1925; and 'Ireland and the International Labour Organisation: I' and 'Ireland and the International Labour Organisation: II' in the issues of March and September 1926. Phelan was subsequently to publish 'Some reminiscences of the International Labour Organisation' in *Studies*, Autumn 1954, and 'The I.L.O. sets up its wartime centre in Canada' and 'The I.L.O. turns the corner' in the issues of Summer 1955 and Summer 1956. These articles and Phelan's *Yes and Albert Thomas* (London 1936) are a major source for the history of the I.L.O. from its foundation in 1919 to 1941. Alfred reviewed Phelan's book in the *Irish Press* in 1936 and reminisced:

'For anyone, who has taken part in its proceedings, this book will recall pleasant memories of the great spirit of fellowship and solidarity which prevails in the I.L.O. One thinks of the Hungarian café where, over goulasche and beer, important resolutions are hastily scribbled; of "camarades" like Jouhaux and Mertens and Third Internationalists from Amsterdam hob-nobbing with Irish Catholics; of old Branting asleep in the chair; of fine Englishmen like Butler, who have become internationalists; of Phelan himself – who while remaining Irish has become a first-class diplomat – buzzing round to repair breakdowns in the machine or reciting Chesterton's poems at three in the morning. Above all, one recalls the outstanding figure of Albert Thomas, greatest of orators and yet most efficient of executives. Even this book does not succeed in bringing out the simplicity and kindliness of the man.'

He set out in great detail the rigorous control to which the I.L.O.'s budget was subjected and suggested to Alfred that, if he considered it worthwhile, he should publicly rebut Gemmell's allegation.[22] Whether he considered it worthwhile or not, Alfred, it seems, neglected to do so.

Government delegate to I.L.O. conference 1925

In the last week of March 1925 Alfred was formally invited to be a government representative on the Irish delegation to attend the I.L.O. conference beginning on 19 May. Besides accepting the invitation, he wrote to Robert C. Ferguson who, it was expected, would also be a government delegate. He proposed that they meet to discuss the business of the conference. Alfred conferred with Ferguson and later with Patrick McGilligan, minister for industry and commerce.[23] Prompted by Phelan, who was engaged in a continuous crusade to persuade all member countries to ratify the maximum number of conventions, he urged the minister to introduce a resolution in Dáil Éireann concerning the ratification of a number of I.L.O. conventions. McGilligan promised that he would do so and have those ratifications registered at the I.L.O. before the opening of the organisation's annual conference. On his initiative eight conventions were passed by Dáil Éireann on 30 April and were registered soon afterwards.[24]

In a letter, dated 17 April, Phelan expressed his pleasure that Alfred was coming to the annual conference. This, he reported, was also the feeling of many other mutual acquaintances at Geneva. He anticipated that Alfred would make significant contributions to the forthcoming discussions on conventions to be finalised on workmen's compensation and night work in bakeries. And he added: 'In all probability you will be regarded

22. O'Rahilly Papers: letter, dated 12 February 1925, Phelan to O'Rahilly.
23. O'Rahilly Papers: letter, dated 25 March 1925, Gordon Campbell to O'Rahilly; letters, dated 27 March, 2 April 1925, Ferguson to O'Rahilly. See also O'Rahilly Papers: International Labour Conference 1925: report to minister of industry and commerce, dated 25 June 1925, appendix.
24. O'Rahilly Papers: International Labour Conference 1925: report to minister of industry and commerce, dated 25 June 1925; letters, dated 12 February, 17 April 1925, Phelan to O'Rahilly; *Dáil Éireann: Díospóireachta parlaiminte, tuairisc oifigiúil: Parliamentary debates, official report*, vol. 11, cols 689-708, 30 April 1925.

as one of the chief authorities on the latter question . . .' Phelan was particularly eager that Alfred should help with solving difficulties in regard to a procedure, which had been introduced by the I.L.O. conference, on the passing of conventions. The procedure involved two readings of a convention in successive years. Some delegates found it unsatisfactory. To meet some of their objections, the I.L.O.'s governing body drafted a new set of standing orders, a copy of which Phelan sent to Alfred.[25]

The full Irish Free State delegation to the I.L.O. conference was:

> *Government delegates:* Alfred and Robert C. Ferguson.
> *Advisers:* Miss Brighid Stafford and Michael MacWhite, representative of the Irish Free State at the League of Nations.
> *Employers' delegate:* Charles McGloughlin, member of the Council of the Federation of Irish Industries.
> *Workers' delegates:* Denis Cullen, vice-chairman of the Irish Labour Party and Trade Union Congress and general secretary of the Bakers, Confectioners and Allied Workers' Amalgamated Union.
> *Adviser:* R. J. P. Mortished.[26]

The conference sat from 19 May to 10 June. Alfred was determined that the Irish Free State delegation would have a considerable impact on the proceedings. He was indefatigable in his pursuit of this goal both in and apart from the formal sessions. With a view to extending the international influence of the I.L.O. he suggested that temporary staff be enlisted from different countries, not fully represented in the I.L.O. In his formal reply to the various debates Albert Thomas stated that, as far as funds permitted, that suggestion had already been implemented.[27] The non-ratification of conventions was one of the major topics discussed at the conference. Speaking on this Alfred referred to the number of conventions already ratified by his country, complained about the lengthy proceedings at Geneva and suggested that a special committee be instituted to

25. O'Rahilly Papers: letter, dated 17 April 1925, Phelan to O'Rahilly.
26. Brian Hillery and Patrick Lynch, *Ireland in the International Labour Organisation*, 30.
27. *Cork Examiner, Irish Independent* 2 June 1925.

inquire into the reasons 'why such and such a country had not ratified such and such a convention'. This suggestion was later to be adopted and became an important element of I.L.O. procedures.[28] He also took a prominent part in the debate on the procedure requiring two readings of proposed conventions. After a prolonged discussion, which revealed considerable dissatisfaction, the matter was referred back to the I.L.O.'s governing body with a recommendation that a *via media* proposed by him might be the best way out of the impasse, as it received widespread support from government, employers' and workers' delegates. Alfred's proposal was accepted by the governing body, and the new procedure, thereafter known as *'système O'Rahilly'*, was adopted.[29] There was a general appreciation of Alfred's interventions. In reporting on the conference the chief British government delegate wrote: 'several interesting suggestions for improving the work of the organisa-

28. *Irish Independent* 1 June 1925; E. J. Phelan, 'Ireland and the International Labour Organisation', *Studies*, March 1926, 18. By virtue of the existing procedure a member state which did not ratify a convention was required to report to the I.L.O. periodically indicating the extent to which effect had been given or was to be given to any of the provisions of the convention and stating the difficulties which prevented or delayed its ratification. This was a development of Article 405 of the Treaty of Versailles which provided that, if the I.L.O. conference adopted a draft convention by a two-thirds majority, the government of each member state was obliged to bring that draft convention for approval before the legislative authority in its particular country before the expiration of twelve, or in exceptional cases, eighteen months. If the draft convention was approved, it was ratified by being then deposited with the secretary-general of the League of Nations. A further article – 408 – of the treaty provided that each member state which had ratified a convention should send it an annual report on the measures taken to secure its application and these reports had to be brought forward each year for the examination of the conference. The new administrative machinery was based on this (see E. J. Phelan, 'The International Labour Organisation', *Studies*, December 1925, 617-18; *Irish Press* 16 April, 9 May 1932).

29. *Irish Independent* 16 June 1925; E. J. Phelan, 'Ireland and the International Labour Organisation', *Studies*, March 1926, 15-17. Alfred's proposal was that there should be consideration of a question at two successive sessions, but that the first session should have before it only a report, and not the text of a convention. This procedure, he argued, would allow the conference to adopt resolutions at the first session on the principles which it considered might be embodied in a convention the following year, but there would be no text on the details or wording, on which opposition could harden during the interval in such a way as to render negotiation at the second session impossible (E. J. Phelan, 'Ireland and the International Labour Organisation', *Studies*, March 1926, 17).

tion were made, particularly by Professor Alfred O'Rahilly (Irish Free State government) and the director promised to take them into consideration.'[30]

The substantive achievement of the seventh I.L.O. conference was the adoption of four conventions and some recommendations. There remained only the automatic submission of these conventions to the legislators of the member states for ratification.[31] Three of these conventions concerned workmen's compensation. One dealt with workmen's compensation in general, a second provided for equality of treatment of foreign workers and nationals in the matter of compensation for industrial accidents, and the third concerned occupational diseases arising from lead and mercury poison and anthrax. The industrial accidents convention came close to not being passed, owing to the opposition of the employers and the British government delegates, but a compromise, proposed by Alfred, enabled the necessary two-thirds majority to be secured. In describing this intervention, the *Manchester Guardian* correspondent referred to Alfred as 'one of the most useful delegates'.[32] The convention which attracted most attention, because it was faced with the stiffest opposition, was one which attempted to prohibit night work in bakeries. This received a first reading at the 1924 conference on a vote of 73 to 15. Subsequently, the master bakers of several countries carried on a persistent campaign against it. But at the 1925 conference it passed its second reading and was adopted by 81 votes to 26. Alfred was chairman of the commission on night-work in bakeries and his contribution to the successful issue of its proceedings was emphasised by Harold Butler, deputy secretary general of the I.L.O., at the closing session of the conference.[33] As in the previous year Alfred ensured publicity at home for the work of the Irish Free State delegation

30. Quoted in E. J. Phelan, 'Ireland and the International Labour Organisation', *Studies*, March 1926, 18.

31. *Irish Independent* 16 June 1925. The Irish Free State ratified three of these conventions, namely, workers' compensation (occupational diseases) 1925, equality of treatment (of foreign workers and nationals in respect of accident compensation) 1925 and night work (bakeries) 1925. Great Britain did not adopt the convention abolishing night work in bakeries, leaving the bakeries of the Irish Free State and later the Republic of Ireland at a disadvantage *vis-à-vis* their competitors in Northern Ireland (see Brian Hillery and Patrick Lynch, *Ireland in the International Labour Organisation*, 27, 49).

32. O'Rahilly Papers: Scrapbook I, press-cutting, dated 20 June 1925.

33. *Irish Independent* 16 June 1925.

10. Copy of photograph of workers' representatives on the Bakery Commission presented to Alfred. The caption read: *Back row:* Schifferstein (Secrétaire International), Zipper (Autriche), Cullen (Irlande), Lagergren (Suède). *Middle row:* Kupers (Pays-Bas), Nielsen (Danemark), Savoie (France), Wilhelm (Suisse), De Roode (Bureau International du Travail). *Front row:* Diermeier (Allemagne), Caballero (Espagne), Banfield (Grande-Bretagne), Hejna (Tchéco-Slovaquie)

by having pictures of the delegation and the commission on night-work in bakeries sent to Dublin.[34] He also briefed journalists reporting on the conference for Irish newspapers. One of the comments in one of the subsequent reports was a direct quotation from him: 'The Free State delegates in three weeks do more in the matter of explaining the position, status and prospects of their country than could otherwise be done in three years.'[35]

Clash with colleagues

Although the Irish Free State delegation and Alfred carried out their briefs with remarkable success, there was considerable bickering between him and the other and junior government delegate, Robert C. Ferguson, and the adviser, Miss Brighid Stafford. He began his report on the conference to Patrick McGilligan, minister for industry and commerce, by stating that the Irish delegation had some success in the objectives set out for them, namely: (1) to take part in the debates on social legislation and to help in raising social standards both in their own country and elsewhere; and (2) to increase the prestige and international status of Ireland. He acknowledged the prompt action of McGilligan in having some outstanding conventions ratified before the opening of the conference and recalled that he had been able to quote with great effect McGilligan's speech in Dáil Éireann in that regard. Next he highly commended Edward J. Phelan for 'the invaluable expert advice' which he provided to the delegation at the 1924 as well as the 1925 conference. In his opinion, R. J. P. Mortished was 'also a great asset, not only from a labour but also from the national point of view'. He regretted that Michael MacWhite, 'our able and courteous representative in Geneva', was unable to act as adviser, as he was engaged in the arms conference of the League of Nations. Here, however, the commendations ceased. The rest of the report was intensely critical of the conduct of Miss Stafford and Ferguson.

According to Alfred's version the differences between the government delegates began when Miss Stafford, without notifying him, decided not to deal with correspondence directed to the Irish Free State delegation. When she, Alfred and Ferguson

34. *Cork Examiner* 11 June 1925.
35. *Irish Independent* 16 June 1925.

had attended the previous I.L.O. conference, she had carried out this role. Alfred learned she was not doing so at the 1925 conference when he missed an important meeting to which he and all other senior delegates had been invited by Dr Eduard Beneš, president of the conference. On complaining to Ferguson, he was informed that Miss Stafford was answerable to her civil service colleague only and had no obligation to assist or take instructions from anyone else. In his report Alfred speculated that the change of attitude of Ferguson and Stafford to him, could, perhaps, be explained by the fact that in 1924 he was a T.D. and, as Ferguson told him, 'a potential minister', whereas in 1925 he was considered to be only 'an outsider without authority'. Because Stafford refused to take instructions from him, Alfred did not appoint her his alternate on the commission on night-work in bakeries. This led to some embarrassment, as it meant he had to act both as a delegate on the commission, as well as its chairman.[36]

The real cause of the friction between Alfred and Ferguson and Miss Stafford was that he regarded them as Anglophiles.[37]

36. O'Rahilly Papers: International Labour Conference 1925: report to minister of industry and commerce, dated 25 June 1925.

37. It is very probable that Miss Stafford was an Anglophile. Her papers (p. 63) which are lodged in the archives department of U.C.D., provide few details of her life and none of her opinions. They indicate, however, that she was a graduate of Dublin University. Her attendance at Trinity College would at least indicate that she was partial to a pro-British ethos. She attended Trinity during the first two decades of its admission of women students. Thereafter she was a prominent member of a number of organisations which aimed at ensuring equality for women, among them the International University Women's Federation. Thus she would not have taken kindly to an assumption by Alfred that as a woman she should automatically act as secretary to the Irish delegation to the I.L.O. By a curious coincidence, in 1926, when omitted from the Irish delegation to the I.L.O., she, with others, represented Ireland at the Labour Conference of the International Women's Suffrage Alliance in Paris from 31 May to 9 June, at which she read a paper on the I.L.O. A further clue to Miss Stafford's opinions may be had from an account of her brother, Fr Laurence Stafford, who for about twenty years was parish priest of Narraghmore, County Kildare, where he was frequently visited by his sister. In the memoirs of Fr John O'Sullivan it is stated that the Staffords originated in Waterford and were strong supporters of John Redmond, M.P., on whose advice Fr Stafford served as a British army chaplain in the first world war. Thereafter, it seems, his colleagues found Fr Stafford to have 'a somewhat soured attitude to nationalism', an English mentality and 'an unIrish respect for British royalty' (John O'Sullivan, 'Fr O'Sullivan's notebook', *Link-Up* (Bulletin for the Dublin diocese), November 1991, 21-2).

He viewed them as ex-British civil servants out of tune with the pronounced nationalist approach which he considered to be essential at Geneva. He was not alone at that time in voicing criticisms of this kind. Suspicions of a lack of commitment by such civil servants tended to surface in the early years of the Irish Free State, although such sentiments were not encouraged by ministers. However, suspicions of that kind once aroused, and whether justified or not, tended to be reinforced by episodes which otherwise would have lacked any significance.

The Irish delegation, Alfred complained, was accommodated in the same hotel as the large British delegation, and his two colleagues had 'constant private conferences' there with British representatives. About these and 'private understandings with the British representatives' Alfred alleged he was not consulted nor was he even aware they were taking place until his attention was drawn to them by 'the unfavourable criticisms of foreigners'. He claimed that no one at the conference got on as well with the British at a personal level but he was adamant that he was not going to be inveigled into situations which in the eyes of foreigners would appear 'compromising and prejudicial to our autonomy'. In fact, he claimed, that before the end of the conference his view of the Irish Free State's relations with the British empire delegation had been adopted by the head delegate of Canada and the two government delegates from South Africa. A further bone of contention concerned an invitation to a dinner of British empire delegates. Alfred maintained that in the League of Nations and the I.L.O. 'British empire' meant

---

Whatever about Miss Stafford it seems that Ferguson was an Anglophile. He died on 4 August 1946, just a week after retiring from the secretaryship of the department of industry and commerce. An appreciation by 'A friend', most probably Robert M. (Bertie) Smyllie, editor of the *Irish Times*, was published in that paper's issue of 6 August. The writer recalled how pleased Ferguson was when he was appointed secretary of the department of industry and commerce, 'realising that, as an Ulster Protestant who never compromised his views or his belief, he had risen to the head of his profession in Dublin solely by virtue of his own merit'. The appreciation continued that, although the government never had a more loyal servant, Ferguson 'reserved to himself the right to hold strong personal opinions which nothing could ever shake'. Ferguson belonged to the Dublin literary circle known as Smyllie's people (see cartoon published in *Irish Times* in 1940 and reproduced in John Ryan, *Remembering how we stood: Bohemian Dublin at mid-century* (Dublin 1975) between pp. 80 and 81). A most affectionate memoir of him by Francis MacManus appeared in the *Irish Times* of 15 September 1945.

Great Britain, Jamaica, Nigeria, Kenya and suchlike colonies. The Irish Free State belonged only to the British Commonwealth of Nations which 'for Geneva purposes' was 'nonexistent'. At the corresponding dinner in the previous year advantage had been taken of hospitality to take a 'British empire photograph' and inflict on Irish delegates unwelcome political speeches. Consequently, he, Denis Cullen and R. J. P. Mortished declined the invitation. Ferguson and Miss Stafford, however, mentioned that they had instructions to attend and did so against Alfred's wishes.

A further cause for a worsening of relations between Alfred and Ferguson arose in connection with the Irish Free State's seat on the commission on workmen's compensation. Alfred maintained that he was responsible for gaining this representation. Ferguson acted as the Irish delegate. Alfred claimed he did not consult nor even apprise him of matters arising from it. He went on: 'Both a representative of the I.L.O. office and a spokesman of the workers on the commission came to me, as head of the delegation, to ask me what were the views of my government and why Mr Ferguson sat next to the British government's representative and supported him automatically.' Alfred further charged that Ferguson refused to assist him when he attempted, on behalf of the Irish Free State delegation and those of Canada and South Africa, to make a very explicit statement that their votes were not 'at Britain's command'.[38]

The most serious difference arose in connection with the business of the commission on night-work in bakeries. Because Alfred, who was chairman of the commission, did not appoint Miss Stafford as his voting substitute initially, he had to act in a dual capacity. Owing to the awkwardness of this situation, he wrote to Dublin for permission to vote for the convention, while safeguarding the reservations made by the Irish government. He had a reply, dated 25 May, from Gordon Campbell, secretary of the department of industry and commerce, informing him that McGilligan had decided to leave to his discretion whether to vote for the convention on night-work in bakeries or to abstain. On foot of this direction Alfred attempted on

38. O'Rahilly Papers: International Labour Conference 1925: report to minister of industry and commerce, dated 25 June 1925. Although Ferguson admitted to refusing to assist in this initiative, Alfred alleged that he 'blocked' it (ibid.).

8 June to propose a strategy to Ferguson, who told him that he would take no direction whatsoever from him. Alfred wired McGilligan, who replied that Ferguson be shown the letter of 25 May. This wire, however, only reached Geneva on 5 June. By that time the crucial vote had been taken. Alfred described in his report the disarray of the Irish delegation as follows: 'When I said "Yes" on the vote on the draft, Mr Ferguson deliberately shouted "abstention", though in my speeches I had explicitly safeguarded our government.[39] On the final vote I answered "Yes" and Mr Ferguson deliberately absented himself.'

Alfred pointed out that in every delegation at Geneva the junior delegate was bound to take instructions from the senior and could not, without reference home, disobey him. To ensure that future delegations would act efficiently and in the national interests he made the following recommendations:

(1) The Dublin end of the I.L.O. work should be strictly supervised by the minister or by the secretary to the minister. The matter is too important to be left largely to subordinates, especially if these subordinates are free to instruct themselves in Dublin as to what they are to do when they arrive in Geneva.

(2) The head of the delegation should be really the head and not an ornamental figure-head. He should previously have direct discussion with the minister or the secretary. No instructions should be issued except through him. His junior delegate and adviser, if any, should be subordinate to him, bound to consult him and to take his advice. The junior delegate should be bound to follow the instructions of his senior, except in case of disagreement and when there is time to refer home.

(3) In general, the head of the delegation should not be a civil servant, least of all a civil servant lacking in a sense of nationality. There are inevitably many political or rather national issues involved in our conduct at Geneva and the head delegate must be one on whose judgement the government can rely in such matters. He should also have

---

39. This referred to a reservation which took account of the Irish Free State government's instructions to its delegates with regard to the convention. These read: (1) oppose the inclusion of proprietors and (2) vote for the convention subject to prior ratification by Great Britain on behalf of Northern Ireland.

character, initiative and ability in order to take a prominent part in the conference.[40]

One's sympathies must go out to McGilligan at this point, engaged as he was in such important projects as the Shannon scheme, the Tariff Commission and the development of civil aviation. It must have wearied him to be presented with such evidence of squabbling among responsible persons sent to Geneva to represent the country at an important international conference. Understandably he did not reply to Alfred's report and some ancillary letters for about three weeks. He was also fully aware of how volatile Alfred could be and probably he hoped that the latter's memory of the contentious incidents at Geneva would by that time have dimmed somewhat. In a letter, dated 14 July, McGilligan agreed that a speech by Charles McGloughlin, the employers' delegate, by which Alfred had expressed himself to have been appalled, 'was grotesque in its inaccuracies' and did not stand as 'any testimonial' to Irish employers. However, he rejected Alfred's view that McGloughlin's address – a tirade against labour – was inspired by Ferguson. He told Alfred that he did not intend to probe into the matters alluded to by him. His main reason for this decision was that a short time previously Phelan had written to him on other matters and in an incidental reference to the delegation had commented: 'All I need say at present is that the record of the delegation was an entirely successful one. The delegation as a whole, in fact, greatly enhanced the credit of the Free State in the organisation.' This assessment, McGilligan continued, he had heard corroborated 'from various quarters'.[41] He informed Alfred that he was keeping his letters as a reminder that for the future there should be a completely organised team sent to Geneva along the lines suggested by him. The attempts by Britain at absorption of Dominion delegates and the meaning of 'British empire delegation', he noted, were problems of which, as minister for external affairs, he had personal experience in the previous autumn at the assembly of the League of Nations. However, he concluded, 'so long as the general result is good

40. O'Rahilly Papers: International Labour Conference 1925: report to minister of industry and commerce, dated 25 June 1925.
41. Ferguson and Miss Stafford would already have communicated their version of the events at Geneva to McGilligan.

and that we can better the details next year, by observing what slight defects there were this year, I am not disposed to be upset.'

Clearly he kept Alfred's letters until the next year, for he himself led the delegation to the 1926 conference, accompanied by a middle ranking official of the department – to the exclusion of both Alfred and Ferguson. Miss Stafford was omitted, ostensibly because her area of expertise, worker safety, was not on the agenda.[42]

Alfred had refused to be mollified. In his reply, dated 18 August 1925, he was particularly angry that McGilligan quoted Phelan's general remark to dismiss any need for an inquiry into the conduct of Ferguson and Miss Stafford in Geneva. Alfred was aware that Phelan had formed the same judgement as himself of the actions of the pair and that he had conveyed this verbally to McGilligan. Alfred protested that the object of his criticism was not to cause any trouble. It was simply to secure guarantees that relations with the I.L.O. should not continue to be exclusively entrusted to those who had shown such discourtesy, disloyalty and insubordination. He concluded that unless satisfactory assurances were forthcoming he would not give any further voluntary service to the department of industry and commerce, as he declined to be associated with those who seriously jeopardised the national interest.[43]

In the light of the saga of his resignation from Dáil Éireann,[44] it would not have been surprising if McGilligan and other members of the cabinet had become weary of what they regarded as Alfred's histrionics. He received no reply to his letter and thereby for the time being his involvement in I.L.O. conferences ended.[45] Although he could have had no complaints in the

42. Brian Hillery and Patrick Lynch, *Ireland in the International Labour Organisation*, 30.

43. O'Rahilly Papers: letter, dated 14 July 1925, McGilligan to O'Rahilly; letter, 18 August 1925, O'Rahilly to McGilligan.

44. See J. A. Gaughan, *Alfred O'Rahilly II: Public figure* (Dublin 1989) 210-15.

45. As already noted, Ferguson and Miss Stafford were not appointed to the Irish Free State delegation to the I.L.O. conference of 1926 and this would seem to have been a consequence of Alfred's report. Apart from 1926 and when Alfred again acted as senior delegate in 1932, Ferguson and Miss Stafford, together or separately, attended every I.L.O. conference which was held from 1923 to 1947 inclusive, except those in 1929, 1944 (held in Philadelphia) and 1946 (a special maritime session) (see Brian Hillery and Patrick Lynch, *Ireland in the International Labour Organisation*, 29-37).

matter, he was very disappointed at this development. He had become a very enthusiastic supporter of the League of Nations and the I.L.O. In particular, the latter, he regarded as having immense potential as a catalyst in the struggle for what he regarded as the necessary antecedent to peace, namely, social justice throughout the world. Furthermore, he viewed it as a splendid forum in which to enhance the international standing of the Irish Free State.

Within a week of Alfred's return from Geneva, Manly O. Hudson, professor of international law at Harvard University, delivered a lecture at U.C.C. on 'America and the League of Nations'. It was a clarion call for support for the League. Hudson congratulated the Irish Free State on its membership and continued:

> I had the very great privilege of being associated in a humble capacity with a very distinguished citizen of Cork and a professor of University College, Professor O'Rahilly, when he was representing the Irish Free State at the I.L.O. conference last year and I would like to pay a tribute to the splendid qualities which he showed at the conference.

He also recalled meeting Michael MacWhite at Geneva and went on: 'No country was better represented and none had more prominent men than the Irish Free State.' In his reply to the lecture Alfred described the League of Nations as 'a great idealistic movement, which was the greatest experiment in world history'. He assured Professor Hudson that in a tribute to him they would establish a Cork branch of the League of Nations' Non-Partisan Association.[46] The Association was subsequently set up with Alfred as its vice-president.

Government delegate to I.L.O. conference 1932

With the change of government in 1932 Alfred was given an opportunity to represent his country once more at the annual I.L.O. conference at Geneva. He anticipated friction between the Irish Free State and Britain, as the Fianna Fáil government attempted to implement its general election programme on issues such as the governor general, the land annuities and the

46. *Cork Examiner* 18 June 1925.

oath of allegiance. In these circumstances he considered it to be crucial that the country should utilise to the full international conferences such as those held by the I.L.O. to counter British propaganda. In mid-March he conveyed these views to Edward J. Phelan and his readiness, if requested by the government, to go to Geneva for the coming I.L.O. conference.

In a reply, dated 24 March 1932, Phelan assured Alfred that the government would 'jump at the chance' of getting him to represent Ireland at the I.L.O. conference. He suggested that Alfred should meet de Valera and Seán Lemass and brief them on the conference and its value as a platform for disseminating propaganda, particularly in the context of the general situation *vis-à-vis* Britain. Next he paid Alfred a remarkable tribute. He stated his eagerness to have set out at the I.L.O. conference 'the whole social problem – including the framework in which it has to be solved, and the heresy of sovereignty, etc.' He declared that he knew no one who could do it as well as Alfred. Above all, Phelan added, he wished the League of Nations to be 'shaken up to a sense of its responsibilities'. He could prepare 'the jolt' required but if it was to be effective it would have to be administered with the intellectual content Alfred alone could give it. Phelan declared that R. J. P. Mortished, who had joined the I.L.O. office in 1930, was also most eager that Alfred would attend the conference. He concluded that, apart from the trouble the government might expect from Britain, a more active policy at Geneva would be 'good politics for Fianna Fáil', as it would be seen as restoring the international influence of the country which their rivals had neglected.[47]

On assuming his responsibilities as minister for industry and commerce, Seán Lemass set about reversing a decision which had been taken by the cabinet of the previous administration on 22 December 1931 not to send a delegation to the I.L.O. conference in 1932 'in view of the need for economy'. On his recommendation the government decided on 18 March 1932 that the country should be represented at Geneva.[48] By that time Phelan and Mortished were strongly urging the Fianna Fáil and Labour leaders respectively that Alfred be chosen as the chief government delegate for the 1932 I.L.O. conference. The government and especially Lemass, whose department had

47. O'Rahilly Papers: letter, dated 24 March 1932, Phelan to O'Rahilly.
48. State Paper Office, Department of Taoiseach, S 6812.

responsibility for the I.L.O., were easily convinced of the merits of the proposal. However, the task of selecting a person to accompany Alfred as the second government delegate proved to be rather delicate. Almost invariably Robert C. Ferguson and Miss Brighid Stafford were members of the government delegation. In 1925 Alfred had placed it on record that he was unwilling to join a delegation of which they were a part. Conversely, they would have been equally reluctant to join a delegation led by him. Lemass resolved the difficulty when on 7 April he sent the following telegram to Alfred: 'Propose you go Geneva sole government delegate.'[49] As far as the minister was concerned this is what was done for the other government delegate was based in Geneva. This was less than a week before the conference was due to open. There was some suspicion that the delay in finalising the delegation reflected opposition within the department to the proposed selection of Alfred. Other factors explaining the delay, however, would be that Lemass was just one week in office, that he had to have the December 1931 decision not to send a delegation reversed by the government and that the department was operating without a secretary since Gordon Campbell retired on succeeding to the title of Lord Glenavy and John Leydon had not yet taken up the post. Before he received the telegram concerning his appointment, Alfred, it seems, was aware that he was to be the government chief delegate at the conference. At the beginning of April he wrote to Frank Gallagher, editor of the *Irish Press*, and volunteered to report on the conference. In a letter, dated 5 April, Gallagher wrote that he was about to ask Alfred to do so when the letter arrived.[50] After Alfred acknowledged Lemass's telegram the full Irish Free State delegation to the I.L.O. conference of 12-30 April 1932 was published as follows:

> *Government delegates:* Professor Alfred O'Rahilly, University College, Cork. T. J. Coyne, secretary to the Permanent Delegation to the League of Nations.
> *Employers' delegate:* Joseph Milroy, president of the Irish National Industrial and Agricultural Development Association.

49. O'Rahilly Papers: telegram, dated 7 April 1932, 'Industry and Commerce' to O'Rahilly.
50. O'Rahilly Papers: letter, dated 5 April 1932, Gallagher to O'Rahilly.

Workers' delegate: Luke J. Duffy, treasurer of the Irish Trade Union Congress; general secretary, Irish Union of Distributive Workers and Clerks.

Adviser: Seán P. Campbell, vice-president, Irish Trade Union Congress; treasurer, Dublin Typographical Provident Society.[51]

At Geneva, it seems Alfred's constructive contributions in the conferences of 1924 and 1925 were vividly remembered. According to press reports even his appearance was enough to cause a ripple of excitement and expectation. At the opening session he spoke in support of a proposal to elect the Canadian, Senator Gideon D. Robertson, president of the conference. On rising he was enthusiastically received by the assembled delegates and applause for his speech came from all parts of the conference hall.[52]

On his return home Alfred published a report of the I.L.O. conference in the *Irish Press.*[53] He explained that the main work of the conference was to draft and pass conventions. These he described as 'an extraordinarily interesting development, utterly incompatible with the older ideas of sovereignty'. They were international treaties between the ratifying states, whereby each guarantees to the others the enforcement of certain social conditions, such as a forty-eight hour week or the abolition of night-work in bakeries, within its own territory. More than thirty of these social treaties had been passed and the Irish Free State had ratified twenty-one.[54] He declared that the national independence of a country arose from a distinctive cultural outlook or social creed. This made it imperative for the Irish Free State to be active at Geneva in working for an ideal of social justice in accordance with that outlook and creed.

Alfred illustrated how the Irish Free State delegation was playing its part at I.L.O. conferences. Apart from ratifying conventions, the Irish delegation proposed the system of two readings for conventions. At the recent conference members of the

51. Brian Hillery and Patrick Lynch, *Ireland in the International Labour Organisation*, 32.
52. *Irish Press* 14, 27 April 1932.
53. *Irish Press* 9 May 1932.
54. In fact, twenty-two. See Brian Hillery and Patrick Lynch, *Ireland in the International Labour Organisation*, 49.

delegation took part in the review of the dockers' convention, the abolition of fee-charging employment agencies, the institution of social insurance and the regulation of admission of children to non-industrial occupations. Luke Duffy was elected vice-chairman of the resolutions committee, while he himself was chairman of the Committee on Article 408 (of the treaty of Versailles), the formation of which he had proposed in 1925. The work of this committee he described as follows: 'This committee . . . was composed of sixteen government, eight employer and eight worker delegates, French, English and German being the chief languages used. We had to inquire into the way in which the various conventions were being carried out in the different countries. Complaints were made against Great Britain – concerning the want of reciprocity in insurance benefits between Northern Ireland and the Irish Free State[55] – and against Greece, Romania, Bulgaria, Cuba, Luxembourg and Hungary. Representatives of these countries appeared before us to give explanations and to promise amendments.'[56] Participa-

---

55. Luke J. Duffy, who was also a member of this committee, took part in the discussion of a complaint of the Irish Trade Union Congress that legislation adopted by the parliament of Northern Ireland in 1928 contravened the provisions of the international convention regarding unemployment insurance. The convention, which was ratified by Britain in July 1921 and by the Irish Free State in September 1925, provided in article 3 that: 'The members of the International Labour Organisation which ratify this convention shall make arrangements whereby workers belonging to one member and working in the territory of another shall be admitted to the same rates of benefit as those which obtain for the workers belonging to the latter.' The Irish contention was that, as Britain ratified the convention, it was mandatory on her to make reciprocal arrangements in regard to unemployment insurance with the Irish Free State. Such arrangements existed as far as Northern Ireland was concerned until 1928, when the Northern parliament altered the Unemployment Insurance Acts in such a way as to preclude Irish Free State citizens working in Northern Ireland from receiving benefit, until they had a three years residence qualification. The British representatives disclaimed responsibility for this development by stating that 'the administration of unemployment insurance in Northern Ireland was transferred to the government of Northern Ireland on 1 January 1922' (*Irish Independent* 16 April 1932).

56. Alfred's attitude while chairing sessions of the committee was universally appreciated. He was most informal and good-humoured, comparing his role to that of a big, kindly Irish policeman confronted with a youthful offender. A few friendly slaps and then release on promising to be a better boy in future. Typically, however, he did not miss the opportunity to emphasise the ameliorative effect of I.L.O. conventions on social legislation throughout the

tion in such activity, he continued, was most valuable as in the light of it 'the crude propaganda of the stage Irishman or the political Kilkenny cats became rather incredible'. The prominence of the Irish delegation in conference activities, he claimed, was not surprising, as it was one of the most influential and popular in Geneva, especially with the I.L.O. office itself and the workers.

Alfred emphasised that the world economic crisis, not the drafting of conventions, dominated the minds of those attending the 1932 I.L.O. conference. This was reflected in the director's annual report. In the discussion which followed, a resolution calling for immediate action was jointly tabled in the name of the workers by trade-union leaders Léon Jouhaux of France, Corneille Mertens of Belgium and Charles Schürch of Switzerland. It soon became clear, however, that the resolution would not be passed. Alfred recalled that the Irish delegation then took the initiative in rewording the resolution which, as thus amended, was passed by 77 votes to 7. In fact, it was Alfred who amended the resolution and in the final vote it was passed by 80 votes to 1.

In urging the amended resolution Alfred repeated some of what he had declaimed on 23 April in reply to the director's annual report. On that occasion a number of the best-known leaders of labour in Europe, including Largo Caballero, the Marxist minister of labour and welfare, who was later head of the Republican government during the Spanish civil war, responded to the report. Alfred, however, upstaged all of them and gave one of the most eloquent addresses ever heard at an I.L.O. conference from brief hand-written notes which survive. That address was published in the *Irish Press*.[57] The reporter began by setting the scene: 'The announcement of the name of Professor O'Rahilly caused the hall to fill rapidly and, as he

---

world. He pointed to the importance of the supervisory function of the committee and its unique character, which was entirely at odds with the older ideas of national sovereignty. In a reference to the lack of progress of the Disarmament Conference sitting a few doors away, he declared that, if discussions on disarmament were to be successful, it would be necessary to establish a supervisory committee like that of the I.L.O., in which he expressed his hope that women and intellectual and manual workers would be included (*Irish Press* 2 May 1932).

57. *Irish Press* 27 April 1932. Parts of it were also reported in *Irish Press* 26 April 1932.

ascended the tribune, he was greeted with applause from all parts of the hall.' A tail-piece to the end of the report of the speech read: 'On the conclusion of his eloquent address the professor was warmly applauded and was congratulated by many delegates.' Such was the feeling with which he delivered his address that it was vividly recalled by at least one person forty years later. In a reference to it, Cornelius Cremin, the former Irish diplomat, wrote in his unpublished memoirs: 'At the third United Nations conference for Trade and Development held in Chile in 1972 I was talking to Mr Michael Noble [a former secretary of state for Scotland], representing Great Britain, when he volunteered the information which very naturally intrigued me that the best speaker he ever heard was Alfred O'Rahilly . . .'[58]

The address[59] was an outspoken attack on the I.L.O.'s failure to improve the general economic situation. Of the I.L.O. he said: 'We are becoming an international bureau of nothing, of zero.' He urged the conference to do something to fight the economic depression and then, referring to the director of the I.L.O. added: 'The head of our little kingdom weeps. But it is our duty to shout, to use this assembly as a megaphone not merely to startle the city of Calvin and Rousseau, but to reach the ears of governments and to awaken hope in the hearts of millions.' The 'soporific droning' of the conference he compared to a meeting of the chamber of commerce at Pompeii just before the eruption of Vesuvius. His peroration ended:

> We are here to voice the mute inglorious Miltons who are suffering. We have to be our brothers' keepers and not mock suffering humanity by discussing minutiae of an employment which does not exist. Let us give this call to action which it is our duty to give and, gentlemen, place your ears to the ground and listen to the heavy tramp of a hundred million of the hungry and unemployed.

The Jouhaux-O'Rahilly resolution

As a result of Alfred's intervention the I.L.O. had what was referred to in the press as the Jouhaux-O'Rahilly resolution placed on the agenda of the next meeting of the Council of the

58. Unpublished memoirs of Cornelius Cremin.
59. For the full address, see Appendix 2.

League of Nations. It called on the Council, which was composed of permanent representatives of the leading allied powers (the great powers) with other rotating members, to take decisions on:

(1) The immediate putting in hand of certain international public works;

(2) Representation of the League of Nations and of the International Labour Office at the forthcoming Lausanne Conference on reparations and debts;

(3) The convocation of an international monetary conference; and

(4) The convocation of a world economic conference to examine 'in a severely practical spirit' the problems of production and international trade.[60]

The great powers were not able to agree on a common financial or monetary policy and were reluctant to agree to an international discussion on this subject, at which the small powers would be represented, until they had reached agreement among themselves. This led to consideration of the I.L.O. resolution by the Council being postponed on two occasions.[61] Eventually a

60. *Irish Press* 27 May 1932.

61. In a letter to Alfred, dated 20 May 1932, Seán Lester described how he had caused the second postponement:

'The Labour Conference resolution came up today. [Salvador de] Madariaga (Spain) was the rapporteur and when the report was circulated a few minutes before the meeting I found it very unsatisfactory with regard to two of the items at any rate. I went to Madariaga and told him I was going to propose that the financial committee be asked to report to the council if the time had not come for a monetary conference, and secondly that the assembly be asked to consider the question of another world economic conference. This, I think, is as far as we can go, but it seems to have been much more than the big powers – England and Italy especially – were prepared for. I notified one or two other members of the council and sat down. It was the first item on the agenda. I saw Avenol, the French under-secretary general, go over to Madariaga who immediately afterwards announced that he wished to postpone this item. During the meeting I got a note from Madariaga asking me to go with him to talk with [Léon] Jouhaux who has come to Geneva to try to push his delegation. I do not know what the result will be or whether I shall get any support in the council or not, but I at least will "keep the flag flying". If I had not intervened, I fear there was every possibility that the report would have been adopted and that meant virtually the council washing its hands "comme Pontius Pilate"!' (O'Rahilly Papers: letter, dated 20 May 1932, Lester to O'Rahilly).

report on the resolution was presented on 21 May. It asserted that the Council was called upon to take no decisions and make no proposals and then somewhat contradictorily concluded by proposing that the committee on public works should be asked to expedite its labours; that the technical services and experts of the League should be placed at the disposal of the Lausanne Conference and that the resolution as a whole should be referred in September to the Assembly which was composed of representatives of all members of the organisation. This represented much less than the I.L.O. conference had desired, but included more than the original proposals prepared by the council secretariat which had envisaged no action at all. Seán Lester, the Irish Free State representative on the Council, successfully urged the acceptance of the proposal. He pointed out that no less than thirty governments had voted for the O'Rahilly proposal at the I.L.O. conference and, in particular, asked the council to refer the question of an international monetary conference to its financial committee. This was opposed by the British and French representatives. However, it was agreed to send the minutes of the meeting to the financial or second committee.

Supporters of the resolution expressed satisfaction that, although somewhat modified, it had been referred to the Assembly of the League. In the Irish press at the end of May it was noted that it would be the turn of the Irish representative to preside over the Council meeting on the eve of the Assembly and that as president he would inaugurate the Assembly's autumn meetings. In such a position it would be possible to turn the attention of the League in the direction to which the resolution pointed. The press also, no doubt at the prompting of Edward J. Phelan, a consummate publicist, speculated on the composition of the Irish delegation to that body, in view of the leading and constructive role which the Irish Free State representatives at the I.L.O. conference had in preparing the resolution.[62]

At the request of Seán Lester, then the Irish Free State's permanent delegate to the League of Nations, Alfred published an article in the *Journal de Genève* of 20 May 1932 on the oath of allegiance, the proposed abolition of which was then becoming a source of acrimony between the Irish Free State and Britain.

62. *Irish Press* 27 May 1932.

The article, which was published on the front page, was a superb summary of the Irish position.[63]

Apart from this foray into the realm of international propaganda, the extraordinary impact which Alfred had at Geneva was generally recognised. In a letter, dated 20 May 1932, Lester wrote: 'We often speak about you and I am still hearing echoes of your work at the Labour conference. "Il a créé une sensation" is the latest remark which has come to my ears, not made direct to me but to a third person.'[64]

Sudden death of Albert Thomas

The satisfaction of the Irish delegation at the success of the I.L.O. conference was tempered by the sudden and unexpected death of Albert Thomas ten days after the conference. Alfred published a memoir of the former director of the I.L.O. in the *Irish Press* of 14 May 1932. He pointed to Thomas's success in shaping the I.L.O. into an efficient organisation for social justice throughout the world. All Irish persons who had gone to Geneva, he continued, would remember him with affection and respect. His obvious concern for Ireland arose from his love of freedom and his reliance on that distinguished Irishman, Edward J. Phelan. Alfred referred to his own dealings with the former director, with whom he had a remarkable rapport. He recalled that on 29 April he had dined with Thomas in his home. The director was worried about the desperate world depression which was likely to wreck all efforts at social amelioration. So anxious was he about the outcome of the vote to be taken next morning on Alfred's resolution that he telephoned the influential Dr Eduard Beneš of Czechoslovakia about it. Thomas considered that the I.L.O. could not continue its work unless the League of Nations took immediate vigorous action concerning reparations, monetary stabilisation and public works.[65]

63. See Appendix 3. Alfred's contribution to the public debate on this subject was already known outside the country. In a letter, dated 4 April 1932, M. Alphand, French ambassador to the Irish Free State, acknowledged to Aristide Briand, French foreign minister, the importance of Alfred's writing on the oath of allegiance and cognate matters (*Collectanea Hibernica: Sources for Irish History* 26 (1984) 155). For more on Alfred's interventions in this public debate, see J. A. Gaughan, *Alfred O'Rahilly II: Public figure*, 248, 261, 263-4.

64. O'Rahilly Papers: letter, dated 20 May 1932, Lester to O'Rahilly.

65. *Irish Press* 14 May 1932. For the full text of the eulogy, see Appendix 4.

11. Albert Thomas, first director of the International Labour Office (1919-32). This picture was taken as he presided at a meeting of the International Labour Conference in April 1932

111

Achievements recognised

News of Alfred's activities at Geneva spread far and wide. He received a number of letters of congratulation. Perhaps the most significant of these was from Michael MacWhite, who served as the Irish Free State's permanent delegate to the League of Nations from 1923 to 1929 and was subsequently Irish envoy extraordinary and minister plenipotentiary to the U.S.A. (1929-1938) and to Italy (1938-1950). In a letter to Alfred, dated 20 July 1932, he wrote:

> I was very pleased when I learned that you were again delegated to the International Labour Organisation conference this year, and still more so as I read of the success that attended the motion on the economic crisis for which I understand you were largely responsible.
>
> I hope the government will justly appreciate the value of your contribution to the cause of international good-will and incidentally the prestige that accrues to the Saorstát because of it.
>
> Experience has taught me and I am sure you will agree that the influence of the larger countries at the League is often negatived by the personality of a delegate from a smaller one whose initiative and integrity cannot be gainsaid. I could cite you numerous examples if it were necessary.
>
> I hope the government will realise the supreme importance of Geneva to us. England will be able for a long time to come to influence the ear of the world because of her control of the press, but she cannot take away from us the facilities for speaking to the world that the Geneva platform affords. Unless we play into her hands by abusing our privileges there, or by sending deadheads to represent us, the prestige of the Saorstát should increase from day to day in the eyes of League members. It would seem, however, that after getting elected to the council we rested somewhat on our oars so that outsiders got the notion that we had no contribution to make to world betterment once our national egotism was satisfied. I should like to see you appointed a delegate to the League assembly as well as to the International Labour Office because there are economic

problems, the various phases of which you have such a complete mastery and which so many others find it most difficult to follow.[66]

Phelan and Mortished were of the same mind as MacWhite. Phelan kept Alfred informed of developments at Geneva. In a letter, dated 7 July, he claimed that Alfred's resolution was prophetic, as it then appeared that the Lausanne Conference would 'ask Geneva to get on with the general economic and financial problems'. He added that he had written to 'Joe Walshe, Hearne, Seán Murphy, Cremins and Rynne, explaining the situation and suggesting, with various formulae, that the Assembly equation will be incomplete unless it includes O'R.' He continued: 'O'R equals author and push and go and imagination and popularity in Geneva.' In addition, Mortished went to Dublin to lobby de Valera and other members of the cabinet to ensure that Alfred would be a member of the Irish delegation to the important meetings of the League of Nations in September.[67]

Mortished did not have to lobby the leaders of the labour movement. They were fully supportive of Alfred's activities at Geneva. The annual meeting of the Irish Trade Union Congress was held in Cork in the last week of July. Congress passed a resolution on the world crisis which welcomed 'the proposals adopted at the sixteenth session of the I.L.O. conference for promoting international collaboration through the machinery of the League of Nations' and asked the government, in virtue of its position as a member of the Council of the League, to urge energetically the adoption by the League of the measures suggested by the I.L.O.[68] In mid-August the resolution was sent to

66. O'Rahilly Papers: letter, dated 20 July 1932, MacWhite to O'Rahilly.

67. O'Rahilly Papers: letter, dated 7 July 1932, Phelan to O'Rahilly.

68. The full text of the resolution read: 'Realising that more than twenty-five million wage-earners throughout the world are being reduced by unemployment to a condition of wretchedness and desperation, owing to the collapse of the present economic system; that the peace and happiness of the world are imperilled by the social unrest produced by years of uninterrupted economic disorganisation; that nationalistic fear and jealousy prompted and cultivated by the manipulators of international finance have delayed the taking of effective measures to restore economic equilibrium throughout the world; that finance capitalism is no longer able to organise internationally the production or distribution of essential and useful commodities; this congress welcomes the proposals adopted at the sixteenth session of the I.L.O. conference for promoting international collaboration through the machinery of the League of Nations and

de Valera for his 'careful consideration'. On 13 September the secretary of the national executive of Congress reminded de Valera of this resolution and pointedly drew his special attention to 'the important resolution passed at the sixteenth session of the I.L.O. conference and since known as the Jouhaux-O'Rahilly resolution'.[69]

Not included in Irish delegation to League of Nations 1932

Alfred was eager to be included in the Irish delegation so as to be able to supervise the progress of his resolution through the various stages of its consideration by the Council of the League of Nations. He wrote to de Valera impressing upon him the importance of the issues to be discussed and the significant advantages to be gained for the Irish Free State if de Valera himself led the delegation.[70] At that stage Alfred and his admirers fully expected that he would be invited by the government to go to Geneva in some capacity. It was reported in the *Irish Press* at the beginning of September that the department of external affairs was finalising the membership of the Irish Free State's delegation to the League of Nations' meetings in Geneva.[71] Alfred, who up to then had heard nothing about the matter, concluded that he was not to be a member of the delegation and expressed his disappointment to Phelan. In a reply, dated 9 September 1932, Phelan suggested that there was no reason why a 'substitute delegate' could not be added later to the listed delegation of three ministers and three civil servants. He indicated his conviction that Alfred was chiefly responsible for persuading de Valera to lead the Irish delegation to Geneva.

calls upon the government of Saorstát, in virtue of its position as a member of the Council of the League, to energetically urge the adoption by the League of the measures suggested by the I.L.O.'

69. *Cork Examiner* 30 July 1932; S.P.O., Department of the Taoiseach, S 6812.

70. See O'Rahilly Papers: letter, dated 9 September 1932, Phelan to O'Rahilly.

71. *Irish Press* 3 September 1932. Eventually the *Irish Press* of 20 September 1932 listed the delegation as follows: *Ministers:* Eamon de Valera (president of the executive council), Senator Joseph Connolly (minister for posts and telegraphs), Conor Maguire (attorney-general), and *Officials:* John Leydon (secretary, department of industry and commerce), Seán Murphy (assistant-secretary, department of external affairs), John J. Hearne (legal adviser, department of external affairs), Frank Cremin (department of external affairs).

Alfred's omission from the delegation he ascribed to de Valera's need to choose his 'supporters'. He advised Alfred not to lose heart and to 'pull any strings' he could and that he would do likewise.[72]

Alfred did not need advice of this kind. He had already written to de Valera complaining that he had made several unsuccessful attempts to meet him. In a letter, dated 6 September, de Valera expressed surprise at this and declared that since he had decided to go to Geneva he had been eager to confer with Alfred about his resolution. He stated that he recognised its importance and 'the opening' it provided. In the meantime he promised to write a week later to arrange a meeting.[73]

In the event Alfred did not have an interview with de Valera and he was not seconded to the Irish delegation. Reasons were not lacking for his exclusion from the delegation. Civil servants would have regarded him as an outsider and would have had no enthusiasm for his appointment. When acting as a delegate at the I.L.O. conference in 1925 Alfred did nothing to win their sympathy. In particular, his formal complaint about Ferguson and Stafford to MacGilligan would not have been forgotten. The omission of Ferguson and Stafford from the delegation to the 1932 I.L.O. conference to convenience Alfred would have been a Pyrrhic victory. The intensive lobbying of the department of external affairs by Phelan, Mortished and Alfred probably caused some resentment. In a letter to Phelan, Alfred disclosed his view that Seán Murphy, assistant secretary in external affairs, 'could poison' him.[74] It is probable that Alfred was apprised of this by Joseph P. Walshe, the secretary of the department and a life-long friend.

Murphy's attitude no doubt reflected that of some of his senior colleagues. The cabinet in general and Lemass in particular would not have been impressed by the intensive lobbying. Moreover, by this time Alfred had clashed in public with Lemass.[75] Finally,

72. O'Rahilly Papers: letter, dated 9 September 1932, Phelan to O'Rahilly.

73. O'Rahilly Papers: letter, dated 6 September 1932, de Valera to O'Rahilly.

74. See O'Rahilly Papers: letter, dated 27 September 1932, Phelan to O'Rahilly.

75. See pp. 51-2. Later he was to severely criticise Lemass on a number of issues, see J. A. Gaughan, *Alfred O'Rahilly II: Public figure*, 319-20, 365, 378, 482. In his 'Pat Murphy's Jottings' in the *Standard* of 11 June 1943 he compiled a piece on the Swiss system of P.R. and concluded: '"A coalition government," said Mr Lemass, "is negation of democracy." This is a piece of hypocritical humbug.'

de Valera, who knew him intimately from his school-days, was fully aware that Alfred was too independent-minded to be a dutiful member of a delegation. This was partially the reason why Alfred was not appointed secretary to the Irish delegation to the treaty negotiations in 1921.[76] But perhaps, most importantly of all, there was de Valera's propensity to be the only light in the firmament. In the ultimate analysis whatever about the views of individual civil servants of Alfred, in selecting delegates to represent the country at international conferences reliability was a factor, of which they had to take account. On that basis Alfred's claim for a place on such delegations would have been regarded by the bureaucratic mind as at best arguable.[77]

Success of Irish delegation to League of Nations

Writing on 27 September 1932, Phelan expressed satisfaction at the results achieved by the meetings of the Council and

76. For more on this, see J. A. Gaughan, *Alfred O'Rahilly II: Public figure*, 104-5, 122-9.

77. Here it is well to reflect on Alfred's strictures on the members of the civil service encountered by him in his representational work in Geneva, and especially on the behaviour of officials inherited by the Free State government from the government of the U.K. in 1922. At the time of the treaty these officials, nearly all Irish, were engaged in administering the range of public services operating in Ireland as part of the U.K. Shortly after the treaty was ratified by the Dáil a British order-in-council was made transferring the various functions of government to the Provisional Government of the Irish Free State and at the same time transferring all officials engaged on the functions covered by the order. By 1 April 1922 the departments of the Provisional Government had taken over the functions and the staff of the various offices. The position then was that civil servants found themselves continuing to do their work, but under a different master. The term 'transferred officer' as applied to these officials carried no connotation of residual loyalty to the U.K.; indeed for the vast majority of them, the opposite was the case. It is not possible to find out what the defence was by the officials about whom Alfred complained to the charges of lack of commitment, etc., or to the less serious charge of incompetence. If they fell short of the standard required, one would expect the minister to take action. However, in the case of the two industry and commerce personnel named by Alfred both survived to represent the government on I.L.O. delegations for several years; and both retired occupying the highest positions to which they could aspire, Robert C. Ferguson as secretary of the department of industry and commerce and Miss Brighid Stafford as chief inspector of factories. As regards the external affairs personnel it would appear that none suffered in his diplomatic career because of his brush with Alfred.

Assembly of the League of Nations. He considered that de Valera's speech to the Assembly was 'very good' and that his presidency of the council was 'quite successful'. Phelan confided to Alfred that he found de Valera a most interesting person who made up his own mind after 'working hard to absorb the facts'. By contrast, he considered that the delegation's officials were 'nervous and timid' and felt that he was not 'quite such a *persona grata* with them as in previous years'. He exempted from this comment 'Hearne, Leydon and to some extent Cremins'. But he described the attitude of Seán Murphy to him as 'silent and polite rather than cordial'.[78]

He speculated that this might have been caused by 'that telegram of mine that you sent on'. This telegram, it seems, implied that Phelan was convinced that Alfred would be far more useful in Geneva than the entire complement of officials in the department of external affairs. Not surprisingly, as Phelan also speculated, this probably caused some 'departmental pique'.

Phelan disclosed to Alfred that he had advised de Valera that the speech given to him by the League secretariat was hopeless. De Valera rejected it as he did the amended version proposed by his own officials.[79] This was quite unusual. The convention was that an incoming president of the Assembly would deliver the speech prepared by the secretariat. This was invariably a bland review of the previous twelve months and an assessment

78. Phelan, it seems, regretted his comment about Murphy. On the following day in a note to Alfred he wrote: 'I may have misled you yesterday about Seán Murphy. I was puzzled at his silence, etc. The fact is that he was absolutely tired out and suffering from strain. He has had to lie up today' (O'Rahilly Papers: letter, dated 28 September 1932, Phelan to O'Rahilly). Generally speaking, Phelan had a high opinion of the civil servants attached to various Irish delegations. In a letter to Alfred, dated 5 October 1932, he described John Leydon as 'a very able and very decent fellow – an excellent appointment, knows his stuff really well and will, I think, do extremely well' (O'Rahilly Papers: letter, dated 5 October 1932, Phelan to O'Rahilly). In addition, throughout the Phelan-O'Rahilly correspondence there were very favourable references to Seán Lester, the Irish permanent delegate to the League of Nations. These three became close friends. Lester's friendship with Alfred, however, did not blind him to the latter's vanity. He liked to describe a visit which he, Phelan and Alfred made to an abbey situated high up in the Swiss Alps. The setting was idyllic. Lester recalled that, on viewing the abbey, he said: 'I could find peace here.' To which Alfred, it seems, replied: 'I could be the abbot here!' (interview with Douglas Gageby, Lester's son-in-law).

79. O'Rahilly Papers: letter, dated 27 September 1932, Phelan to O'Rahilly.

of the work confronting the Assembly. De Valera, however, delivered a speech prepared by himself. It caused a sensation and received considerable publicity all over the world. De Valera spoke of the threat of conflicts and pointed out that, after conflict and war, the contestants must eventually get together to negotiate terms of peace and agreement. Why not seek agreement now and avoid all the horrors of war and the destruction accompanying it? In the final third of his address he dealt with the possibility of impending economic collapse and the radical changes required to obviate it. he called for 'the deliberate shaping of economic activity to an ethical and social end'. In this part of his address he was clearly influenced by Alfred's major contributions at the I.L.O. conference of 1932 and the subsequent resolution placed under his name and that of Léon Jouhaux on the agenda of the council of the League of Nations.[80]

In his letter of 27 September[81] Phelan told Alfred that he found Senator Joseph Connolly interesting but had difficulty in understanding his radical ideas on credit and economics, the senator himself not being very clear on these.[82] De Valera, however, he noted, was influenced very much by Connolly, although he tended to adapt and modify his advice. The third cabinet member of the delegation, Conor Maguire, the attorney-general, he found likeable, but interested solely in legal questions.[83] Phelan told Alfred that de Valera in conversation with

80. Maurice Moynihan, *Speeches and statements by Eamon de Valera 1917-73* (Dublin 1980) 219-23.

81. O'Rahilly Papers: letter, dated 27 September 1932, Phelan to O'Rahilly.

82. In a letter to Alfred, dated 5 October 1932, Phelan wrote that Connolly wished to nationalise the banks (O'Rahilly Papers: letter, dated 5 October 1932, Phelan to O'Rahilly).

83. In a letter to Alfred, dated 5 October 1932, Phelan wrote of the attorney-general: 'I think you are wrong in thinking he has anything against you. He strikes me as the attorney-general of the old or classic style, that is, not regarding himself as a politician but only as a legal adviser on the small day to day legal problems. I talked to him about *inter se*, etc. He does not pretend to know anything about it, nor to have followed the 1926 report, etc. All that seems quite outside his line and I imagine he regards that as Dev's business and as pertaining to external affairs and as not being the attorney-general's function.' Phelan continued: 'I have not been able to talk to Connolly about that side of things yet but I will try to before he goes. Dev, I think, understands. I hope he will make a treaty in *proper form* with South Africa so as to hit *inter se* with one good precedent' (O'Rahilly Papers: letter, dated 5 October 1932, Phelan to O'Rahilly). The reference here to *inter se* concerned the conviction of Alfred and Phelan that every opportunity should be availed of to ensure that the Anglo-Irish treaty

his fellow delegates referred to him as 'intellectually far and away the best-equipped man in Ireland' and 'a man with ideas, personality and energy'.[84] Phelan described de Valera's method of procedure as wise: 'he listens to the department [his external affairs] officials, to the senator, to Seán Lester and to me and then makes up his mind alone'. He conveyed his delight to Alfred that de Valera was 'inclined to follow our line', as evidenced by his speech to the general assembly.

In a further letter of 5 October[85] Phelan's comments on de Valera were most favourable. He found him 'very pleasant and approachable'. De Valera's speech at the assembly he judged to be 'a great success', as was his tenure as president of the Council. Phelan noted with approval that de Valera prepared not only his speech to the Assembly but also an address from the League of Nations broadcasting station on 2 October. In this de Valera disposed of suspicions that he was opposed to the League of Nations[86] by emphasising that in his inauguration of the current session of the Assembly he had spoken 'not as an enemy of the League but as one who wishes the League to be strengthened and developed as the best visible means of securing peace among the nations and of solving the major political and economic problems which face the world today.'[87]

Phelan informed Alfred that de Valera would be coming out again to Geneva in mid-November to preside over the discussion of the Lytton report on the Sino-Japanese conflict. In a letter of 17 October he told him that Senator Connolly at a meeting of

would be recognised by Britain as an international agreement. It is very likely that Maguire's coolness to Alfred was due to somewhat insistent advice and promptings from the latter that the attorney-general should be more active in this regard. For the background to this, see J. A. Gaughan, *Alfred O'Rahilly II: Public figure*, 225-31.

84. In a letter, dated 5 October 1932, Phelan told Alfred that de Valera on the occasion of a formal visit to the I.L.O. office 'covered' him with praise (O'Rahilly Papers: letter, dated 5 October 1932, Phelan to O'Rahilly).

85. O'Rahilly Papers: letter, dated 5 October 1932, Phelan to O'Rahilly.

86. It is not difficult to find the source for such suspicions. Senator Joseph Connolly wrote in his memoirs that at the conclusion of de Valera's speech: 'The Assembly was slightly stunned . . . There was a momentary pause of silence and then a loud burst of applause, but the temporary pause enabled some of the less scrupulous of the British journalists to report that the speech was received in stony silence' ('Unpublished memoirs of Joseph Connolly', 236; see also Maurice Moynihan, *Speeches and statements by Eamon de Valera 1917-23*, 219).

87. Maurice Moynihan, *Speeches and statements by Eamon de Valera 1917-23*, 219.

the Second Committee had made 'an excellent speech' on his resolution and had been supported by Léon Jouhaux. In so doing they had thwarted a move 'to bury it in the Assembly' and ensured that it went forward to the world economic conference. Phelan assured Alfred that Connolly had 'a high opinion' of him. Connolly, it seems, suggested at that time that Alfred should be added to the Lausanne Committee dealing with problems arising from war reparations.[88]

World economic conference 1933

Alfred was very disappointed that he was not invited to be a member of the delegation to the meetings of the Assembly and Council of the League of Nations in September 1932. This was compounded when no call came to him to go as an adviser to the world economic conference which opened in London on 12 June 1933. The decision to convene this conference had been taken almost a year earlier, on 15 July 1932. The Council of the League of Nations made the decision after a resolution to that effect was placed before it by the Lausanne Conference. By that time the great powers who took part in that conference had anticipated that the pressure building up for a world economic conference made it virtually certain that such a conference would be held. They realised that if it were convened as a result of a discussion of the Jouhaux-O'Rahilly resolution, then on the agenda of the Assembly, the small powers would have had an opportunity to influence the thrust of the ensuing conference. Consequently, at a session of the Lausanne Conference, they took the initiative which ensured that it would be organised along lines which coincided with their national interests. It was left to Sir John Simon, the British foreign secretary, to persuade the Council members to agree to the resolution which effected this.

This initiative by the great powers was unexpected. The reaction of Seán Lester, the Irish Free State delegate, was typical. He expressed surprise both at the form and the substance of the proposal. Continuing, he pointed out that the council had before it in May the Jouhaux-O'Rahilly resolution of the International Labour Conference. But, although he had then urged that something should be done, the council had considered that

88. O'Rahilly Papers: letter, dated 19 October 1932, Phelan to O'Rahilly.

the matter required wider consideration and had referred the resolution to the Assembly in September. Nonetheless, he was not opposed to immediate action, as the matter was certainly no less urgent now than it had been then. He urged, however, that adequate participation should be afforded to the small powers, whose economic destinies were going to be affected, that the interests of agriculture should be taken into consideration, and that representation should be secured for the International Labour Organisation through which organised workers and employers could be brought into full consultation. Although the subsequent discussion indicated that Lester's views were widely shared, Sir John Simon succeeded in persuading the Council to call and finance an economic conference to be, in effect, organised and conducted by the six great powers represented at the Lausanne Conference. This development prompted the Geneva correspondent of the *Irish Press* to make the following comment: 'We pointed out that the inaction of the Council in May was to be explained by the reluctance of the great powers to agree to a general discussion of economic and financial questions until they were agreed among themselves. The methods now proposed are a further indication of the desire to secure for the great powers a sort of international economic dictatorship.'[89]

In mid-April and, again, on 1 May 1933 Phelan urged Alfred to come to Geneva as a delegate to the 1933 I.L.O. conference. He wrote that, given Alfred's agreement, he and Mortished were eager to lobby to that end. Alfred did not reply to Phelan's letters.[90] By that time he had become disillusioned with the manner in which persons were selected for delegations to Geneva. Earlier he had ignored a request to draft an official report on the I.L.O. conference of 1932. Eventually this was prepared by an official of the department of industry and commerce. In presenting the report to de Valera on 1 March 1933, John Leydon, secretary of the department, noted that 'a letter forwarding a copy of the report was issued to Professor O'Rahilly on 20 February to which no reply has been received.'[91] The announcement in mid-May that Robert C.

89. *Irish Press* 20 July 1932.

90. O'Rahilly Papers: letters, dated April, 1 May, 17 June 1933, Phelan to O'Rahilly.

91. S.P.O., Department of the Taoiseach, S 6812.

Ferguson was to join Seán Lester in representing the government at the I.L.O. conference of 8-26 June was a clear signal that Alfred's career as a government representative or adviser at I.L.O. conferences had ended.

By 14 June 1933 the fanfare with which the world economic conference was inaugurated had attracted immense public interest. On that date Frank Gallagher, editor of the *Irish Press*, sent a telegram to Alfred: 'Please write 1000 words on "what I would propose to the economic conference".'[92] By return of post Alfred replied:

> As representative of this country at last year's International Labour Conference, I took a leading part in proposing such a conference. Subsequently the big powers, led by Sir John Simon, succeeded in completely distorting and diverting the proposal.
>
> This year the Fianna Fáil government decided on choosing for Geneva a representative who presumably represents its views more accurately than I do. The government has also appointed its advisers to the economic conference. I have therefore nothing further to do with the matter. But, as you ask me, the first thing I would do would be to scrap Fianna Fáil's 'advisers' and to substitute for them men with an independent national outlok, neither academically nor economically tied to the support of mass capitalist production or our system of currency and credit. After that – well, let us wait till it happens.[93]

Alfred's dismissive comment about 'Fianna Fáil's advisers' was unwarranted and no more than an expression of the strong resentment he felt against the 'bureaucrats' of the department of external affairs and of industry and commerce. Senator Joseph Connolly, in effect, led the Irish delegation to the world economic conference.[94] In his unpublished memoirs he recalled

92. O'Rahilly Papers: telegram, dated 14 June 1933, Gallagher to O'Rahilly.
93. O'Rahilly Papers: copy of letter, dated 14 June 1933, O'Rahilly to Gallagher. In the event Gallagher published articles under the heading 'What I would propose to the world economic conference' by Robert C. Barton, H. T. Gallagher, George O'Brien and Louie Bennett in the *Irish Press* of 16, 20, 24 and 28 June 1933 respectively.
94. The Irish delegation to the world economic conference was listed in the press as: Eamon de Valera, president of the executive of the Irish Free State, minister

that before travelling to London he and Frank Cremins of the department of external affairs, who was responsible for League of Nations' matters, spent a week preparing for the economic conference. Cremins acted as secretary to the delegation which included a few advisers. On 15 June, the fourth day of the conference, Connolly expressed the determination of the Irish Free State to co-operate and work for world peace and security based on justice and with due regard for the rights of others. He expressed disappointment with the report of the agenda committee for suggesting that a solution had to be found within the conventional orthodox fiscal system.[95] Connolly was no less ready than Alfred to be critical of current economic wisdom. The kernel of his statement read:

> It may not be inopportune to ask ourselves at this stage if our whole basis of money, exchange, credit and distribution has not broken down and, if we allow that it is functioning, is it not merely staggering along? Yet the position in which we are endeavouring to survive today has been built on the system of production, credit and finance that still seems to be accepted as inevitable. Must we accept it as inevitable? Has it worked? Is it working? These are the questions that we may well ask ourselves when we are warned by the drafting committee that we must do nothing *'to diminish confidence in the banking system'*, that the *'machine is delicate'* and so forth. My feeling is that the 'machine' is so 'delicate' that it has ceased to be effective, and as regards 'confidence' I ask where is that confidence to be found, to what extent does it exist today and if there is any indication of its early return?[96]

Connolly and presumably the officials who advised him were no less inhibited in referring to the then uneasy relations

for external affairs, and head of the delegation; Senator Joseph Connolly, minister for lands and fisheries; Seán Lemass, minister for industry and commerce; Seán MacEntee, minister for finance, and Dr James Ryan, minister for agriculture (*Irish Press* 6 June 1933). Connolly and Frank Cremins, of the department of external affairs, effectively represented the Irish Free State at the conference, the attendance and involvement of the rest of the delegation being not more than cursory.

95. 'Unpublished memoirs of Joseph Connolly', 272, 274; *Irish Press* 16 June 1933.

96. 'Unpublished memoirs of Joseph Connolly', 274.

between Britain and the Irish Free State. Another part of his address read:

> Reviewing broadly the present position, it is not easy to escape the feeling that the situation has been aggravated by the political and international conflicts of the past. These are not necessarily confined to wars, whether long past or recently experienced, but include so-called treaties of peace imposed on weaker states, divisions of territories, border impositions and the like.
>
> I am not referring to the position of any particular country – neither my own nor others – but I think it cannot be disputed that, when might or power exercises its superior force in either the military or economic sphere, then the results are fear, bitterness and a spirit of antagonism that make impossible any cooperation or any approach to a fair and reasonable solution of the problems.[97]

Alfred's reply to Frank Gallagher's telegram of mid-June 1933 was a sad postscript to the heady days of April 1932 when at Geneva he and his international-minded admirers and colleagues proposed a radical way forward out of the economic and financial chaos throughout the world. The hopes they then kindled of a solution arising from a new approach to national sovereignty and world trade were firmly dampened down by the great powers, such as Britain, France and especially the United States of America at the conference and thereby the slide towards world war two continued.[98] However, the impact

97. 'Unpublished memoirs of Joseph Connolly', 275.
98. The cynicism exhibited by the great powers, not least the United States of America, is captured in Senator Connolly's recollection of the conference:
'From the outset, there seemed little likelihood of any worthwhile harmony or agreement being reached. In the monetary sub-commission, many of the Central and Southern European Nations wished to have the discussions confined to the problem of indebtedness. France, Germany, Italy, Spain, Poland and a number of others pressed for this course, but they were defeated on a vote. Efforts were made to secure temporary stabilisation of currencies but this was turned down, the Americans arguing that any such move would cause a violent price recession. Their qualification of their refusal was to me somewhat bewildering. It read: "The American delegation has already introduced a resolution designed for ultimate world-wide stabilisation of currencies and is devoting itself to the support of measures for the establishment of a coordinated

Alfred had made at the I.L.O. conferences of 1924, 1925 and especially 1932 was not forgotten. In his letter to Alfred of 17 June 1933 Phelan wrote: 'although you remain buried in Cork your resolution goes working on as I knew it would'. He was optimistic about the thrust towards social justice in the future: 'I think the world will be struggling along the O'R[ahilly] resolution lines for some time to come so that you may get another opportunity to lead a great cavalry charge.'[99] Alas for his optimism; by 27 July the world economic conference had been adjourned *sine die*, having become an embarrassing fiasco for those participating in it.

---

monetary and fiscal policy to be pursued by the various nations in cooperation for the purpose of stimulating economic activity and improving prices.'' The French representatives were keen to have currency stabilisation and regarded it as a necessary preliminary to restore price levels. There was a threat of deadlock in the monetary sub-committee and this probably accounted for the American promise of "*ultimate* world-wide stabilisation". It can hardly have satisfied the French representatives, but with it they had to rest content' ('Unpublished memoirs of Joseph Connolly', 275).

99. O'Rahilly Papers: letter, dated 17 June 1933, Phelan to O'Rahilly. Phelan also informed Alfred (ibid.) that his resolution had been mentioned in the director's report to the I.L.O. conference of 1933, at the world economic conference then in session in London and in an account of Alfred's formulation of it at the I.L.O. conference of 1932 (see E. J. Phelan, 'Industrial and social aspects of the economic crisis', *Problems of peace* (seventh series) – lectures delivered at the Geneva Institute of International Relations 1932 – published by Allen and Unwin, London, 1933, 110-17).

ANTI-COMMUNIST CRUSADER

A split in the Labour Party and the emergence of a remarkable system of workers' education at University College, Cork, led to Alfred becoming the effective leader of an anti-communist crusade from 1944 to 1952. On 7 January 1944 the Irish Transport and General Workers Union disaffiliated from the Labour Party. Of the seventeen Labour T.Ds, eight were members of the I.T.G.W.U. On 14 January five of these followed the lead of their union, seceded from the Labour Party and formed the National Labour Party. In a joint statement, dated 26 January, they declared that their action was due to communist influence in the Labour Party.

The 'Larkin issue'

Notwithstanding this statement and subsequent protestations by National Labour Party T.Ds, the split was essentially a new flare-up of what in Labour Party circles was known as the 'Larkin issue'. A legendary figure in the struggle of Irish workers for their rights, James Larkin was a vital, pugnacious, egotistical, blustering genius who found it as easy to quarrel with his own side as to attack those whom he regarded as his own and the workers' enemies. His contribution to the working-class movement up to 1913-14 was outstanding, but thereafter his activities bedevilled the trade-union movement and the fortunes of the Labour Party. As a result of his clash with the leadership of the I.T.G.W.U., a dissident union, known as the Workers' Union of Ireland, was set up in his name by his brother, Peter. It was made up of former members of the I.T.G.W.U., who regarded themselves as supporters of Larkin, and for four years a bitter feud continued between its members and those of the parent union. From 1923 onwards Larkin had conducted a continuous campaign against Thomas Johnson, T.D., leader of the Labour Party, and was largely responsible for Johnson losing his seat for County Dublin in the September 1927 general election. For his disruptive activities Larkin was excluded from the Labour Party and his union from the Irish Trade Union Congress. As a result of libel actions against him by the I.T.G.W.U. and later by Johnson, he was declared to be bankrupt on two occasions. But perhaps the most damaging result, for the labour movement, was that he attracted the undying enmity of William O'Brien, the influential secretary of the I.T.G.W.U.

The events which led to the split in the Labour Party began in December 1941, when, in the backlash of the trade-union opposition to the Wages Standstill Order, Larkin, his son Jim, and a large number of Larkinites successfully applied for admission to the Labour Party. In August 1942 Larkin was elected to Dublin City Council. With a general election due in 1943, Larkin and his followers began to take steps to ensure that he would be a Labour candidate in Dublin North-East. Mainly at the instigation of William O'Brien, these efforts were thwarted by the I.T.G.W.U. However, at the beginning of May 1943 a Dublin selection conference of the Party nominated Larkin as a candidate. The seventeen-member Administrative Council declined to ratify the nomination, by eight votes to seven, all eight members of the I.T.G.W.U. on the Council voting against ratification. This decision was not accepted by the Dublin Labour branches, and Labour candidates for Dublin City and County, acting in conjunction with the Dublin executive of the Party, nominated Larkin as an official candidate for Dublin North-East. Larkin was elected. At the first meeting of the Administrative Council after the election, the I.T.G.W.U. members moved that the chairman, Jim Larkin junior, and the secretary of the Dublin executive, John [E. de Courcy] Ireland, be expelled from the Party on the grounds that, in promoting the candidature of Jim Larkin senior, they had acted in defiance of the Party constitution. Discussion of the motion continued over a period of five months. Eventually the I.T.G.W.U. members insisted on a vote on the motion on 3 December 1943. The motion was defeated, the eight I.T.G.W.U. members voting for it, but the remaining members voting against it. Just over a month later came the disaffiliation of the union from the Labour Party.

In the months before the disaffiliation the union's leaders, including William O'Brien, realised that there was not much support from the membership for such a drastic move. In the labour movement as a whole there was an eagerness to lay the 'Larkin issue' to rest. Thomas Johnson, the Party's elder statesman, who had been much maligned and treated outrageously by Larkin, saw little merit in harking back to old controversies. William Norton, leader of the Party, was eager to see an end to the squabbles and damaging divisions of the past. To this end, he made numerous efforts to placate the opposition of the I.T.G.W.U. to the acceptance of Larkin into the Party, which the latter in former years had been so determined to destroy.

William O'Brien raises the issue of Communist infiltration

At the beginning of 1944 William O'Brien had a circular prepared explaining the reasons for the union breaking with the Labour Party. In this, which was dated 15 January and sent to every branch of the I.T.G.W.U. for distribution, O'Brien and his colleagues on the union's executive charged that communists had taken over the Labour Party in Dublin, that the Party had allowed communism to permeate it to such an extent that there was no hope of its recovering its independence and that Norton was fully aware of these facts. The irony of O'Brien, who as a young man had claimed to be a revolutionary socialist, warning against a communist take-over was not lost on his former colleagues. They regarded his ideological conversion as mainly due to a determination to retain control over the I.T.G.W.U. and thereby considerable influence over the labour movement. For them O'Brien's ploy was all the more blatant in that during the bickering on the 'Larkin issue' at meetings of the Administrative Council from April to December 1943 the 'communist bogey' was never raised. The only indirect reference to it was when Jim Larkin junior, who had been an important figure in the Communist Party of Ireland, made a clear declaration of his acceptance of the Labour Party programme and was understood thereby to have rejected his past affiliations.[1]

In fairness to O'Brien it should be noted that in 1937 he had written a preface to a pamphlet by Norton, *Cemeteries of liberty: communist and fascist dictatorships.*[2] However, the enthusiasm with which he 'played the red card' had little to do with a fear of increasing communist influence in the labour movement. It was rather an indication of his accurate knowledge of the prevailing attitudes of the rank-and-file members of his union. While they had no sympathy with what they regarded as the continuation of the feud between Larkin and O'Brien, they had even less for communism. Patrick J. O'Brien, who was

1. J. A. Gaughan, *Thomas Johnson (1872-1963): first leader of the Labour Party in Dáil Éireann* (Dublin 1980) 258-77, 372-80.

2. William Norton, *Cemeteries of liberty: communist and fascist dictatorships* (Dublin 1937) 2.

one of those responsible for the Cork office of the I.T.G.W.U., was not untypical in this regard. Initially, at least, his main preoccupation was the tension in the labour movement between trade-unionists and non-trade-unionists and between the I.T.G.W.U. and the much smaller craft unions, a number of which were really branches of British unions. In a letter to O'Brien, dated 7 January 1943, he noted that in the selection of candidates in the Meath-Westmeath constituency for the coming general election Captain Peadar Cowan had 'knocked out' a trade-unionist, named Charles McGurk. He also reported a threat by Larkin and his followers to mount a 'vast volume of protest' at a meeting of the Administrative Council to be held on 12 January 1943. And P. J. O'Brien added 'the gents [representatives of the craft unions and others on the Administrative Council] who justified Dublin Central twelve months ago [in assisting on the re-admission of Larkin to the Labour Party] will hardly be over happy with their "nestling".'[3]

Comment on I.T.G.W.U. circular

The *Standard* of 28 January 1944 carried a report of the circular issued by the I.T.G.W.U. and called upon the leadership of the Labour Party to deal urgently with the alleged communist infiltration of the organisation.[4] It stated: 'By good fortune we

3. O'Brien Papers: MS 13960, letter, dated 7 January 1943, P. J. O'Brien to William O'Brien.

4. It gave the following analysis of recent and current communist activity:

There are two schools of communism in Ireland – those who have adhered to the Third International (called by themselves, Stalinists) and those who have adhered to the Fourth International (called Trotskyites). The Third Internationalists were organised as the Communist Party of Ireland; the Fourth as a secret society.

The Communist Party of Ireland claims direct descent from Saor Éire, formed in 1931. At the outbreak of the war, after several years hard work, it had in the whole of Ireland about 1,000 members – 400 in Dublin, 500 in Belfast and 100 scattered through the rest of the country. Amongst the 1,000 members there was only one who had any pretensions to education. He was a cautious Englishman . . .

The Communist Party of Ireland was no menace. Still it contrived to place at least three of its members in positions as honorary secretaries of branches of the Labour Party in Dublin and to secure for two of its members places on the Dublin Constituencies Council of the Party.

The Fourth International came on the scene at the conclusion of the Spanish civil war. Prior to September 1939, four of its emissaries, who

have in the files of *Torch* and the *Irish Workers' Weekly* (defunct organ of the C.P.I.) abundant evidence of the thorough-going faith of practically all the communist leaders now allied to labour.' The editor expostulated that it was impossible to understand how, 'in the face of their public professions, the Labour Party was able within its rules to admit them to membership'. He described the split in the Labour Party as 'a national disaster', as it dashed hopes that an influential workers' party would succeed in furthering significant social reforms.[5]

had belonged to the International Brigade, arrived in Dublin and proceeded forthwith, undisguised, to make their way into the councils of the Labour Party.

With amazing speed they wormed themselves into the good graces of persons in the office of *Torch*, organ of the Dublin Constituencies Council of the Party. The ground broken, three of the four went back whence they came and sent a man from Glasgow to work with the Trinity College, Dublin, Irishman they left behind.

The Glaswegian was an extraordinary person, for within a period of a few months (or maybe weeks) he had made himself chairman of one of the most important Labour Party branches in Dublin. During the years that he was in Dublin (he disappeared as mysteriously as he arrived), he was 'unemployed', but he was, it was observed, always in comfortable circumstances.

Thenceforward the Labour world began to buzz with activity. New branches of the Party were formed in Dublin. One of the first of these was a 'dummy' – a branch without members, or with only a fictitious list of members – but as an instrument of penetration it was powerful. It made the first real breach in the Labour walls, and in a short time there were five representatives of the Fourth International on the Dublin Constituencies Council of the Party. The communism of *Torch* became blatant. Several members of the Fourth International wrote for the paper, sometimes over their own names, sometimes over pseudonyms, and openly preached communism.

The Communist Party of Ireland, watching, beheld itself being beaten in the race for power, and, to counter its rivals, dissolved the Party in August 1941. Its members were instructed to join the Labour Party and carry on their propaganda from within. The executive committee of the Party, however, did not dissolve itself.

In the meantime, the Third International has been officially dispersed, and in Ireland the Fourth International holds the field. But old Third and Fourth appear, exteriorly anyway, to work in harmony from the Labour platform. Prominent communists from both camps appear at Labour meetings. What the full extent of the influence of these men is *within* the Labour Party, the present writer does not profess to know, but the I.T.G.W.U. circular gives one to understand that it is a dominating influence.

5. *Standard* 28 January 1944.

In the *Standard* of 4 February Alfred commented on the I.T.G.W.U. circular under the heading 'A showdown is overdue'. At the outset he indicated that he had no desire to discuss the withdrawal of the I.T.G.W.U. from the Labour Party and the reasons therefor. His concern was with the charge that 'a majority of the Administrative Council allowed and encouraged admission into the Party of people who have been active members of, and well-known propagandists for, the Communist Party'. He declared that the majority of the members of the I.T.G.W.U. did not see any incompatibility between their religion and their advocacy of social justice and that they abhorred totalitarianism, be it of the left or the right. Union members and leaders realised that any flirting with communism would produce a vigorous reaction which would reduce labour to political impotence. It would be self-delusion, he continued, to attribute this to clericalism. If this issue were not clarified it would be the lay people who would act vigorously and spontaneously.

Alfred then turned his attention to a number of the allegations in the I.T.G.W.U. circular. It referred to an article in a British newspaper, the *New Leader*, of 14 August 1943. Under the heading 'Ireland will one day do what Russia did' was a profile of Larkin. Before the Irish labour leader addressed the summer school of the British Independent Labour Party he was introduced by James Maxton, M.P., as being responsible for 'the liberation of the Catholic working-class in Ireland from clerical domination'. In his address Larkin dealt with his sterling work in organising unskilled workers in Liverpool and Belfast. Referring to the foundation of the Irish Labour Party, he continued: 'Its first policy was the same as that of the I.L.P. . . . . The group of militants which formed the Labour Party subsequently established the Irish Socialist Republican party.' He regretted that more progress had not been made in achieving the social ideal advocated by himself and his comrades, but the influence of religion was opposed to it and this could not be got rid of in a day. But, he assured his listeners, 'what the Bolsheviks did in Russia socialist workers would do in Ireland one day'.

At the end of his address Larkin was offered the co-operation of the Independent Labour Party, to which Alfred next turned his attention. He cautioned against confusing it with the British Labour Party with which it had ceased to have any connection.

From the same issue of *New Leader* he quoted from an address by James Maxton at the concluding session of the summer school. Maxton wanted a revolution and maintained that 'a measure of control and a measure of punishment might be very justifiable and very necessary against counter-revolutionaries'. Alfred pointed out that, as was only too clear from recent history, the definition of counter-revolutionary was very elastic and inclusive. It meant anybody opposed to or even distasteful to 'the clique with the guns'. Maxton then gave his view of religion: 'Roman Catholicism, Episcopalianism, Presbyterianism, Mohammedanism, Shintoism, Confucianism and all other religions were, in his view, out of date . . . From a purely scientific point of view Catholicism should have disappeared with the end of feudalism . . .' Alfred pointed out that, in the presence of all the religions in the world, 'this half-educated ranter' might have suspected that there was something wrong with his 'purely scientific point of view'. But not at all, Marxist dogmatism was impervious to argument and to facts alike.

Alfred then referred to *Irish Freedom* of December 1943. This he explained was published in London and he drew attention to a particular heading as follows: 'J. Larkin junior, T.D., urges that Ireland must publicise its case, contact other small nations and make contact with the Soviet Union', the last seven words being printed in large capital letters. He added that, according to the I.T.G.W.U. circular, the same J. Larkin junior was chairman of the Dublin executive of the Communist Party of Ireland.[6] Alfred acknowledged that *Irish Freedom* was not openly communist, but maintained it was part of a scheme for indoctrinating Irish people in Britain so that they might return home 'pink if not red'. He noted a few other news items in the paper, such as the establishment in Dublin of a section of the International Brigade Association, 'composed of Irishmen who fought in Spain for the democratic government'. A booklet, *Russia's gift to the world*, issued by the Ulster Soviet Committee, was strongly recommended.

Looking nearer home, Alfred declared that there was a

6. The charge that James Larkin junior was a communist was plausible. He attended the elitist Lenin college in Moscow, and in June 1922 presided at a congress of workers' revolutionary groups in Dublin for the purpose of forming a Communist Party. Throughout the 1930s he was a prominent member of the Party and stood as a communist candidate for the Dáil in February 1932.

communist bookshop in Dublin, that communist meetings were held in the city and that he had a detailed report of one such meeting, attended by 'several prominent labour men'. He concluded that it was high time for Irish Catholics, especially trade-unionists, to make a determined stand against the campaign of penetration and undermining that was going on. All friends of labour would regret the secession of the I.T.G.W.U., but the time had come for drastic action and he hoped that, as a result of it, a re-invigorated Irish Labour Party would arise.[7]

Intervention by Patrick J. O'Brien

Patrick J. O'Brien, of the Cork office of the I.T.G.W.U., wrote to Alfred on 12 February. On behalf of James P. Pattison, T.D., chairman of the National Labour Party, he requested Alfred's permission to republish the article in the *Standard* as a pamphlet. He acknowledged Alfred's 'very great service to the movement' in the past and conveyed the appreciation of his colleagues for Alfred's current action 'which it is hoped will help all of us to continue on in the best interests of our people, clear and definite on fundamentals, intertwined with faith and nationality'.[8] On receipt of O'Brien's letter, Alfred, it seems, had a short conversation with him during which he indicated his intention to write a number of articles and suggesting that all of them could be included in the proposed pamphlet. He subsequently sent him a short note by hand repeating this suggestion and advising that the I.T.G.W.U. should not 'increase the personal element'. If the union, he wrote, considered that Larkin should not be a member of the Labour Party, it should give the reasons objectively. Above all it should point to the reforms required and these should not include 'complete control by the I.T.G.W.U.' He suggested that the proofs of the proposed pamphlet should be submitted to him as 'a friendly critic' so that he could help in this regard. It was essential to avoid damaging the labour cause as much as possible. Yet it was better to clear up the problems in the Labour Party then rather than when 'a crowd of communised emigrants return'.[9]

7. *Standard* 4 February 1944.
8. O'Brien Papers: MS 13960, letter, dated 12 February 1944, P. J. O'Brien to O'Rahilly.
9. Ibid.: note, O'Rahilly to P. J. O'Brien.

Alfred wrote again to P. J. O'Brien on 14 February. He informed him that he had just read the official statement of the Labour Party which was practically all devoted to the I.T.G.W.U. versus Larkin. On this aspect of the row, he asked O'Brien to keep him posted. He asked for information on two assertions contained in the Labour Party press release with which he would have to deal before the end of the week. The first was that 'the constitution of the Labour Party was framed to exclude the possibility of communists or members of similar organisations being members of the Party'. He regarded this as amazing and added: 'Surely you and I know that communists and near-communists are in fact in the Labour Party and are bent on controlling it?' The second was that 'the I.T.G.W.U. was a union affiliated to a Marxist International and whose officials have served with Marxists on that International'. In addition, he asked for any information, even of a confidential kind, from P. J. O'Brien or his 'headquarters', with regard to 'the accessibility of the Labour Party to communists and communist influence'. He noted that *Torch* had been careful and irrelevant in its comments on the Labour Party split and he was contemptuous of its claim to be the 'weekly organ of the labour movement'.[10]

A letter, dated 16 February, from P. J. O'Brien to William O'Brien, general secretary of the I.T.G.W.U., and enclosing Alfred's letter, indicated clearly that the latter was privy to the discussions his Cork official had with Alfred. P. J. O'Brien wrote that he would be conferring with Alfred on the following Sunday, 20 February, and asked the general secretary to send on any information which he considered might be useful. He stated to William O'Brien what, it seems, he had already reported, that Alfred had offered to confer with him when in Dublin on Thursday, 24 February, should an appointment be made. The wily William O'Brien, it appears, did not avail of the offer. In his letter, the Cork official informed his general secretary of developments in branches in the Labour Party in the Cork area and went on to report that on Sunday, 13 February, Dean Sexton had preached 'in strong terms about the Communist Party and praising the action of those who broke' and that it had been reported that several other priests in outlying parts were beginning to speak.[11]

P. J. O'Brien wrote to William O'Brien again on 21 February.

10. Ibid.: letter, dated 14 February 1944, O'Rahilly to P. J. O'Brien.
11. Ibid.: letter, dated 16 February 1944, P. J. O'Brien to William O'Brien.

He referred to a discussion he had on the previous day with Alfred who, he declared, was 'very pleased with the talks he had with our friends during the week and is prepared to go a long way to ensure our success on this issue'. The friends in question, it seems, were leaders of the National Labour Party and he went on to report that Alfred was eager 'to help in the drafting of a constitution and is prepared to act in the capacity of adviser, recognising in the last analysis our right to reject, accept, or alter in this matter'. The Cork labour official added that, such was Alfred's enthusiasm, that he offered to travel to Dublin at his own expense, as often as was required, presumably to confer with William O'Brien and others, and had indicated that he did not expect to dominate the discussions. In view of Alfred's previous service to the labour movement,[12] P. J. O'Brien strongly urged that this offer be taken up. In this view he was supported, he stated, by Thomas D. Looney, T.D., who was working closely with him.[13]

It seems that on the previous day P. J. O'Brien, Looney and some associates had also extensive discussions with 'representatives of the Republican movement'. In his letter, P. J. O'Brien wrote that, as a result of these, he was convinced that 'there is a golden opportunity for a Party veering closer to national issues, with men who have favourable national records, not just mere opportunists, or parish-pump politicians'. He did not regard it to be 'a big job' to harness that group with 'the many who take their inspiration from Alfred O'Rahilly'.[14]

12. In a reference to these, P. J. O'Brien indicated the respect which the workers of Cork had developed for the integrity and moral courage shown by Alfred over the years: 'he has been at all times a very great friend of ours here and in no uncertain way has stood openly with us when strong forces were ranged against us and when he could easily have kept out of issues. He is a great nationalist in its widest sense and a good lay Catholic who has asserted himself in many matters in very high places and in the present issue we owe him a debt that will take a long time to repay.'

13. O'Brien Papers: MS 13960, letter, dated 21 February 1944, P. J. O'Brien to William O'Brien.

14. Ibid. This comment by P. J. O'Brien was prophetic. Two years later Clann na Poblachta was founded, mainly with Republican support, and less than a further two years on a non-Fianna Fáil inter-party government was formed. In the light of O'Brien's reference to the feasibility of 'harnessing' the Republican group and 'the many who take their inspiration from Alfred O'Rahilly', it is interesting to note that Alfred was given credit for preparing the climate for the general acceptance of the coalition. For more on this, see J. A. Gaughan, *Alfred O'Rahilly II: Public figure*, 375-85.

Before concluding, P. J. O'Brien acknowledged that Alfred might subsequently state publicly that he had drafted or helped to draft the National Labour Party's constitution or that he might make some claim which the Party could not concede without loss of principle. Yet he urged once again that Alfred's offer be availed of and informed William O'Brien that Looney was prepared to go to Dublin to enlighten him further on the matter if that was considered necessary.[15] The I.T.G.W.U. leader, however, was far too cautious even to entertain such a proposal.

Reply to Peadar Cowan

In the meantime Captain Peadar Cowan, a solicitor who stood unsuccessfully as a Labour candidate for the constituency of Meath-Westmeath in the general elections of 1943 and 1944, replied to Alfred in the *Standard* of 11 February 1944. Alfred responded in the following issue.[16] At the outset he dismissed a considerable amount of abuse which the captain had directed towards him. He declared that his views were his own and that he declined to become involved in the domestic dispute between the I.T.G.W.U. and the Labour Party. To Cowan's contention that Larkin had been elected by a 'Catholic constituency', he replied that, had he been returned by a bench of bishops, he would still have considered it his duty to direct the attention of his fellow-Catholics to Larkin's 'open avowal of communism'. He objected to what he described as an attempt to present him as an enemy of the Labour Party, because he was anti-communist. His credentials as a long-standing friend of the labour movement he set out as follows:

> I have the highest respect for men such as Mr Corish, T.D., Mr Murphy, T.D., and Senator Seán Campbell; I am quite certain that they agree with me in social principles; their influence in the Labour Party will be excellent. I have never hesitated to denounce maldistribution, malnutrition and the financial racket; I was twice chosen to lecture at the Labour summer school; at the last election I was officially

15. O'Brien Papers: MS 13960, letter, dated 21 February 1944, P. J. O'Brien to William O'Brien.
16. *Standard* 18 February 1944.

asked to become a Labour candidate; for a quarter of a century I have been arbitrating in labour disputes.

He deplored the split in the Labour Party, but expressed his conviction that the time had come for a showdown as regards communism and 'its various camouflages' and for that reason only he was drawing the attention of the public to 'the vacillations and weakness of the Labour leadership and rules'.

An attempt by Cowan to dismiss the 'bogey of communism' prompted Alfred to refer to James Hogan's *Could Ireland become communist?* (Cork 1935). He quoted a passage[17] which he hoped 'would explode the complacent smugness of some of our labour leaders'. Then he quoted a member of the Labour Party to the effect that the branch movement, in which communists were active, was attempting to gain control of the Party.[18] This, Alfred declared, was not surprising as the Irish Labour Party, unlike the British Labour Party, placed no bar on communists. And one of the official aims of the Communist Party of Ireland was 'to co-operate with all other sections of the labour movement to win the majority of the people, North and South, for the aim of a socialist Ireland'. To this end its members were urged to belong to a trade union, a professional organisation or a co-operative society and with the assistance of the Communist Party of Ireland do everything possible to improve an understanding of Marxist theory and win support for it. To the objection that such persons were only a small minority, he pointed out that the Communist Party in Russia numbered only two million out of a total population of one hundred and seventy million.

Alfred next turned his attention to *Unity*. This was published in Belfast between 14 November 1942 and 14 December 1946

17. 'The presence of the relatively large and semi-communist minority in the councils of the Labour Party and of the trades councils represents a danger to the Labour movement which it would be a mistake to minimise. While no one will think of questioning the basic soundness and integrity of the Labour Party leadership, neither is there any use in closing our eyes to the fact that communist influences are at work within the Labour movement and that the communists have managed to push themselves into positions of vantage in Labour councils out of all proportion to the amount of communistic sentiment or doctrine to be found amongst the rank and file of Irish workers.'

18. The long passage was taken from an article 'Labour doings' by Patrick Cunningham in the *Irish Rosary*, Jan.-Feb. 1944.

with the sub-title 'for victory over fascism'. The victory in question, he charged, was not so much over fascism in foreign countries as in 'Éire' which was described in *Unity* as in bondage to 'fascism masquerading as nationalism'. The issue of 25 September 1943 contained two advertisements – one for an address by Harry Pollitt, general secretary of the British Communist Party, and the second for a *History of the Communist Party of the Soviet Union*, prepared 'under the guidance of Stalin himself'. The book was available at the 'International Bookshop' in Belfast, head office of the Communist Party of Ireland, and at 'New Books', the communist bookshop then in Pearse Street in Dublin. The same issue contained a report of the Party's annual congress which praised 'the progressive anti-fascist policy adopted by the Irish trade union congress'. This, Alfred pointed out, referred to the fact that at its annual meeting in 1943 the I.T.U.C. had not had the courage or the principle to condemn both communism and fascism. The Belfast Congress called on the southern labour movement to advocate certain reforms. These included 'systematic planning of agricultural production', with not a hint, added Alfred, about 'the liquidation of the Irish kulaks'. The congress singled out one trade union for special mention: 'A serious campaign must be undertaken to win the rank and file of the I.T.G.W.U. for progress; and thus to activise the whole trade-union membership in the twenty-six counties'. In the issue of *Unity* for 29 January 1944, side by side with an article headed 'Our debt to Lenin', the rejection by the I.T.G.W.U. leadership of Larkin's suggestion that Irish workers should emulate the Bolsheviks was treated with derision. To a personal attack on William O'Brien: 'And this from a man who in Dublin in 1917 welcomed the Russian revolution', Alfred replied: 'Rubbish; early in 1917 a lot of us were fooled; the Bolsheviks (numbering only about 27,000) promised democracy and peasant ownership and succeeded in seizing power only in November 1917.'

Using a pamphlet *The Irish in Britain* by Patrick Dooley of the Connolly Association, Alfred focused his attention on that organisation. Among its objectives was 'democracy against all forms of fascism'. This was based on the assumption, Alfred noted, that the only alternative to communism was something called 'fascism'. He alleged that, although the association sheltered under the name of Connolly rather than Marx, its aim

138

was to indoctrinate Irish men and women in Britain in communism. Then they could return home after the war to Irish labour organisations 'communised' by Irish-based 'comrades'. The *New Leader* of 15 May 1943 stated that the Connolly Association's paper *Irish Freedom* was controlled by the Communist Party, that Desmond Greaves, secretary of the Connolly Association, and Patrick Dooley were members of the British Communist Party, and that according to Dooley's pamphlet 'the leadership of the Irish in Britain' was 'attributed' to Greaves.[19] The same pamphlet indicated that John Nolan 'was asked by the committee of the Dublin branch of the Labour Party to convey their hearty greetings' to the Connolly Association. No mention, Alfred continued, was made of the fact that he was manager of 'New Books', the communist bookshop in Dublin. Harry Craig of the 'Dublin Labour Party' was quoted, but his membership of the Communist Party was not noted. Dooley's pamphlet contained a picture of T. A. Jackson making 'an impassioned plea' for 'full freedom and independence for Ireland'. Alfred reproduced a quotation from 'this same Englishman' of the British section of the League of Socialist Freethinkers from James Hogan's *Could Ireland become communist?* It read: 'I have had so many inquiries for dates to speak at meetings of the Friends of the Soviet Union on atheism that my Fridays are full for many weeks ahead.' But, added Alfred, 'No atheism or communism from Mr Jackson at the Connolly Association. Oh no! This Englishman, a frequent contributor to *Irish Freedom*, made an impassioned plea for Irish freedom!' Alfred's article was a source of considerable satisfaction to the protagonists of the National Labour Party. In a letter, dated 23 February, P. J. O'Brien drew the attention of William O'Brien to it and added: 'He will go non-stop for a considerable time. I am sure the captain's friends are gnashing their teeth on what has been provoked.'[20]

---

19. For more on Greaves, see A. Coughlan, 'C. Desmond Greaves, 1913-1988: an obituary essay', *Saothar* 14 (1989).

20. O'Brien Papers: MS 13960, letter, dated 23 February 1944, P. J. O'Brien to William O'Brien.

Labour Party's committee of inquiry

In the meantime the Labour Party had moved swiftly to limit the damage caused by the disaffiliation of the I.T.G.W.U. and its circular justifying that action. At a joint meeting of the parliamentary party and the Administrative Council on 13 January 1944 a committee was set up 'to enquire into the position of the movement in Dublin in regard to the allegations that there were communists in the branches and that they were using the Labour Party for communist activities'.[21] On 5 February the Party published what was, in effect, an interim report of the committee, dismissing the allegations. About the same time the Administrative Council appointed a sub-committee to investigate the membership and administration of the Liam Mellows branch in Cork city. It emerged that Michael O'Riordan, the secretary, and William Nagle, the vice-chairman, had been in Belfast during the annual congress of the Communist Party of Ireland. Their denial that they attended the congress was not accepted and their membership of the Labour Party was cancelled.[22]

Alfred dealt with the report of the Labour Party of 5 February in the *Standard*.[23] He dismissed its main thrust that the split in the labour movement was 'really due to the fact that the Transport union wants to boss all the other unions and it dislikes Jim Larkin'. This he characterised as a mere tactical ploy 'to prevent several other unions from seceding as soon as they hold their annual congresses'. As regards the promotion of Larkin as a Labour Party candidate, he noted the admission that 'the action of the Dublin Executive of the Party was "technically wrong".' However, the issue he wished the Party to address itself to was: 'Are the avowed aims of Jim Larkin compatible with membership of the Labour Party?' He provided a number of quotations to illustrate that Larkin had impeccable credentials as regards commitment to communism. From *The attempt to smash the Irish Transport and General Workers' Union* (Dublin 1924) he reproduced the following statement made by Larkin in court on 19 February 1924: 'I represent the city of Dublin in the Soviet of Moscow.' He drew attention to

21. I.L.P., 1943 *Report*, 15-16.
22. *Standard* 10 March 1944; I.L.P., 1943 *Report*, 16.
23. *Standard* 10 March 1944.

passages in the *Annual Report of the Irish Labour Party and Trade Union Congress* for 1925. One dealt with the disruptive tactics of Larkin's Workers' Union of Ireland the other cast a cold eye on 'the Workers' International Relief Organisation directly associated with persons, such as Messrs Larkin and [Patrick T.] Daly who had not the confidence of trade unionists' and whose proceedings gave 'some colour to the belief current outside this country that it is used as a medium of communist propaganda'. Then from *The Worker's Voice* of 19 August 1930 he took this extract from an article by J[ames]. L[arkin]:

> At the fourth congress of the Red International of Labour Unions, held in July 1928, a policy for the followers of the R.I.L.U. in Ireland was worked out. At the time of the fourth congress the Workers' Union of Ireland was the only Irish union affiliated to the R.I.L.U. and consequently the Irish delegation was only representative of the W.U.I. . . . This union as the representative of the R.I.L.U. in Ireland was charged with carrying out certain tasks covering the whole trade-union movement in Ireland . . . The mass of the Irish trade-unionists were to be drawn nearer to the R.I.L.U. by the organisation of a left-wing trade-union movement in Ireland . . . a national movement embracing revolutionary workers of all organisations.
>
> The left-wing movement would be composed of individual members and of affiliated unions, Labour bodies, co-operative guilds and unemployed organisations; and by building up militant groups in all unions by participating in and leading the economic struggles of the workers, by providing a new revolutionary leadership from the ranks and by ousting the reformist leaders.

Next Alfred gave a detailed account of a meeting in Dublin on 5 November 1943 to celebrate the twenty-sixth anniversary of the Bolshevik revolution. Seán Murray, formerly secretary of the Communist Party in Dublin, delivered an address 'From Tsarism to Stalin'. The meeting was attended by 'well-known labour personalities'. In dismissing any danger of communist infiltration, the report of the Labour Party pointed to the Party's constitution which was 'framed to exclude the possibility of communists or members of similar organisations becoming

members'. The constitution, however, Alfred argued, did not
prevent individuals in trade unions (which were corporate
members of the Labour Party) from being active communists.
Nor did it prevent members from openly advocating socialism
and communism at Labour Party meetings and congresses. It did
not guard against the numerous camouflaged communists who,
technically and for the purpose of penetration, might not be
'members' of the Communist Party. Above all, he pointed out,
it seemed the constitution was not sufficient to reckon with the
notorious disregard of moral considerations in the interests of
communism. This was essential to communism, as he illustrated
with the following quotation from Lenin: 'We must be ready for
sacrifice of every kind, and even, if need be, to practise
everything possible – ruses and tricks, illegal methods – be
ready to be silent and hide the truth. In short, it is from the
interests of the class war that we deduce our morality.'

The Labour Party's committee of inquiry refused to disclose
evidence submitted to it. Alfred declared this to be unsatisfactory and demanded that an independent tribunal of inquiry be
established. This was necessary, he argued, because the public
required a number of questions to be answered. Then he gave
a sample of a number of queries which he suggested such a
tribunal could address. John Ireland had just been re-elected
honorary secretary of the Dublin Executive of the Labour Party.
He was a prominent member of the Party's central branch, was
at the same time a director of 'New Books' in Dublin, and was
reputed to be the Dublin correspondent of *Irish Freedom*. Was
it he also who wrote under the name Peter McQuillan in two
communist organs, the *Workers' Voice* and the *Irish Workers'
Weekly*? Did he operate in Britain as John Maxwell and in
Northern Ireland as Robinson?[24]

24. John de Courcy Ireland had directed a considerable number of barbs at
Alfred in the columns of *Torch* from 1940 onwards. In an article in the *Standard*
of 10 March 1944 Alfred selected two of the most recent and proceeded to give
Ireland a lesson in unrestrained polemics. In the *Torch* of 19 February 1944
Ireland wrote: 'The *Standard*, in its last issue, is still very evasive as to the
degree with which this witch-hunting blatherskite is blessed by the editor.' And
in the issue of 4 March he continued: 'We referred to his statements as drivel
and blatherskite . . . *Torch* would be guilty of unpardonable scurrility in apply-
ing such a term to any individual . . .' After drawing attention to the slipshod
nature of this prose, Alfred commented that the examples he had given would
provide readers with 'a measure of the startling stupidity which graces the

The public inquisition continued. John Nolan was director of elections in North-West Dublin having acted as a delegate of the Central branch at the constituency selection conference. He was manager of 'New Books'. Alfred asked: 'Is he in direct contact with William McCullough, of Belfast, secretary of the Communist Party of Ireland, and with agents throughout Ireland?' Did the typewritten monthly *The Spark*, published 'by the Waterford Labour Party Divisional Council', obey the Communist Party line? Where had the equipment for issuing the monthly been obtained? The Dublin delegates to the Communist Party Congress in Belfast in October 1943 were John Nolan, John Ireland, Robin N. Tweedy and Charles Kenny. Did they

---

columns of that strangest of strange organs'. He acknowledged *Torch*'s charge that he was guilty of 'offensive snooping' into the private affairs of others. But, he urged, was it not the right and duty of citizens who envisaged the day when John Ireland would be the supreme commissar of an Irish Workers' Republic to 'snoop' into his 'private affairs'? Despite considerable 'snooping', Alfred declared, no one seemed to know who he was or where he had come from. What Alfred did discover about Ireland he shared with the public as follows: '(1) That he dropped into Muff, County Donegal, in the summer of 1939 and today, after a very short novitiate, he is honorary secretary of the Dublin Executive of the Irish Labour Party, and his wife, Mrs Betty Ireland, is chairman of the women's branches of the Dubin Labour Party; and (2) That he has masqueraded under the names of McQuillan, Maxwell and Robinson.' With the help of quotations, Alfred demonstrated that '"Peter McQuillan" wrote communism for *Torch* under the nose of Mr Norton. At the same time,' he continued, '"John Maxwell" was discoursing on communism for the *Irish Workers' Weekly* cheek by jowl with Comrade Robin N. Tweedy, who learned a lot on the banks of the Volga . . .' He concluded by advising Norton that he should be much more curious as to the identity of John de Courcy Ireland, alias John Ireland, alias John Maxwell, alias Robinson.

In the *Bell* of July 1945, to which he contributed an article entitled 'The founder of the Olympic Games', a thumbnail sketch of John Ireland read: 'Educated at Oxford, history scholar of New College. Has travelled in Europe and South America. Written widely on Irish and international affairs, chiefly in the labour press. He is now teaching.'

In the *Irish Times* of 24 August 1991 Kevin Myers quoted John de Courcy Ireland: 'I am a red. What that means anymore, I am not sure, but I am not going to go back on my principles. I know what I am against. Violent empires, racism, injustice, poverty.' During the course of his tribute to de Courcy Ireland's work in the Maritime Institute, Myers noted that the latter was born in Lucknow, India, in 1911, was educated in England at Anglican preparatory schools and Marlborough and, on leaving Oxford, was a teacher in Manchester. He settled in Ireland in 1938 and a few years later resumed his career as a teacher, taking up his first appointment in this country at St Patrick's Cathedral School in Dublin.

143

confer on the eve of their departure with Jim Larkin junior on the premises of 'New Books'? Did the vice-president of the Liam Mellows branch of the Labour Party in Cork city attend the congress of the Communist Party of Ireland in Belfast?

Alfred next referred to a pamphlet *Ireland looks to Labour* by W. H. McCullough giving an account of the Second National Congress of the Communist Party of Ireland. The delegates included 'two from the W.U.I., three from the I.T.G.W.U., eleven from the A.E.U., etc.' McCullough declared that the task facing the people of Ireland, particularly the labour movement, was to campaign to change the neutrality policy of the Irish Free State. Alfred pointed out that, before the Soviet Union was attacked by Germany, the same Communist Party of Ireland was 'violently anti-war'.

On 20 April 1944 the Committee of Inquiry into communist infiltration set up by the Labour Party submitted what was, in effect, its final report to the Administrative Council. Its main thrust was no different from the report published on 5 February. However, it set out in some detail its method of procedure. It acknowledged that in the Dublin branches there were members who at one time or other were active in the Communist Party. But it argued that by their acceptance of the constitution of the Labour Party such persons had positively renounced their former political associations.

Then it stated that at an early stage of its inquiries an allegation was made that John (Seán) Nolan, Charles Kenny, John Ireland and Robin N. Tweedy attended the annual congress of the Communist Party of Ireland, held in Belfast the previous October. It was also alleged that the four were communists. It summarised its investigation (1) into the relationship of the four with the Communist Party of Ireland and (2) the nature of their contacts with elements working for communist objectives. On the first issue, the committee declined to express a view, but on the second declared that the four persons in question were present in Belfast during the period of the congress of the Communist Party of Ireland, that they attended functions organised by the C.P.I. and that they were in contact with the promoters and organisers of the congress and thereby had held themselves out as persons sympathetic to communism. For such 'improper' and 'irregular' conduct the committee recommended that the four be expelled from the Labour Party and the

144

four subsequently had their membership of the party cancelled.[25]

The report was signed by William Norton, T.D., chairman of the committee, and by William Davin, T.D., Michael J. Keyes, T.D., and Luke J. Duffy, secretary. However, the fifth member of the committee, Alderman Martin O'Sullivan, the lord mayor of Dublin and T.D. for Dublin North-West, where John Nolan had acted as his election agent, provided an addendum. In this he stated that he did not lightly dismiss the suggestion that, as far as Dublin was concerned, there was a small group of people in the movement whose activities were inimical to its best interests.[26] He suggested that the Administrative Council set up a committee to supervise closely the branch organisation and stated that, with the support of his colleagues on the Committee of Inquiry, he would submit detailed proposals to that end.[27]

Eamon de Valera called a general election for May 1944. He was eager to secure an overall majority in Dáil Éireann. His prospects of doing so were enhanced by a popular rejection of

25. Most members of the Administrative Council would have had no regrets about expelling John Ireland. He was identified with *Torch* which had caused them considerable unease. According to the *Annual Report of the Administrative Council for 1943*, early in that year the council reviewed its attitude to *Torch*. This was prompted by complaints from members of the council, branch secretaries and active members of the Party that, although described as the weekly organ of the Irish Labour movement, the content of the paper did not represent the standpoint of the Labour Party. In July the council decided that, unless a change could be effected in the paper, no further financial support would be extended to it. No attempt, it seems, was made to meet the viewpoint of the council which, as a result, declined to make a payment to *Torch*. The *Annual Report* was at pains to point out that at no time was the paper an official organ of the Labour Party. A grant was made to the proprietors on two occasions merely in consideration of facilities given by them for the publication of Party reports, the last payment being made on 21 November 1942 (I.L.P., 1943 *Report*, 7). The first issue of *Torch* appeared on 6 May 1939, the last on 29 April 1944. After *Torch* failed, the Labour Party published the weekly *Irish People* from 20 May 1944 onwards (ibid., 1944 *Report*, 4).

26. In a further comment O'Sullivan, in effect, drew attention to the secretiveness of proponents of communism. For some time Labour leaders and officials were exceedingly distrustful of their conspiratorial activities. In a letter, dated as early as 1 November 1931, to R. J. P. Mortished, Thomas Johnson, in a reference to the draconian Constitution Amendment Bill of 1931, wrote: 'Those of us, who know something of how the Communist Party does its work, can appreciate the dangers, if there were to be no counter move.' (J. A. Gaughan, *Thomas Johnson (1872-1963): first leader of the Labour Party in Dáil Éireann* (Dublin 1980) 471).

27. Johnson Papers, MS 17267.

pressure exerted on him by the governments of the U.S.A. and the U.K. to end the country's policy of neutrality. The split in the Labour Party also guaranteed some electoral advantage to Fianna Fáil, as did some uncertainty in the ranks of Fine Gael, following the retirement of its leader, William T. Cosgrave. In the event the government Party improved its representation from 67 to 74 seats. Mainly because of the disarray in the movement the combined Labour vote dropped by one-third compared with the 1943 general election and only eight of the twelve Labour T.Ds and four of the National Labour T.Ds were returned. During the election campaign spokesmen from both sides of the split in the labour movement attempted successfully to play down their internal division. This tendency was probably accentuated by Fianna Fáil's determined effort, spearheaded by Seán MacEntee, T.D., to exploit the Labour Party's internal divisions. It showed also that in most parts of the country the rank and file of the Party were not at all as disunited as were the leaders, although according to Walter McGrath, who covered the election for the *Cork Examiner*, they were completely bewildered in the Cork area.[28]

'The Vanguard'

The *Standard* of 28 July 1944, however, reminded the public once more of the serious divisions in the labour movement. It was prompted to do so by a piece of communist propaganda issued anonymously to 'all members of the labour movement'. After a progress report on the class struggle in Costa Rica and elsewhere the author in the course of further comments deprecated:

(1) 'The breakaway of William O'Brien and the I.T.G.W.U. from the Labour Party on the grounds that communists had been allowed into membership of, and were exercising a big influence "on the affairs of, the Labour Party".'

(2) 'The campaign of slander and manipulation against the Labour Party by Seán MacEntee, the *Standard* and the so-called National Labour Party.'

28. James B. McKevitt, 'The split in the Irish Labour Party and the general eleciton of 1944' (thesis presented, as part requirement, for M.A. degree at University College, Dublin, September 1984); interview with Walter McGrath.

(3) 'The weak-kneed behaviour of Labour Party leaders in face of these attacks, especially shown by the expulsion of members in Cork and Dublin and the cringing statements of leading Labour Party spokesmen, notably Mr William Davin, T.D.'[29]

In August Captain Peadar Cowan, a solictor who had stood unsuccessfully as a Labour candidate for Meath-Westmeath in the two previous general elections, resigned from the Party to promote 'an organisation for socialist propaganda' known as 'The Vanguard'. His public statements indicated clearly that the socialism he had in mind was revolutionary socialism or communism. To a public query whether membership would be considered compatible with that of the Labour Party, a spokesman for the latter organisation replied that this would depend on the constitution of Vanguard.'[30]

The *Standard* of 29 September 1944 carried a detailed report of the inaugural meeting of Vanguard, held a week earlier. Addressing some fifty people, Captain Cowan declared that his purpose was 'to obtain control of returning Irish workers and demobilised Irish soldiers for a revolutionary class-war'. He embarrassed his former colleagues by suggesting that the Labour Party had no objection to its members joining Vanguard. This was seized on by adversaries of the Labour Party. Only too typical was the partisan comment of James Everett, T.D., of the National Labour Party, who declared that the Labour Party's attitude 'to the new communist organisation, The Vanguard, showed how helplessly the Party leaders were caught in the communist web'. He went on: 'The individuals running The Vanguard were the same people who crashed into the Party in 1942, formed the notorious Dublin City Central branch and caused the Party constitution to be torn up.'[31]

Early in October the Labour Party banned its members from

29. *Standard* 28 July 1944.

30. The *Standard* of 29 September 1944 was severely critical of the attitude adopted by the Labour Party to 'The Vanguard'. It regretted that, though the Party had declared Cowan's manifesto to be rubbish, it had not recognised it to be 'dangerous rubbish' or Cowan and his associates to be 'the disruptionists' they were. It pointed out that Cowan had interpreted the official reply of the Labour Party to the question, whether members of the Party could also be members of Vanguard, as implying that the Party had no objection to Vanguard.

31. *Standard* 29 September, 13 October 1944.

147

joining Vanguard. The organ of the Communist Party of Ireland, *Unity*, in its issue of 19 October 1944, greeted this with derision, and as indicative of the lengths to which Labour leaders such as 'Duffy and Davin' were prepared to go 'to do whatever they were ordered to do by the Catholic *Standard* and when urged by the National Labour Party'. With remarkable prescience the editor of *Unity* speculated that, if Vanguard 'developed into a non-party educational association, the Labour leaders will look more foolish than ever'.[32]

The *Standard* of 3 November carried a report of a further meeting of Vanguard held on 27 October. Captain Cowan told the twenty persons who attended that a draft constitution which he read had been prepared only as a matter of tactics, as the Labour Party had requested one. He expected that the organisation would receive 'a quota of newsprint to start a newspaper'. Vanguard should be developed by groups of four or five persons. Cowan, who was addressed as comrade, as were all present, was declared to be chairman of the organisation's provisional committee. The rest of the committee consisted of Comrade O'Reilly, vice-chairman, and Comrades Eager, Ireland, Nolan, Mulally and Palmer. The *Standard* concluded its report: 'And there Vanguard rests, safe in the arms of the communists!'[33]

32. *Unity* 19 October 1944.

33. *Standard* 3 November 1944. Thomas Johnson, elder statesman of the Labour Party, in a letter to R. J. P. Mortished, dated 13 November 1944, presented the following cameo of Vanguard:

'[Peadar Cowan] issued a manifesto to the people purporting to come from a committee, but I have not learned who his collaborators were. They were not, I think, in the early stages at any rate, the late C[ommunist]. P[arty]. members, though some of them joined at a later stage. The manifesto was socialist or communist in intention . . . It was certainly revolutionary in phraseology and nationalistic in sentiment . . . And it sets out boldly that the new organisation is to be based on "Democratic Centralism" with "a leader who is to be obeyed" after being elected. I gather that already a change has been made from the original scheme, that, instead of a mass organisation, they are to confine their activities to socialist education and propaganda and this change has been due to the left-wing or C.P. members . . . Its origins will prevent its success' (J. A. Gaughan, *Thomas Johnson (1872-1963): first leader of the Labour Party in Dáil Éireann*, 380). (Captain Peadar Cowan was an Independent T.D. for Dublin north-east from 1948 to 1954.)

For a revealing account of communist activity at that time, see Mike Milotte, *Communism in modern Ireland: The pursuit of the Workers' Republic since 1916* (Dublin 1916) 182-215. A measure of the author's bias, however, can be

Emphasis on difference between Christian and Marxist view of society

In the *Standard* of 15 December 1944 Alfred reviewed *The plan of society* (Dublin 1944) by Peter McKevitt, professor of Catholic Action and sociology at St Patrick's College, Maynooth. He recommended the work as an excellent introduction to Catholic social principles. However, he took issue with McKevitt's seeming acceptance that sociology was the study of 'the transformations of social groups in so far as the course of life of these groups is moulded by the time and space conditions in which it unfolds itself'. This implied that sociology was a factual study of human social life, a historical and statistical science, independent of philosophy. Although acknowledging the possibility of such a science, Alfred argued that in practice it was difficult to eliminate value judgements from it. He declared that he tended to be suspicious of the alleged neutrality of economists and sociologists and he showed that in fact Rev. Dr McKevitt's treatment of his subject was normative and assumed Catholic philosophy.

Alfred stated this was the manner in which he interpreted sociology. At his course in U.C.C., having enunciated ethical and social principles, he proceeded to discuss economic and social life in detail. He argued that most treatments of economics implicitly assumed 'a false philosophy, a wrong system of values'. Indicating his main preoccupation, he continued: 'our job, in an opposite sense to that of the Marxians, is to tear aside this pretence of pseudo-neutrality'.

Alfred broadcast eight talks on social principles from Radio Éireann each Sunday night from 25 February to 15 April 1945. In the fifth talk he dealt with property and liberty.[34] He pointed to capitalism and communism as being equally destructive of

gathered from his comment on the anti-communist crusade: 'As the Labour Party started its inquisition, the right-wing *Standard*, with a weekly circulation of around 80,000, began a series of lurid exposés concerning the alleged communists in the Labour Party. Numerous aliases and photos appeared alongside a graphic account of each of the accused's sins. Professor Alfred O'Rahilly, president of U.C.C., and a colleague of the former Blueshirt ideologue, James Hogan, wrote most if not all of the *Standard* articles and he did so with a minutely detailed knowledge that some alleged – as they had done over Hogan's earlier "exposures" – had its source in Special Branch files.'

34. See Appendix 5.

economic liberty, declaring that neither capitalists nor communists had any desire to decentralise economic power or to democratise private property. He quoted Pope Pius XI denouncing the 'immense power and despotic economic domination' of a few capitalists and financiers 'so that no one can breathe against their will'. And he drew attention to a radio address of Pope Pius XII on 1 September 1944 in which he denounced 'the dictatorship of a political group which will, as the ruling class, dispose of the means of production and at the same time of the daily bread and hence of the will to work of individuals'. These two denunciations, he argued, removed all ambiguity from the Catholic defence of private property.

Alfred declared that capitalists and communists were animated by a profound distrust of ordinary men and women. The argument for 'chain-stores' and 'the Chain-State' was the same, namely, anti-libertarian pessimism. It was better for men and women not to be free, lest they give way to their bad tendencies. Thus it was necessary to remove temptation, to deprive people of responsibility and control. According to capitalists ordinary workers would be better behaved and better disciplined under a handful of directors and managers. For communists the same result is aimed for under a small clique of 'keepers and commissars'. He warned that, once workers had opted for the latter in the name of collectivist security, they might never be able to escape from it. As contemporary history testified, their children could easily be trained by the State to like that kind of servitude.

Critical of Harold J. Laski

Alfred was given the opportunity to conclude his anti-communist crusade with a flourish when requested by the *Standard* to review *I believe* (ed. H. Macmillan, London 1940 and reprinted 1944) and a pamphlet *The rights of man* (London 1940). Professor Harold J. Laski of the London School of Economics contributed to the first and was the author of the second. Towards the end of world war two and immediately afterwards Laski was one of the best known apologists for the 'socialism of the Soviet Union'. To this end, he made a number of broadcasts to the U.S.A. He was chairman of the British Labour Party and, following the Party's decisive victory in the general election of July 1945, toured Europe advocating that social democrats should as far as possible co-operate with communists, though on no account to accept fusion with them. Laski presented his message to congresses of workers in various European cities, including Paris and Oslo, and urged it in articles in serious journals and popular newspapers.

In the *Standard* of 14 September 1945, under the title 'A short guide to Laski', Alfred first focussed his attention on the left-wing professor's contribution to *I believe,* which, he explained, was published in 1940, containing statements by twenty-three 'eminent men and women of our time' to remind the world 'of the tradition' for which the war was being fought. He declared that, with the exception of the contribution by Jacques Maritain, this could be summarised as 'atheism plus communism'. Alfred quoted Laski that he had been an atheist from childhood and commented that clearly then his rejection of theism was not based on any research or investigation. Laski had asserted that the main religions were not interested in social justice and Alfred responded that this conclusion was based solely on a Marxist understanding of that term. This excluded religion's insistence of the maintenance of man's unique personal status and such teaching as was to be found in the social encyclicals. Laski's socialism, like his irreligion, had not been the outcome of adult investigation, as he claimed to have been a socialist since his schooldays. Alfred admitted the contention that 'no class voluntarily abdicates from the possession of power', but objected to the failure to apply this principle to the privileged bureaucracy which ran the Russian managerial State. He described as academic rhetoric, divorced from reality, the statement that the State power in Russia had been captured by one hundred and seventy million workers. In fact, he pointed out, the State power in Russia had been taken over by middle-class intellectuals like Laski himself. Alfred dismissed Laski's Marxist and simplistic explanations of the origins of armaments and war as examples of 'a myopic dogmatism acquired in childhood'. He was savage when commenting on the manner in which Laski condoned the barbarism associated with the Spanish civil war: 'These gullible intellectuals like Laski are at heart very bloodthirsty fellows; they should be psycho-analysed'.

In the same article in the *Standard* Alfred's critique of Laski's

The rights of man was even more devastating. Therein Laski set
out his objections to Naziism. Alfred pointed out that nowhere
did he give a hint of being aware that the very features of
Naziism to which he objected he applauded in the Soviet Union
and was, to a large extent, proposing for Britain.[35]

From the beginning, Alfred claimed, Laski undermined his
attempt to champion the rights of man when he wrote: 'The
rights of man meant, and were understood increasingly to
mean, that the popular will, and only the popular will, was the
effective source of power. This implied the total subjection of
the individual to the majority, or to a sufficiently powerful
clique masquerading as such. In this context no objective moral
order or law was envisaged. Consequently Laski was unable to

35. This he did as follows: 'In *I believe* Professor Laski refers deliriously to
"the magic of that day when Lenin inaugurated the victory of the first socialist
revolution in the world". Well let us have a look at "the Nazi method" as
described in his pamphlet, bearing in mind (a) the Soviet method and (b) the
Laski method proposed for Great Britain:

(1) "No opposition to the government is permitted . . . There is only one
political party . . .; all others without exception have been suppressed".
Exactly as in Russia.

(2) "All trade unions have been abolished . . . There is no right to strike".
As in Russia, witness Sir Walter Citrine and others who have shown up
the Russian trade-union camouflage.

(3) "Organised religion has been fiercely attacked by the government
wherever it has failed to accept the aims of Naziism . . . The leaders of the
Nazi Party are openly contemptuous of Christianity." It is rather unexpected to find Laski a champion of Christianity! For "Naziism" read "Communism", for the "Nazi Party" read the "Communist Party" and you have
a picture of the Russian system which Laski is backing. Is he consciously a
hypocrite in thus trying to humbug his readers?

(4) "There is no longer any freedom of opinion . . . All newspapers,
periodicals, books, plays, music, art, the wireless and the films, are under
censorship . . . It is a serious offence to listen to foreign broadcasts".
As it is in Russia.

(5) "All forms of education have been strictly subordinated to Nazi purposes . . . The purpose is to produce a well-regimented mass obedient to the
discipline imposed from above".

For "Nazi" read "Communist". Let us omit the further objections – con-
cept of law, treatment of minorities, persecutions – which are equally
applicable to Russia. Here is the final objection:

(11) "The state is all . . . The individual has no rights, but only duties. He
is not an end in himself . . ."

This too occurs in the totalitarianism advocated by Professor Laski. It is
inevitable; for, rejecting God and a spiritual soul, he has no basis for supporting the claims of personality.

defend convincingly the human person or the family against 'the popular will'.[36]

In February 1948 the split in the Labour Party was effectively ended when the leaders of the Labour Party and the National Labour Party joined a non-Fianna Fáil inter-party government. Just over two years later the two parties formally reunited under the leadership of William Norton, T.D. Other divisions were to last longer, however. The trade-union centre, the Irish Trade Union Congress, was split when certain nationally-minded unions, including the I.T.G.W.U. (but not Larkin's Workers' Union of Ireland) seceded before the end of the second world war to form the Congress of Irish Unions (C.I.U.). It was 1959 before both congresses were induced to re-unite to form the Irish Congress of Trade Unions (I.C.T.U.). It took another forty years, and, more significantly, the passing on of all the personalities involved, for the I.T.G.W.U. and the Workers' Union of Ireland (both unions having in the meantime absorbed a number of smaller unions) to come together in 1989 to form the Services, Industrial, Professional and Technical Union (S.I.P.T.U.).

While the Irish trade-union movement was so divided, major events were happening in the world. The cold war was intensifying. With the backing of the Red Army, communist governments, which were no more than Soviet puppet regimes, were installed in the countries of eastern Europe. The continued existence of the European democracies which remained was by no means certain. In 1949 they joined with the U.S. and Canada

---

36. In the *Standard* of 27 November 1942 Alfred had already published a comprehensive critique of *The rights of man*. This prompted the following letter in the *Glasgow Observer* of 11 December 1942:

> I fear that the Dublin *Standard* is not widely read in this country, and it may be that Professor Laski will fail to see the devastating argument directed against his 'Macmillan war pamphlet' by Professor O'Rahilly in the issue of November 27. I would like to see Laski answer for he is no fool, and a great deal of his political writing is first-class. I remember years ago meeting him in his West Kensington house, where he discoursed at length and with both learning and true sympathy about French religious history. He is perfectly capable of seeing the force of Professor O'Rahilly's contention that the will of the majority, untaught by morality, is likely to be as despotic as any one man dictatorship. Indeed in Hitler's Germany it probably was, for, however cooked the plebiscites, it is generally recognised that Hitler would have obtained a handsome majority under any form of ballot at any time between 1933 and 1939.

in a mutual pact, known as the North Atlantic Treaty Organisation.

Education of workers in social teaching of Christianity

Alfred was gravely disappointed that the country did not become a member of N.A.T.O.[37] Moreover, he considered that a military alliance would not be sufficient to halt the onward march of communism. The struggle for the minds and hearts of men and women had to be won. Communist ideology, which he regarded as militant secularism, had to be challenged. To attempt to do so merely with a secularism of the liberal or socialist genre, he regarded as futile. For him, the task to be undertaken was to convince workers and their leaders that Christianity and its social imperatives was a far better option than communism. An essential requisite to this end, was to make workers and especially their leaders familiar with the social teaching of Christianity.

By a curious coincidence the emergence of the remarkable system of workers' education at U.C.C. enabled Alfred to demonstrate what should and could be done in this regard. On 14 October 1946 he inaugurated the first course. All taking it were trade-unionists. It extended over two years, during which the subjects studied were sociology, economics, accounting, secretarial and business practice and modern social organisations. Alfred and Professor John Busteed took the classes in sociology and economics respectively.[38]

Twenty-four out of an original thirty-four completed the course successfully and were conferred with their diplomas by Alfred on 23 June 1948. He declared that democracy had placed great responsibility in the hands of workers, and by their votes and powerful organisations they could now sway the fate of nations. Trade-union congresses discussed and decided such problems as the cost of living, nationalisation, education, natural rights, the family, the State, democracy and, above all, communism. The claim that trade unionists could be neutral on those fundamental issues was either the result of a delusion or mere hypocrisy. For that reason and to avoid 'the humbug of neutrality', in the course at U.C.C. they made no deceitful

37. J. A. Gaughan, *Alfred O'Rahilly II: Public figure*, 385-7.
38. *Cork Examiner* 15 October 1946.

154

pretence of being neutral. They made an open profession of Christian values and social principles, such as were embodied in the papal encyclicals and the constitution. In particular, they openly took their stand against communism in all its disguises and subterfuges. To this end, they were determined to retain their autonomy, but, if invited to do so, U.C.C. was ready to extend the system of workers' education outside the Cork area.[39]

Following an invitation from Limerick Vocational Education Committee and the local trades council, Alfred addressed a public meeting in Limerick on 28 September 1948. He emphasised the importance of education for workers. Apart from equipping them to deal with day to day issues concerning wages and working conditions, it enabled them to participate to the full in democracy. Trade unionists had to adopt an attitude to all the great issues of the day, including communism. He concluded with a flourish:

> We are in a unique position in this country, where the mass of the workers are faithful to their religion and have resisted subversive ideologies. But let us beware of complacency and apathy. Hostile forces are at work, all the more dangerous because they disguise themselves as neutral and liberal. Irish Catholic workers must bestir themselves lest leadership pass out of their control. Limerick has a glorious place in the struggle for faith and fatherland. But it must not rest in the romantic past. There are difficult times ahead.[40]

Alfred was in Waterford on 5 October. In an address to the city's Vocational Education Committee and trade-union leadership, he described in detail the workers' course at U.C.C. He declared that the 'opprobrious epithet "sectarian"' had been applied by those who, with their 'humbug of neutrality', were attempting to delude Irish workers, 98 per cent, of whom were Catholics. It was not possible, he claimed, to be neutral. They had to make up their minds to be either for or against communism, totalitarianism and secularist materialism. Issues such

39. *Cork Evening Echo, Cork Examiner* 24 June 1948.
40. *Cork Examiner* 29 September, 1 October 1948; *Standard* 1 October 1948.

as private property, the family and the functions of the State could not be ignored. The constitution was not neutral. Nor were they in U.C.C. He warned that there was a grave danger that an attempt would be made by a determined metropolitan minority to mislead workers with a scheme of 'undefined' education which could be used as a vehicle for alien propaganda.[41]

On 10 November 1948 Alfred inaugurated a workers' course in Limerick. His address was far more homiletic in character than those of the Catholic or Church of Ireland bishops who also spoke. He stressed the importance of education for workers and their role in ensuring the survival of democracy. The great need in the country was for a small select class of men who, in spite of being engaged in daily toil, would act as leaders of their fellow-workers. This, in fact, had happened in Cork. The workers who gained the diploma in social and economic science had not only become more active and efficient in their trade-unions, but had also begun lecturing to their fellow workers. He continued: 'Let us learn a lesson from the communists, who work through a small well-trained minority. Indeed, it was the method of Our Lord, who sent out twelve apostles to win the world.' Such were the conditions in the world that everyone was in the front line. No one could afford to be neutral. The lesson from events in eastern Europe was that they were faced with the choice of the early Christians – Christ or Caesar.[42]

On 16 November Alfred was again in Waterford inaugurating a workers' course. He declared that working men and women needed education in social and political principles, as in every democratic country it was the workers who were predominant. This was due to their sheer weight of numbers and to powerful organisations. It would not be an exaggeration to say that the fate of the Western World was in the hands of the trade unions. Little hitherto had been done to equip workers for their great responsibility. Were it not for the influence of religion, alien and hostile forces would have played havoc with Irish workers, as they had done elsewhere. The goal of the workers' courses was an educated Christian democracy. This was the positive fulfilment of their struggle for national freedom. A generation ago they knew very well from what they wished to be free. Let

41. *Cork Examiner* 30 September, 6 October 1948.
42. *Cork Examiner, Limerick Leader* 10 November 1948.

12. Bishop Patrick O'Neill, speaking at the inauguration of the diploma course in social and economic science at the Technical School, Limerick, on 10 November 1948. *Left to right*: M. B. O'Malley (mayor of Limerick), Most Rev. Patrick O'Neill (Catholic bishop of Limerick), P. V. Twomey (Technical School), Most Rev. Evelyn Charles Hodges (Church of Ireland bishop of Limerick), Fr Athanasius, O.F.M., Alfred

them now concentrate on for what they achieved freedom. He pointed out that in many countries workers once as fervently religious as in Ireland had in large numbers reneged on their faith and adopted a false soul-destroying social creed. 'Let us,' he concluded, 'betimes take measures to avoid this disaster in our own beloved country. Workers of Waterford, it is up to you to produce your quota of pioneer leaders in this great crusade for faith and fatherland.'[43]

Such was the enthusiasm of those who attended the workers' courses provided by U.C.C. that they insisted on having an annual conference. The first was held at U.C.C. on the weekend of 9-10 July 1949. It was attended by over two hundred students. In a concluding address Alfred spoke about the practical merits of the courses and then referred to Cardinal Mindszenty, Archbishop Stepinac, and Archbishop Beran as martyrs for ideals, the fundamental decencies of life, education and the right to organise. There was a clear lesson to be learnt from what was happening on the continent. If the Catholic Church went down in Ireland, trade-unions would not survive. He declared that he regarded himself as 'ultimately more revolutionary than some of those communists', for he stood for bringing the Church into the world and religion into every aspect of their lives.[44]

The second annual conference of worker-students was held on 15-16 July 1950 at U.C.C. Lectures were given by General Michael J. Costello, general manager of Comhlucht Siúicre Éireann Teo.; R. J. P. Mortished, chairman of the Labour Court; Rev. Dr Cornelius Lucey, professor of mental and moral philosophy, St Patrick's College, Maynooth, and Michael P. Fogarty, specialist in industrial relations at Nuffield College, Oxford. In his address to the conference Alfred recalled that, in a private audience which he had been recently granted with the pope, the latter had asked him about the workers' courses and had imparted his blessing on them. The pope, Alfred explained, 'realised that if Ireland was not to go communist, it was necessary to have educated Catholic labour leaders'.[45]

These annual weekend conferences were attended by students from the U.C.D. extra-mural studies programme,

43. *Cork Examiner* 17 November 1948; *Standard* 19 November 1948.
44. *Standard* 15 July 1949.
45. *Cork Examiner* 10, 17, 18 July 1950; *Standard* 14 July 1950.

13. Second annual conference of worker students at U.C.C., July 1950. *Front row, left to right*: Unidentified, unidentified, Seán McCarthy (lord mayor of Cork), Alfred, Patrick F. Parfrey, General Michael J. Costello, unidentified, R. J. P. Mortished (chairman of Labour Court), unidentified, Michael P. Fogarty (Nuffield College, Oxford)

directed by Fr Edward Coyne, S.J. The impact Alfred had on them, it seems, was considerable. Maureen MacPartlin, then Dublin representative of the telephonists in the Post Office Workers' Union, attended the 1950 conference. Her most abiding memory of it after some forty years was of Alfred presiding over seminars, calling delegates to their meals, pouring out tea for everyone and attending to visitors with the utmost kindness. She also judged that his was the most impressive lecture of the conference.

Effective Anti-Communist campaigner

Apart from his addresses inaugurating workers' and other courses in different parts of Munster, Alfred availed of other speaking engagements to highlight the communist threat. On 9 May 1948 he spoke on 'Christ and society today' in University College, Galway, to commemorate the social encyclicals. He declared that the choice before the world was Christ or Stalin, Christianity or communism. Men killed and died for communism, because it was a religion. To counter it, a virile practical Catholicism was needed, whereby Irish people were aware of, and observed the social implications of their creed.[46]

A week later Alfred addressed the annual convention of the National Council of the Catholic Young Men's Society in Cork. He stated that, in the general activities of trade unionism, they had to be guided either by Catholic social principles or else slip into communism which was being thrust forward by small, well-organised minorities. In Czechoslovakia the crucifixes were being taken down and pictures of Stalin put up. Just as the early Christians had to decide between Christ and Caesar, so now the choice was between Christ and Stalin. The most important challenge facing them was their ability to prove to people who called themselves socialists that they could either go up towards Christ and carry out all that was good in their programme or else go down and develop into communists. It was ridiculous to expect the Catholics of the country who constituted 95 per cent of the population to put their religion in their pockets, for fear they might offend the other 5 per cent. Indeed, if they did so, they would merely disedify those compatriots.

46. *Standard* 14 May 1948.

What was required in Ireland was plurality, diversity, different associations to ensure as many centres of liberty as possible. Under no circumstances should they allow the country to become monolithic as Russia had become, where everything was ruled by the bureaucrat. The Catholic Church was the only organised corporate defender of the fundamental principles on which trade unions and other free associations rested. If the Church were to be suppressed did they think that trade-unionism would survive for very long? Those who thought that individualistic capitalism could continue were living in a fool's paradise. They were at the parting of the ways and something was going to replace the present system. The worker was going to have a new role, a new status, and the only choice ultimately was between receiving him as a brother and co-operator in a vocational order, or else the worker would sell the pass and his liberties for the sake of security in a regimented communism.[47]

On 19 August 1948 Alfred addressed the Annual Summer School of the Christus Rex Society[48] on 'Trade union leadership today'. In every country, he declared, the labour movement was concerned not only with the immediate problem of hours and wages but with fundamental issues – State control, the family and education, socialism and communism – upon a right handling of which western civilisation depended. The idea that men with nothing but an elementary education acquired in childhood could competently cope with such questions was an obvious delusion. Moreover, there was a general assumption that religion and even a sound philosophy were irrelevant to social and professional life. Exhortation to the contrary from the outside, it seemed, was ineffective. To cope with that grave situation, he suggestion that they learn from the communists who worked from the inside through a vigorous minority with a clear objective. It was essential to equip and train men and women who would influence their fellow-workers. He expressed satisfaction at the fact that, of the twenty-four trade-unionists who had successfully completed the workers' course

47. *Standard* 21 May 1948.

48. This organisation was founded in 1941 by Rev Professor Cornelius Lucey of St Patrick's College, Maynooth (later bishop of Cork). Its first chairman was Dr Cahal B. Daly of Queen's University, Belfast (later bishop of Ardagh and Clonmacnoise, subsequently bishop of Down and Conor and eventually archbishop of Armagh and a member of the college of cardinals). The purpose of the society was to promote the study of social issues among priests.

14. Christus Rex Society's Annual Summer School at U.C.C., August 1948. *Left to right:* Fr Peter McKevitt (St Patrick's College, Maynooth), Fr James P. Bastible (dean of residence, U.C.C.), Fr Thomas Morris (St Patrick's College, Thurles), Alfred, Fr Michael Walsh, C.C. (Roundstone,

at U.C.C., two were already secretaries of their respective trade-unions and a third had been appointed secretary of the Railway Clerks' Association.[49]

At Alfred's invitation Douglas Hyde lectured on 'Communism from the inside' in the Opera House, Cork, on 20 February 1949. The lecture was under the auspices of the U.C.C. Extension Movement and Alfred presided. Hyde had been news editor of the communist *Daily Worker* and was the best known and most articulate critic of communism in the U.K. His address was mainly autobiographical and included a first-hand account of communist conspiratorial tactics and the intensity of the commitment of communists to their cause. Alfred, in a letter to the press, dated 21 February 1949, expressed his regret that many were unable to gain admission to the lecture, but stated that he hoped to induce Hyde to pay a return visit to Cork.[50]

Alfred was in Kilkenny on 6 March lecturing on 'Catholics and communism' at the invitation of the local C.Y.M.S. He stressed the importance of Catholic social philosophy, a knowledge of which, he stated, was essential to persuade those outside the Church that only by having a Christian outlook could the world conserve its liberties. He pointed to the growing power of trade unions and the responsibilities of the worker in the modern democratic world. Workers should be fitted for the great powers thrust upon them. He urged that Kilkenny should adopt training courses for Catholic leaders among the workers, such as had been done in Cork, Limerick, Waterford and Dublin. Ireland had to play its part in the latter-day struggle between Christ and Stalin.[51]

On 22 May Alfred was the principal speaker at the national centenary celebrations in Carlow of the founding of the C.Y.M.S. In his address on 'Social action', he referred to communism which he described as a rival religion to Christianity

49. *Cork Examiner* 20 August 1948; *Standard* 20, 27 August 1948. See also *Cork Examiner* 17, 18, 19 August 1948. Alfred again addressed the annual congress of Christus Rex in April 1963. Then a monsignor, he was the only cleric to address the congress which discussed the lay apostolate. In 'Catholic social action, the layman's part' he urged that religion become personalised, really assimilated into the depths of one's being so as to become part of one's way of thinking and living. He also emphasised the importance of encouraging lay-initiative (*Standard* 26 April 1963).

50. *Cork Examiner* 22 February 1949.

51. *Cork Examiner* 7 March 1949.

and not merely a system of production and distribution. The crucial issue on the continent was: Could Catholics persuade the socialists to implement what was good in their outlook in association with Catholics without giving way to the materialistic creed of communism? He reminded trade unionists that the Catholic Church was a bulwark of freedom, especially of the principle of the right of association. Consequently, if the Church were suppressed, trade unions would inevitably meet the same fate. He warned that there were communist cells in three Irish cities. He concluded: 'It is our job to get ready and put Catholic social principles into practice . . . We must educate our workers. I do not mean mass education; we must take them in small groups. From these we must select our leaders, and prepare to face the struggle that lies ahead.'[52]

On 12 November 1950 Alfred delivered a public lecture on 'Religion for the layman' in the Olympia Theatre, Dublin. The lecture was organised to raise funds for a retreat house, which had been opened by the Marist Fathers in St Doolagh's Park, County Dublin. In the chair was Senator Séamus O'Farrell, in the absence through illness of Frank Fahy, Ceann Comhairle, Dáil Éireann, and the supporting speakers were: James Everett, T.D., minister for posts and telegraphs; Peter McLoughlin, member of the Labour Court; and Leo Crawford, secretary of the Congress of Irish Trade Unions (C.I.U.). Such was Alfred's popularity as a public speaker that the theatre was full half-an-hour before the lecture was due to begin and the press reported that hundreds of people had to be turned away. He stressed the social dimension of Christianity. The country, he then added, had achieved its freedom, but was not at all clear as to what that freedom was for. They could take pride in the Legion of Mary, already a world-wide association, and their Irish missionaries. Otherwise, not much had been achieved except for a pale imitation of British socialism. The most important task before them was to root out the modern heresy that religion was irrelevant to social life. Communism was a creed and the only way in which it could be fought was with a counter-creed; one could not be neutral. They must train their people, have their own Catholic leaders and cultivate their own lay spirituality. This

52. *Cork Examiner* 24 May 1949; *Standard* 27 May 1949; *The Nationalist and Leinster Times* 28 May 1949.

was the age of the laity, and it was the laity who could make or unmake the Church.[53]

Alfred's reputation as an effective anti-communist campaigner spread beyond the shores of Ireland. In November 1948 the archbishop of Westminster, Cardinal Bernard Griffin, then anxious about communist attempts to infiltrate the British trade-union movement, announced that he was inaugurating a scheme of workers' education in his archdiocese. It was acknowledged in the English Catholic press that the scheme was based on the courses at Cork, Limerick and Waterford.[54] In addition Alfred had requests for information on the workers' courses from priests involved in Catholic Action in a number of other countries.[55] The courses received considerable attention in the Catholic press. Douglas Hyde contributed articles on them to the English *Catholic Herald*.[56] In the struggle against communism, he vouched for their effectiveness, stating that their purpose was 'to turn out trade unionists who are equipped to become really efficient leaders, armed with the social teaching of the Church . . .' Alfred's zest for attacking communism was, to a large extent, influenced by the activities of communist regimes in eastern Europe and the progress of the Korean war. At times, however, the intensity and appropriateness of his oratory, while admired from a distance, was not appreciated even by colleagues and friends. At the inauguration of a class in a social and economic diploma course at Mallow on 19 November 1950, Professor John Busteed, who spoke after Alfred, pointedly remarked that to describe the course as one to combat communism was to give it a very limited objective. Even if there was no Marxist philosophy in the world, the course would be of immense value in the cultural education of the people.[57]

53. *Irish Independent* 11, 13 November 1950; *Cork Examiner* 13 November 1950.

54. *Cork Examiner* 23 November 1948.

55. Interview with Canon James P. Bastible. See also *Cork Examiner* 23 November 1948.

56. *Catholic Herald* 11, 18 March 1949.

57. *Cork Examiner* 20 November 1950.

EDUCATIONALIST

Alfred considered the initiation of the courses in workers' education and their subsequent organisation and development under his inspiration as one of his major contributions to U.C.C.[1] The courses were the beginning of a remarkable growth of continuing education throughout the country and enabled him to influence strongly the new courses which were established.

Course in Rathmines College of Commerce

One of the first was inaugurated at the Rathmines College of Commerce. On learning of the intention of Alfred and his colleagues at U.C.C. to initiate a course in workers' education, Dr John F. Burke, of the department of education, made a detailed study of the proposed course. Within a few months of the beginning of the course in U.C.C., Dr Burke supervised the inauguration of a similar course in the Rathmines College of Commerce. In so doing he had the assistance of his colleague, Joseph Hackett, and the co-operation of the authorities of the college. He also had the full support of Archbishop John Charles McQuaid who made Fr James Kavanagh[2] available to conduct lectures on social and economic theory from 1947 to 1950.[3] The course was an outstanding success, with an enrolment of 250 students and an average attendance at lectures of about 200. At a meeting on 10 March 1947 of the Joint Committee on Adult Education established by the Irish Trade Union Congress (I.T.U.C.) the success of the course was noted, but the committee reported that it fell short of its aim, namely, the training

1. For more on this, see J. A. Gaughan, *Alfred O'Rahilly I: Academic* (Dublin 1986) 92-102; Denis O'Sullivan (ed.), *Social commitment and adult education: essays in honour of Alfred O'Rahilly, an Irish adult educator* (Cork 1989).

2. Fr James Kavanagh, born in 1914, was a lecturer in political theory and social science at U.C.D. from 1956 to 1963, professor of social science from 1963 to 1973 and an auxiliary bishop of the archdiocese of Dublin from 1973 to 1990. (For more see pp. 185-8 and *Irish Times* 2 January 1991.) In a letter to Alfred, dated 7 October 1948, referring to Fr Kavanagh's appointment to the Rathmines College of Commerce, Fr Edward Coyne, S.J., wrote: 'His Grace had this priest trained in Oxford and I understand that he is first-rate' (Coyne Papers: letter, dated 7 October 1948, Coyne to O'Rahilly).

3. Interview with Bishop James Kavanagh: Coyne Papers: letter, dated 27 September 1948, Coyne to O'Rahilly, letters, dated 12, 20 October 1948, O'Rahilly to Coyne.

of well-informed propagandists for the labour movement.[4] In spite of this luke-warm official reception, the course continued to be well-attended and supported by trade unionists.[5]

The attitude of Dr Burke to the workers' course at U.C.C. was not universally shared. Some of Alfred's academic colleagues considered that the course and their proposed attendant diploma would tend to depreciate the value of the college's academic degrees and distinctions.[6] The national executive of the I.T.U.C. regarded them as unsuitable for trade unionists. They argued that the courses for trade unionists should be secularist, as trade unions were secular organisations, and they objected to the Christian and denominational emphasis in the sociology taught, based as it was on the papal social encyclicals.[7]

The People's College

From 1925 onwards the national executive of the I.T.U.C. had attempted to organise continuing education for its members. Despite the dedicated efforts of a number of persons, these attempts were largely unsuccessful. By the spring of 1947 renewed attempts to provide continuing education for trade unionists at U.C.D. had ended in failure.[8] At the annual meeting of Congress in 1946 James Barry, a Cork delegate, disclosed that the Cork Trades Council and representatives of U.C.C. were to launch a course for workers in the college that autumn. Then,

4. R. Dardis Clarke and Ruaidhrí Roberts, *The story of the people's college* (Dublin 1986) 9-10.

5. Interview with Bishop James Kavanagh.

6. See J. A. Gaughan, *Alfred O'Rahilly I: Academic*, 94.

7. See R. Dardis Clarke and Ruaidhrí Roberts, *The story of the people's college*, 26.

8. R. Dardis Clarke and Ruaidhrí Roberts, *The story of the people's college*, 1-6. In 1945 a joint meeting of the Labour Party and the Irish Trade Union Congress requested George O'Brien, professor of political economy in U.C.D., to provide continuing education for trade unionists. He organised a course in economics and social science, beginning in October 1945. However, he wound up the course during the following academic year when attendance at classes dropped to seven or eight. According to Fr Edmond Kent, S.J., George O'Brien's sensitive and highly-strung disposition was also a factor in the abandonment of the course, as he found exchanges of opinion with the trade-union students, who tended to be aggressive and committed socialists, to be altogether too uncongenial (ibid., 4-6; interview with Fr Edmond Kent, S.J.).

at congress in the following year, he and other Cork delegates reported on the progress of the course and were unstinting in their praise of it and of Alfred's role in organising and sustaining it.[9]

The national executive of the I.T.U.C. showed no interest. But, when it became generally known that Alfred was preparing to extend the workers' course to Limerick and Waterford and elsewhere in Munster, the executive set about organising workers' education under its own aegis throughout the country with a new urgency. To this end, it invited Ernest Green, secretary of the Workers' Educational Association in Britain, to help with the establishment of adult education facilities along W.E.A. lines in Ireland. He addressed a public meeting and conferred with the I.T.U.C. executive on 23 and 24 March 1948. At that time he also met representatives of T.C.D. and U.C.D. to ensure their co-operation in making university lecturers available. After some further preparatory meetings the educational programme was inaugurated in mid-October 1948. The organisation adopted the title People's College of Adult Education Association or in short the People's College.[10]

Alfred was disappointed that the U.C.C. course did not receive what he considered to be due recognition from the national executive of the I.T.U.C. His disappointment was shared by Peadar O'Curry, editor of the *Standard*. In the issue of 26 March 1948 O'Curry endorsed a front-page article, written by a correspondent, which was dismissive of what it described as the latest attempt to establish the British Workers' Educational Association in the country. The writer of the article argued that the U.C.C. course was a far more appropriate model for Irish workers' education.[11]

9. R. Dardis Clarke and Ruaidhrí Roberts, *The story of the people's college*, 5-6.

10. Ibid., 11-18.

11. The article declared that a number of attempts had been made to introduce the W.E.A. into Ireland and continued:

'While it was also sought very often to inoculate the workers here with the doctrine of Karl Marx, the failure of these efforts was mainly due to the fact that our viewpoint in social and political questions differs fundamentally from that of the majority of the people of Britain. There the struggle has been between the old capitalistic system and the doctrine of Karl Marx; and the activities of the adult education movement in Britain have been largely directed towards propagating Marxism. This is a position which we here in Ireland cannot support.

15. Group at U.C.C. after conferring of diploma in social and economic science on 23 June 1948. *Front row, left to right:* Joseph Nolan, Seán Ó Murchú, Professor John Busteed, Alfred, Michael Sheehan (lord mayor), William McAuliffe, Diarmuid O'Donovan. *Middle row:* John McCarthy, D. Jones, Frank O'Sullivan, J. Hurley, Patrick Crowley, Eamonn Wall, M. Hennessey, Seán Doyle, J. Meade. *Back row:* R. Kennedy, P. Hickey, J. C. Hennessy, J. C. Kelly, C. O'Meara, Denis Long, J. Ridgeway (Seán Casey, one of those conferred, is not in the group)

In a letter in the *Standard* Alfred reacted to the proposed People's College and suggested that: 'It is certainly high time that we, Irish Catholics, inaugurated a co-ordinated movement for adult education. If we do not we shall be forestalled by forces hostile to our faith.' He continued: 'The only W.E.A. official I ever met was from Belfast and he made no secret of his being a communist. A university institution such as U.C.C. can help but cannot create an adult education movement. We have Christus Rex, the Legion of Mary, An Ríoghacht, Muintir na Tíre, etc. Let us unite for the job.'[12]

By a coincidence the annual meeting of the I.T.U.C. was held in Cork in the second week of July 1948. Louie Bennett took over as president and delivered the customary address. She declared that it had become increasingly evident that the trade union was no longer merely an organisation to secure higher wages and defend the workers against injustice. It was involved in fundamental moral and social issues on which members had to make up their minds. The movement, she complained, was hampered in its development because it had not yet adopted a defined objective. Beyond a vague reference to 'spiritual values', she did not elaborate further on the trade-unions' ultimate objective.

In the *Standard,*[13] under the heading 'The humbug of

We believe that the social and economic structure of society must be based on the moral law, and that most of our economic ills have sprung from the violation of the ten commandments and a disregard of the principles of Christianity; and that these ideas must be the root of all our activities in the field of adult education. These are the principles that have been so often laid down in the encyclicals, but they cannot be too frequently repeated nor too strongly emphasised. Our difficulty here in Ireland was that until recently we had no organised effort to put these principles into operation in the matter of adult education. The university is the natural home of such education.'

In this regard the writer described the University Extension Movement at U.C.C. and charted its development down to the inauguration of the course for workers. He concluded:

'There is, however, a gap still to be bridged – this feature of the work of the university must be brought, as has been done in other countries, within reach of the vast body of the people. Fortunately the machinery by which this may be accomplished is now also in existence. The parish councils and Muintir na Tíre, if they set themselves to the task, can devise plans by which the specialised teaching of experts in such subjects as social science and economics can be brought within easy reach of their members' (*Standard* 26 March 1948).

12. *Standard* 2 April 1948.
13. *Standard* 16 July 1948.

170

neutrality', Alfred declared that he found Miss Bennett's position utterly illogical. She asserted that trade unionism, then so politically and socially influential, should have principles for dealing with such issues as the function of the State, the family, education, nationalisation, management in industry, strikes, relative wage-levels, vocational organisation, socialism, communism, etc. Yet the way to deal with these issues, she suggested, was to increase the power of the I.T.U.C. and enlarge the office staff. He characterised as ludicrous and insulting her assumption that Irish workers were living in a vacuum devoid of 'spiritual values', without a religious creed or social code and groping after undefined objectives. It was no more than a blatant attempt to relegate religion to being a private affair irrelevant to social issues. He suggested that Miss Bennett who had called for 'a great objective to inspire enthusiasm and loyal service' should be reminded of the social encyclicals and the programme of the International Federation of Christian Trade Unions.[14]

14. In the same article Alfred took issue with the refusal of the I.T.U.C. to affiliate with the International Federation of Christian Trade Unions. He was at his most abrasive in rejecting the reasons adduced by Miss Bennett and her colleagues on the executive for this decision:

'(1) The T.U.C. was already affiliated to the World Federation of Trade Unions. Well, why not affiliate to both? If the so-called World Federation, or the Russophile elements thereof, object, then have we not a clear demonstration that its alleged neutrality is anti-Christian?

'(2) The Christian Federation "represents a small minority movement" of two and a half millions, whereas the World Federation is swollen by an enormous number of Reds – and our "mission" is to these "unconverted".

'Now affiliation to the Christian Federation simply means acceptance of its programme. (This was published for 2d. last April by the Catholic Social Guild, Oxford, under the title "Light and Life for Trade Unionists".) Does or does not the Irish T.U.C. accept this programme or even its principles? That is the real issue. The T.U.C., as Miss Bennett declared, "is hampered because it has not yet adopted a defined objective". So it cannot in any practical sense declare itself Christian. After this, to talk of having a mission to convert the Reds is just bluff or hypocrisy.

'(3) Miss Bennett, while willing to accept the ideal of "the social system in this country being built on Christian principles" (undefined), declared it necessary "to accept Jews, Indians and others with their religion and . . . their spiritual principles". She forgot to add Communism which is also a religion. What does she mean by "accept"? Are the 98% Catholic workers being advised by Miss Bennett (who belongs to the 2%) to put their religion and their social principles in their pockets and to pretend to be in agreement with Hindus and Communists? (And by the way, how many Indians are members of the Irish T.U.C.?) As to the programme of the Christian trade unions, it should be acceptable to every genuine Christian, and indeed to any orthodox Jew.'

The delegates to congress were briefed by the National Executive Education Committee of the I.T.U.C., of which Miss Bennett was also president, of the steps which had been taken to organise continuing education modelled on the courses conducted by the Workers' Educational Association. In spite of the opposition of delegates from Cork, Congress passed a resolution proposed by the executive to proceed with the plan in this regard. Alfred recalled that Ernest Green, in addressing a public meeting, had advised 'neutral or secularist education' for Irish workers. He complained that no advice had been sought from him and others at U.C.C. who had been active in a workers' education movement since 1915. The reason, he suggested, was that their views on neutral or secularist education were well known. He noted that in the proposed course workers were to be taught not only economics but also sociology and philosophy. What sociology, what philosophy?, he asked. Was it to be that of Aquinas or Marx?

At congress Ruaidhrí Roberts, secretary of the National Executive Education Committee, declared that, although the new educational scheme was to start in Dublin, 'it was their intention to develop it all over the country, and when they came to Cork they hoped to have the co-operation of the College in Cork'. In this remark Roberts ignored the division in the trade-union movement from 1945 onwards. The division resulted in two congresses; the I.T.U.C., rump of the original organisation, and the Congress of Irish Unions (C.I.U.); which did not reunite until 1959. In reply to Roberts Alfred asked what right had the I.T.U.C to speak for the workers of the country. He pointed out that it catered for only half of the trade unionists in Ireland. Whereas the workers' course in Cork, he declared, had 'the fullest support from both parties of Irish Labour'. He charged Roberts with impertinence 'to talk of this Dublin-sponsored mushroom movement extending to Cork and demanding our co-operation' and he concluded.

> Miss Bennett declared her 'conviction that they stood today at a cross-roads in the history of trade unionism'. We do indeed. And she proposes to stay at the cross-roads for she is unable to make up her mind which road to take. Within another generation all the neutrals will be en route for Moscow. Irish Catholic workers, study the signposts!

Alfred did not exaggerate when he declared that he had the support of both parties of Irish Labour. From the outset he received the fullest co-operation of the Congress of Irish Unions (C.I.U.) in general and in particular the I.T.G.W.U., the largest union in the C.I.U. Formal votes were passed at the annual congresses of the C.I.U. in 1948 and 1949 thanking him and his associates for providing adult education for workers. He was given an opportunity to make an impassioned plea for support for the workers' courses at the 1949 congress.[15] The courses centred in U.C.C. also enjoyed the support of trade unions affiliated to the I.T.U.C., as well as prominent members of the Labour Party, as distinct from the National Labour Party.

The People's College was not so fortunate. There was a great deal of antipathy between the two congresses. As a result, the leadership and membership of the C.I.U., almost without exception, adopted a hostile attitude to the People's College which they viewed essentially as a product of the I.T.U.C.[16] Alfred was aware of this and avoided becoming involved in it. Although eager to draw attention to, and rally support for, the workers' courses, he declined an invitation to speak at the annual dinner of the I.T.G.W.U. on 14 October 1948, because, as he informed Michael Tierney, in a letter at that time, the People's College was being established on the following day.[17]

In a review of *British trade unionism: six studies* (London 1948) in the *Catholic Herald* Alfred gave a further airing to his view of 'the humbug of neutrality'. He acknowledged the merits of the treatment of the origins of the British trade-union movement. But for him the view that the movement was a great empirical achievement, with no creed beyond a striving for justice and a sense of social solidarity, was superficial, as in the past it had been inspired largely by a non-conformist Christianity. The current stance of neutrality towards basic human values, he declared to be as out of date as Victorian liberalism. The shallow treatment of live problems, such as the closed shop, trade unionists in parliament, nationalised industries, strikes, education, arose from an absence of a definite philosophy. They were moral issues and could not be solved

15. C.I.U., 1948 *report*, 112, 1949 *report*, 18. For his address to the 1949 Congress, see Appendix 6.
16. R. Dardis Clarke and Ruaidhrí Roberts, *The story of the people's college*, 30.
17. Coyne Papers: letter, dated 12 October 1948, O'Rahilly to Tierney.

without recourse to a code of ethical and social principles. He regretted that the British Trade Union Congress was in favour of 'the public ownership and control of natural resources and services'. To the comment that 'official trade union thought – though perhaps not that of the left wing of the movement – now accepts the continuance, at least for some time, of a large part of industry in private hands', he countered: 'So at least for some time the movement will not go communist!' He decried the absence of an awareness that private property and the pluralism of economic control were linked to human liberty. He was exceedingly critical of the determination of British trade unions to evade fundamental issues such as the inconsistency between complete collectivism and personal freedom and independent trade unions.

Alfred recalled that in 1945 the British Trade Union Congress (T.U.C.) took the initiative in forming the World Federation of Trade Unions (W.F.T.U.) which professed to include all the trade unions of free countries on a basis of equality, regardless of race, creed or political faith. The free countries included Russia and her satellites, but not Spain or Portugal. The T.U.C. was under the impression that there were free trade unions in the Soviet countries, with which it could form a joint body. Perhaps, he continued, the opposition of the W.F.T.U. to the Marshall Plan would show British trade unionists that it was not so easy to form a body 'regardless of creed or political faith'. Such a dangerous façade of impossible neutrality was a serious weakness in British trade unionism.[18]

Alfred's challenge in the *Standard* of 16 July 1948 to those organising the W.E.A. courses was left unanswered. In the *Standard* of 17 September he availed of an opportunity to re-state his objections by commenting on an article in the current issue of *The Irish Tobacco Workers' Review* by Christy Ferguson. A national organiser of the Workers' Union of Ireland, Ferguson was one of the most active members of the Provisional Committee organising the W.E.A. in Ireland. In describing the preliminary steps taken to establish the courses, he dismissed the course in workers' education at U.C.C. as 'not quite the type of liberal education envisaged by the pioneers of the movement, being of necessity sectarian in character and limited in scope'. By that comment Ferguson, in effect, declared Alfred, was

18. *Catholic Herald* 10 September 1948.

telling Irish workers, 98% of whom were Catholics, that their religion had nothing to do with questions such as, the family, the rights of the State, education, strikes, totalitarianism, etc. According to that way of thinking the Constitution was sectarian, because it contained social principles which could have been culled from papal encyclicals. Moreover, it was a viewpoint which considered that the only sects which were by definition unsectarian were socialism and communism. Alfred concluded by dismissing Ferguson's comment that the Provisional Committee included many distinguished persons, most famous of whom was Professor Erwin Schrödinger, Nobel prizewinner in physics. Schrödinger would obviously not be teaching higher mathematics to workers and, 'as for his own incursion into semi-popular biology, the result was lamentable'.

During his address at a conferring of degrees at U.C.C. on 9 November 1948, Alfred made it clear that the courses for trade unionists which had begun in Dublin were not far from his mind. At the outset he declared that the Queen's Colleges had been founded on the supposition or pretence that education could be purely secularist or neutral. Whatever plausibility that view had in the heydey of laissez-faire liberalism, when economics and business were divorced from ethics and social ideals, it was now an exploded anachronism. Over a large part of the world universities had become the mouthpiece of a State-imposed materialist philosophy. In U.C.C. they stood for the philosophy enshrined in the constitution and for the religious ideals of the overwhelming majority of the people. They differed from their predecessors of a hundred years earlier in that they were not an alien body foisted on the people. He continued: 'To use a term recently and erroneously invented in Dublin, we are the People's College.'[19]

Not surprisingly, the Council of the People's College in general and Christy Ferguson in particular were stung by the tone and content of Alfred's criticisms. At that particular time Fr Coyne appealed to the I.T.U.C. for support for his proposed course at U.C.D. In reply, as Coyne reported to Alfred, he was summoned to a meeting of the Council of the People's College on 27 October and asked his opinion of Alfred's article in the

19. *Cork Examiner* 10 November 1948.

Standard of 17 September.[20] On disclosing that he had not read it, Coyne was informed that it attacked 'non-sectarian, undenominational education'. Coyne indicated that he also was opposed to that kind of education. A few days later he received a letter from the council stating that, as the trade unions were undenominational, any educational system set up by them would have to take account of that fact. In a reply, dated 4 November, Coyne pointed out that members of the council were mistakenly confusing the interdenominational nature of the trade unions and undenominationalism. By virtue of their membership the trade unions were not undenominational but interdenominational, consisting of members of various religions. Subsequently Coyne conferred with Ruaidhrí Roberts on the matter. After further discussions the council passed a resolution that it had no wish to set up an undenominational system but wished each denomination to have its own interests and requirements looked after.[21] The publication of the resolution in the press of 13 November prompted Alfred to comment in a note on the same day to Peadar O'Curry, editor of the *Standard,* that the People's College 'proposes now to become as sectarian as Cork'.[22]

Despite an unimpressive beginning, the People's College survived, due in no small measure to the commitment of Ruaidhrí Roberts and Christy Ferguson, to provide a variety of courses and lectures for trade unionists.

---

20. At the meeting Coyne was accused of attempting to 'sabotage' the work of the People's College by announcing in the *Standard* that a diploma course in social and economic science was to begin at U.C.D. in the following January. Coyne rejected the accusation, showing that the proposed course was different in scope, price and length to that organised by the People's College.

21. R. Dardis Clarke and Ruaidhrí Roberts, *The story of the people's college,* 25-9; Coyne Papers: letter, dated 15 November 1948, Coyne to O'Rahilly.

22. Coyne Papers: copy of note, dated 13 November 1948, O'Rahilly to O'Curry. Ruaidhrí Roberts subsequently complained (*The story of the people's college,* 29) that the *Standard* did not give credit to the People's College for this change of policy. Alfred was responsible, at least in part, for this. In the note to O'Curry, of 13 November, he informed him that the change of policy was far from spontaneous and suggested that the People's College should not be given too much credit for it (Coyne Papers: copy of note, dated 13 November 1948, O'Rahilly to O'Curry; see also copy of note, dated 15 November 1948, O'Rahilly to O'Curry, in which Alfred expressed further reservations about the resolution passed by the Council of the People's College).

Extra-mural Courses at U.C.D.

In his contribution to the debate on the respective merits of interdenominational education and that of the neutral or secularist variety, Alfred by his vigorous polemical style unduly raised the level of acrimony. In a letter to Fr Coyne, dated 16 November, he felt obliged to explain his attacks on the People's College. His intention, he declared, was to ensure that there would be a positive rather than a negative response to this new scheme of workers' education. However, by this he meant that opponents of the scheme should not rest content with being critical of it, but should organise an alternative system in the metropolitan area.[23] In the event, Alfred was most active in urging such a system and exercised a significant influence in the establishment and development of the extra-mural courses at U.C.D. and the Catholic Workers' College at Sandford Road in Ranelagh.

Alfred was not alone in the mid-1940s in regarding workers' education to be of the first importance. At the general chapter of the Society of Jesus in Rome in September 1946 one of the major decisions taken was that Jesuits should, wherever appropriate, become involved in adult education and especially the teaching of social science throughout the world. Members of the Society were already active in this way in the U.S., where they staffed labour schools in New York and elsewhere; in Canada, where they organised social study courses on an extensive scale and in England, where, in association with Oxford university, they had established the Catholic Workers' College in 1922. Towards the end of 1946 Fr Thomas Byrne, S.J., the Irish provincial, appointed a committee, consisting of Frs Joseph Canavan, Thomas Counihan and Edward Coyne, to implement the decision of the Society's general chapter. In 1947 the committee, in effect, recommended the establishment of a Catholic Workers' College. Frs Counihan and Coyne set about canvassing the support and co-operation of the trade unions for this new adult education venture and the newly-ordained Fr Edmond Kent, S.J., was sent to the U.S. to gather information on workers' colleges and other adult education courses conducted by the Jesuits.[24]

23. Coyne Papers: letter, dated 16 November 1948, O'Rahilly to Coyne.

24. Interview with Fr Edmond Kent, S.J. For more on this, see M. W. Ó Murchú, 'The role of the universities and university-level institutions in continuing education' (a dissertation submitted for the degree of Ph.D. to the department of education, U.C.D., N.U.I., 1986) 72-4.

At various times in 1947 and 1948 Alfred had appealed to Fr Byrne to involve some of his colleagues in workers' education. He urged that in the conditions then prevailing such a ministry was far more important than teaching secondary school-boys, to which the Society in Ireland had allocated most of its personnel and resources.[25] At the end of September 1948 Alfred learned from Fr Coyne that he had been requested by the provincial, with the enthusiastic approval of Archbishop John C. McQuaid, to organise a Catholic Workers' College.[26] Alfred immediately conferred with Fr Byrne.[27] With the memory of the successful completion of the first workers' course at U.C.C. still fresh in his mind, he convinced the provincial of the importance of linking workers' education with U.C.D. Fr Byrne pointed out that such an initiative could come only from Michael Tierney, president of U.C.D. Alfred promised to ensure Tierney's co-operation. A few days later he met with the president of U.C.D. who subsequently reported of the meeting: 'President O'Rahilly harrangued me on the role of U.C.D. in workers' education and on the suitability of Fr Coyne to initiate Extra-Mural studies in the college to that end.'[28]

From the outset President Tierney had little enthusiasm for courses in adult education at U.C.D. Besides, he had a most independent temperament and found if difficult to co-operate even with the sister colleges of the National University. When Alfred attempted to convince him of the merits of jointly organising courses with other bodies, as U.C.C. had done with vocational educational committees, Tierney remained unconvinced. By the end of September 1948, however, Tierney must have felt somewhat isolated in his lack of enthusiasm for adult education. There was much favourable comment about the workers' course at U.C.C. Fr Coyne had been appointed to establish a Catholic Workers' College. The People's College was proposing to inaugurate its scheme of continuing education in the following month, with the support of T.C.D. Then one of the reasons adduced by Tierney for not agreeing to U.C.D.

25. Interview with Fr Edmond Kent, S.J.
26. Coyne Papers: letter, dated 27 September 1948, Coyne to O'Rahilly.
27. He was enabled to do this when he and Fr Byrne attended the funeral of one of the Jesuit fathers attached to St Francis Xavier church, in Gardiner Street, Dublin (interview with Fr Edmond Kent, S.J.).
28. Interview with Fr Edmond Kent, S.J.

16. Alfred, Fr Edward Coyne, S.J., and Professor Michael Tierney, August 1941

involvement with the People's College was his declared intention that such a system of continuing education should be established independently in the college.

Alfred continued to exhort Tierney to take a lead in the provision of adult and workers' education in the Dublin area.[29] Fr Coyne was aware of this and, in a letter to Alfred, dated 7 October 1948, wrote: 'I want to tell you how grateful I am for all the trouble and care you have shown in helping us in this delicate matter.' In a reply to Alfred's offer of advice on the details of organising a workers' course, Fr Coyne continued: 'I assure you that no definite steps will be taken without the fullest consultation with you and that your advice will always weigh most heavily in any decision taken.'[30] Tierney bowed to the inevitable. A Board of Extra-Mural Studies was established at U.C.D., to which Fr Coyne was appointed director. He was given the responsibility for the content and organisation of courses to be inaugurated in January 1949. As soon as he learned of his appointment he informed Alfred who thereafter plied him with advice. Tierney also informed Alfred of the developments at U.C.D. In a reply, dated 12 October 1948, after congratulating him on his decision, Alfred continued: 'There is one point on which I would advise you to think again, namely, co-operation with the vocational education committee.' Conscious of how sensitive Tierney could be to even an appearance of dictation from anyone, he concluded: 'Please do not think I wish in any way to interfere with your full liberty. You may decide to go on different lines from ours here.'[31]

Fr Coyne was fully appreciative of Alfred's help in rallying Tierney's support. In a letter, dated 10 November 1948, he reported that the college was ready to do all it could to make the course a success. He continued that if the course did turn out well 'it will be due to your timely intervention with Michael Tierney and to your invaluable advice and help'.[32] Coyne himself was very successful in rallying the support of the trade-union movement. In a letter to Alfred, dated 2 December, he declared that the preparations were going well and that 'the

29. Coyne Papers: copy of letter, dated 12 October 1948, O'Rahilly to Tierney.
30. Ibid.: letter, dated 7 October 1948, Coyne to O'Rahilly.
31. Ibid.: letter, dated 12 October 1948, O'Rahilly to Tierney.
32. Ibid.: letter, dated 10 November 1948, Coyne to O'Rahilly.

trade unions and the congresses have given me great moral support as well as financial help'.[33] From September 1949 onwards Coyne had the help of Fr Edmond Kent, S.J., who, on returning from his fact-finding mission in the U.S., was appointed to be Coyne's assistant in the work at U.C.D.

Some 400 trade unionists signed on for the first course – a two-year diploma course in social and economic science – which went ahead on schedule in January 1949. In response to a demand for an alternative, Fr Coyne and the Board of Extra-Mural Studies introduced a two-year diploma course in liberal arts from October 1950 onwards.[34] Almost from the outset there were requests for courses in other centres in Leinster. Alfred urged Coyne to provide these, as U.C.C. had in various parts of Munster. Coyne indicated his eagerness to do so but pointed out that only Tierney could make such a decision. Tierney was reluctant to authorise the expansion of the U.C.D. programme outside Dublin. During the early 1950s after representatives of centres elsewhere in Leinster had sought in vain to be included in the U.C.D. Extra-Mural Studies programme, they appealed to Alfred for his assistance. Invariably they would invite him to speak on the subject of adult and workers' education. In his address he would announce that the centre was within the jurisdiction of U.C.D. and subsequently he would appeal formally on their behalf to the U.C.D. Board of Extra-Mural Studies. This and considerable covert pressure from the centres persuaded Tierney and the U.C.D. Board to provide courses at Athlone, Carlow, Drogheda, Dundalk, Kilkenny, Mullingar, Naas, Portlaoise and Wexford.[35]

33. Ibid.: letter, dated 2 December 1948, Coyne to O'Rahilly.
34. Interview with Fr Edmond Kent, S.J.
35. Coyne Papers: letter, dated 15 March 1949, O'Rahilly to Coyne; interview with Fr Edmond Kent, S.J. Tierney was well aware of Alfred's connivance in the pressure being exerted on him and Alfred was equally conscious of his friend's resentment in the matter. In a letter to Fr Edmond Kent, S.J., dated 19 December 1950, Alfred advised Fr Kent to ensure Tierney's support for the Catholic Workers' College, but warned him when seeking it '*never* mention me or Cork' (Coyne Papers: letter, dated 19 December 1950, O'Rahilly to Kent). Notwithstanding his irritation at what he described as Alfred's 'habit of interfering', Tierney was never other than magnanimous in acknowledging Alfred's contribution to the establishment of centres throughout the country. Typical was his remark when conferring diplomas in social and economic science at Carlow on 21 September 1951: 'These courses began in Dublin under the inspiration of Professor Alfred O'Rahilly, of Cork, and the need for them was quickly felt all

Alfred O'Rahilly III: Controversialist

Fr Coyne continued as director of the U.C.D. Extra-Mural Studies programme from 1949 until his death in 1958. As Tierney recalled:

> Though his main work lay outside the college, Fr Coyne never lost his lively interest in its well-being, and willingly undertook the direction of its Extra-Mural courses in addition to his other onerous duties. It is safe to say that without him the Board of Extra-Mural Studies would have found its task, in the circumstances in which it was established, next to impossible. Fr Coyne's early death was recognised as a great national loss.[36]

over the country' (*Standard* 28 September 1951). In a letter to Tierney, dated 24 September 1951, Alfred demurred at the favourable mention of his name and protested that he had 'no copyright on the business' and that all he desired was to 'see U.C.D. forging ahead and beating U.C.C. to a frazzle' (Tierney Papers).

36. Michael Tierney, *Report of the president, University College, Dublin 1958-1959* (Dublin 1959) 66. Tierney did not exaggerate. Fr Coyne (1896-1958) was an indefatigable champion and exponent of the social encyclicals. He was a protégé of Fr Thomas Finlay, S.J., professor of political economy in U.C.D., who, with Sir Horace Plunkett and R. A. Anderson, founded the Irish Agricultural Organisation Society (I.A.O.S.), cornerstone of the co-operative movement in Ireland. Coyne absorbed the philosophy of co-operation and self-reliance of his mentor. In 1931 he assisted Fr John M. Hayes in founding Muintir na Tíre and in 1934 he prepared, with Thomas Johnson, the Labour leader, the pamphlet *Planning for a new order in Ireland* which was published by the I.T.G.W.U. By the time the Commission on Vocational Organisation was set up in 1939 he had become well known for his lecturing and writing on social questions and was an automatic choice for inclusion on the Commission to which he rendered sterling service for over four years. From 1943 onwards he was president of the I.A.O.S. He was a member of a number of the organisation's Joint Labour Committees and of the Fisheries Advisory Council. As well as his involvement in adult and workers' education from 1946 until his death, he was professor of moral theology at Milltown Park and was occasionally directed by his superior to conduct week-long retreats in convents and institutions around the country. As if the duties Coyne already had were not enough, at the beginning of 1949 Alfred set about having him appointed professor of rural sociology at U.C.C. However, he was thwarted by the governing body where, as he saw it, the 'jealous mediocrities who made up the anti-clerical and the anti-O'Rahilly factions', as well as the Capuchin fathers, united to block the appointment. Coyne's work-rate was comparable to that of Alfred's and probably led to his death at the relatively young age of sixty-two. It was almost certainly the cause of a quite uncharacteristic irritability noted by friends and acquaintances in his last years.

The Board of Extra-Mural Studies discontinued its two-year diploma courses in 1960. This decision was prompted mainly by an ever-increasing demand for a wide variety of lecture courses. By that time the future of continuing education at U.C.D. was assured.[37]

Catholic Workers' College

In a letter to Alfred, dated 7 October 1948, Fr Coyne speculated that President Tierney might authorise courses under the supervision of U.C.D. and combine them with the vague scheme for a Catholic Workers' College which the provincial and himself were trying to elaborate. In the event, that very week Tierney authorised the establishment of a Board of Extra-Mural Studies with Fr Coyne as its director. As a result, all of Coyne's preparations to establish a Catholic Workers' College were directed towards the successful inauguration of a two-year diploma course in social and economic science under the auspices of the new Board.[38] While Alfred was eager that workers' courses in Dublin should be linked with the university as in Cork, he wrote to Coyne on 30 November 1948 that, in addition, there was 'room' for a Catholic Workers' College. He considered that the role of such a college and that of the other initiatives in workers' education would be to ensure that workers in Ireland would not become disenchanted with, or disengaged from, the Church as had occurred in Catholic Belgium and France.[39] In a reply, dated 2 December, Coyne confirmed that the only scheme likely to come into effect was the course at U.C.D., the Workers' College having merged its proposed course with that to be inaugurated in the college. He informed Alfred that, although the provincial and the archbishop had bowed to the inevitable, they considered that the Catholic Workers' College should remain in existence even if for the time being it did not run a separate system of education from the course in U.C.D.[40] Alfred conferred on these develop-

37. M. W. Ó Murchú, 'The role of the universities and university-level institutions in continuing education', 84, 91. For a more detailed account of the two-year diploma courses, see ibid., 72-84.

38. Coyne Papers: letter, dated 7 October 1958, Coyne to O'Rahilly. See also ibid.: letter, dated 12 October 1948, O'Rahilly to Tierney.

39. Ibid.: letter, dated 30 November 1948, O'Rahilly to Coyne.

40. Ibid.: letter, dated 2 December 1948, Coyne to O'Rahilly.

ments and other aspects of the organisation of the U.C.D. course with Fr Coyne in Dublin on 8 and 9 December. Subsequently both met General Richard Mulcahy, minister for education, and Michael Tierney on 9 December to discuss funding for the workers' courses.[41]

With Fr Coyne fully occupied in organising the U.C.D. courses, his assistant, Fr Kent, took over responsibility for establishing the Catholic Workers' College. He wrote to Alfred for advice. This was freely given as well as exhortations on the crucial importance of such a college at that particular time.[42] An opportunity to inaugurate the Catholic Workers' College arose when forty-two worker-students, who had successfully completed the first diploma course at U.C.D., indicated their desire to continue the study of social and economic questions. Fr Kent organised a course for this purpose early in 1951 and thereby the C.W.C. was inaugurated. From the outset the main aim of the college was to improve industrial relations. This was evident when in the late autumn of 1951 the college organised a successful pilot course for employers. This concern to create a climate of respect and understanding between employers and workers has remained a feature of the college. It was situated in Sandford Lodge,[43] Ranelagh, and initially it was mainly staffed by Jesuits from Milltown Park nearby. In 1966 it was renamed the College of Industrial Relations and in 1987 became the National College of Industrial Relations.[44]

U.C.G. Programme of Adult Education

Alfred's influence in continuing education extended to U.C.G., where a two-year diploma course in social and economic science was inaugurated in the autumn of 1949.

41. See ibid.: letter, dated 20 November 1948, O'Rahilly to Coyne; letter, dated 2 December 1948, Coyne to O'Rahilly.

42. Ibid: letter, dated 19 December 1950, O'Rahilly to Kent.

43. Before the acquisition of Sandford Lodge, Fr Coyne had appealed to colleagues for rooms, where he could conduct his course for workers. The response was mixed, varying from an outright refusal from the rector of University Hall, Hatch Street, to a generous offer from the rector of Belvedere College.

44. Interview with Fr Edmond Kent, S.J. See also Declan Byrne, 'Placing the Catholic Workers' College 1951 to 1958 in its societal context' (thesis for Bachelor of Arts degree in industrial relations, National College of Industrial Relations, March 1989).

Subsequently courses were organised in other centres in Connacht and County Clare such as Sligo and Ennis. The courses were modelled on those at U.C.C.[45] In the *Standard* Fr Felim Ó Briain, O.F.M., director of the U.C.G. courses, acknowledged the debt to Alfred of himself and others involved in adult and workers' education.[46] Alfred's influence continued over the organisation of adult education at U.C.G. In 1968 the governing body authorised an intensive survey to determine the nature and extent of the demand for extra-mural education in Connacht and County Clare. During the winter of 1968-69 the survey was carried out by Cornelius (Con) Murphy, who had been Alfred's assistant in organising and promoting adult and workers' education. Murphy's report *Proposals for Extra-Mural Adult Education Programme in University College, Galway* was presented in May 1969. The report was adopted and has since remained the blueprint for extra-mural studies at U.C.G.[47]

Dublin Institute of Adult Education

Alfred cast his shadow over what is now known as the Dublin Institute of Adult Education. In 1945 Archbishop John Charles McQuaid sent Fr James Kavanagh to Campion Hall, Oxford, to study social and economic theory with a view to developing a scheme for social education, in effect, courses in Catholic sociology, in the archdiocese.

On his return to Dublin in 1947, Fr Kavanagh and others reviewed the activities of groups involved in social education. This kind of activity was not very extensive but neither was it entirely lacking. A Catholic social reform movement had been sparked off by a memorable address by Fr Charles D. Plater, S.J., in St Patrick's College, Maynooth, in 1912. This prompted Fr James Dempsey, C.C., Fr John Flanagan, C.C., and Fr Lambert McKenna, S.J., to establish the Leo League that same year. The Priests' Social League, which is dated from that time, also promoted the study of Leo XIII's *Rerum Novarum*. The social

45. M. W. Ó Murchú, 'The role of the universities and university-level institutions in continuing education', 94.

46. *Standard* 10 August 1951.

47. M. W. Ó Murchú, 'The role of the universities and university-level institutions in continuing education', 94-5.

movement was quickened by the chaos and hardship caused by the lock-out in Dublin in 1913. In 1926 Fr Edward Cahill, S.J., co-founded An Ríoghacht (League of the Kingship of Christ) to popularise the social encyclical. When he was president of Blackrock College, Fr John C. McQuaid, C.S.Sp., was associated with the establishment, in 1933, of the Guilds of Regnum Christi, which enabled past pupils to study Catholic social teaching with a view to putting it into practice. The Catholic Societies Vocational Organisation Conference was founded in 1945 to promote this important aspect of the teaching of the social encyclicals. Other individual study groups, some praesidia of the Legion of Mary and some branches of the St Joseph's Young Priests' Society also concerned themselves with the 'social question'. In 1950, on Fr Kavanagh's recommendation, all these groups were given accommodation at 14 Gardiner Place, which was named the Dublin Diocesan Social Study Centre. In 1951 Fr Kavanagh was appointed its director and courses were organised along the lines pioneered at U.C.C.[48]

Alfred was responsible for one of the courses, that for journalists. In the first week of December 1951 Pádraig Ó Dargáin of the *Wexford People* suggested that such a course be organised. In a reply, dated 12 December, Alfred welcomed the suggestion, promised to air it at a forthcoming lecture to the Catholic Writers' Guild and advised Ó Dargáin to inquire as to the level of interest in the course. On 2 January 1952 Alfred emphasised to Ó Dargán the need for a knowledge of Catholic sociology and elementary economics and sent him the outline of a programme of instruction on these subjects. On 11 February 1952 Ó Dargáin reported an interest by journalists in Dublin and the provinces in the proposed course. All of them, it seems, were members of the Guild of Irish Journalists, founded in 1949 as an Irish controlled trade union. Subsequently Ó Dargáin sent Alfred a letter which he had received from James J. Mac-Sweeney, vice-president of the National Executive Council of the Guild, pledging the support of the Guild.

By 23 February 1952 Alfred and Ó Dargáin had agreed that it would not be feasible to organise the course at U.C.C. and

48. Souvenir brochure of official opening and blessing by Archbishop Dermot Ryan of the Dublin Institute of Adult Education, December 1980; R. Burke Savage, S.J., 'The Church in Dublin 1940-1965', *Studies* 54 (1965) 301; interview with Bishop James Kavanagh.

Alfred promised to do his utmost to have it started in Dublin. On the same date he sent his correspondence with Ó Dargáin to Archbishop McQuaid. After an exchange of letters between Alfred and Archbishop McQuaid, Ó Dargáin was in contact with the archbishop and Fr James Kavanagh. In a letter, dated 17 May 1952, Ó Dargáin informed the archbishop that officers of the Guild of Irish Journalists would be writing to Fr Kavanagh about the course, but that he did not know if any member of the National Union of Journalists would be interested in taking it.

The course was announced in the *Standard* of 13 June 1952. Alfred commented on the announcement as follows:

> In view of recent discussions on social principles, for example, in the mother-and-child scheme, tenure of farms, etc., and of future problems confronting this country, it seems to me most important that Irish journalists should be equipped in social principles. Furthermore, a more systematic study of Irish economic realities would be of great help to them.
>
> Irish journalists have not yet secured a proper professional status and there appears to be no regular course of training and no minimum standard of qualifications. Hence, in addition to helping this influential body of persons to guide the country, a diploma in journalism or sociology would help their professional status.

The course was inaugurated in October 1952 and was conducted by Fr James Kavanagh until 1954.[49]

From 1952 onwards an annual social study week was held. Alfred's contribution to the development and expansion of social education was acknowledged when he was invited to be the principal speaker at the first of these social study weeks. He struck a spiritual note. Our religion, he declared, must be paramount, practical and personal, and he continued that the greatest need was for a deepening of lay spirituality. He also emphasised the importance of Catholic sociology in the ideological struggle which lay ahead. Soon afterwards Archbishop McQuaid had the diocesan centre renamed the Dublin Institute

49. Dublin Archdiocesan Archives, Alfred O'Rahilly file, correspondence on course for journalists; *Standard* 13 June 1952; interview with Bishop James Kavanagh.

of Catholic Sociology. With Frank Sheed, Douglas Hyde and Lt-General Michael J. Costello, Alfred made up the panel of lecturers at the annual congress of the Institute in June 1956.[50] Alfred continued to take an active interest in the Institute. This ended in the early 1960s. Apart from his advanced years, he incurred the disfavour of the archbishop. This arose from a complicated, three-cornered wrangle after Alfred had given President Michael Tierney the mistaken impression that McQuaid was behind a proposal to link courses at the Dublin Institute of Catholic Sociology with U.C.D.[51] In the meantime and subsequently Fr Kavanagh's successors ensured the continuing development of the Institute which was renamed the Dublin Institute of Adult Education in 1967.[52]

50. Souvenir brochure of official opening and blessing by Archbishop Dermot Ryan of the Dublin Institute of Adult Education, December 1980; *Standard* 31 October 1952; 4 May, 22 June 1956.

51. Interview with Rev. Dr Michael O'Carroll, C.S.Sp. By this infelicitous intervention Alfred caused McQuaid and Tierney to be at odds and earned the grave annoyance of both. At that time Tierney was reported to have said that it was disastrous to have Alfred on one's side in a controversy because he threw so much mud that some of it spattered those on his own side (ibid.).

52. Apart from Fr James Kavanagh, much of the credit for the subsequent success of the D.I.A.E. is due to Fr George Thomas Fehily (1923-   ) who was director of the institute from 1954 to 1963. Adept at securing sponsorship, Fr Fehily developed the annual social study week into a major event in Dublin's civic calendar. Under the auspices of the institute, he organised highly publicised public debates on social issues, for which he was highly commended by the Taoiseach, Seán Lemass (Fehily Papers: letter, dated 19 January 1963, Lemass to Fehily). One such issue was the plight of the itinerants. As a result, the commission on itinerancy was set up in 1960. It reported three years later but, owing to the apathy and, occasionally, outright hostility of the public, it was not possible to have any of its important recommendations implemented. With Victor Bewley, a fellow-member of the commission, Fr Fehily formed the Dublin Itinerant Settlement Committee with a view to changing public opinion, so as to make it possible for local authorities to implement the commission's recommendations. This became the Dublin Committee for Travelling People which encouraged the establishment of local committees throughout the country to assist in providing amenities for itinerants. These committees, under the direction of the National Council for Travelling People, were relatively successful in providing accommodation and facilities for itinerants. Nearly thirty years later there has been no improvement in the accommodation and facilities that had been available in the mid-1960s. In the meantime, itinerants have greatly increased in number and the difficulties associated with the relationship between the settled and the travelling communities continue (Interview with Mgr G. Thomas Fehily; *Report of the Commission on Itinerancy* (Dublin 1963); Victor Bewley (ed.), *Travelling People* (Dublin 1974)).

Reaction to Workers' Courses

Reaction from abroad to the workers' and other courses at U.C.C. was varied. On the positive side a number of priests who were involved in Catholic Action on the continent visited U.C.C. to observe the courses at first hand. Cardinal Bernard Griffin of Westminster also showed interest. In the summer of 1947 he conferred with Alfred who persuaded him that the U.C.C. scheme was far more practical and less expensive than sending young workers to the Catholic Workers' College in Oxford. As a result, the cardinal inaugurated a scheme of workers' education in the autumn of 1948 on the model of that at U.C.C.[53] At Alfred's invitation, Douglas Hyde was in Cork to deliver some public lectures in February 1949. He also addressed those taking the workers' course at U.C.C., Limerick and Waterford and, on returning to London, he helped to organise a similar course.[54] On 8 July 1951 Alfred addressed a meeting at the National University of Ireland Club in London on the workers' courses. He stated that, if such courses for Irish expatriates could not be organised by the club in conjunction with London University or some similar body, he would ensure that U.C.C. took responsibility for them. A committee, comprised of members of the club, was set up to consider this proposal. Although it took no action in the matter, it extended a warm welcome to the proposal.[55]

On the negative side an article 'Workers in Ireland: The New Educational Movement' in the *Times Educational Supplement* was most unsympathetic. Alfred replied to the anonymously written article, in the *Standard*. The first criticism directed at the workers' courses was that too much attention was paid to the winning of a diploma which encouraged a narrow approach to the subject. Alfred pointed out that the diploma provided a psychological incentive for hard work and was a public recognition that the students had been accepted by a university institution. Moreover, an examination ensured that the students could express themselves in writing. The second criticism was: 'The

---

53. Interview with Canon James P. Bastible; Coyne Papers: letter, dated 30 November 1948, O'Rahilly to Coyne; *Cork Examiner* 23 November 1948.

54. *Cork Examiner* 21 February 1949; Coyne Papers: letter, dated 26 February 1949, O'Rahilly to Coyne. See also *Catholic Herald* 11, 18 March 1949.

55. *Catholic Herald* 13 July 1951.

impression given is that the Catholic Church is seeking to train a cadre of disciplined enthusiasts, who will be able to take over the trade-union movement.' In urging this, the author quoted Alfred as follows: 'Our object is to train leaders. It is not our function to run trade unions or to undertake rural co-operation. We are equipping our students to do this. Here we have taken a leaf out of the communists' book.' Alfred acknowledged that the main purpose behind the courses was to disseminate as widely as possible a knowledge of Catholic social principles. In that way workers would not be easily convinced by the facile allure of communism and would not be enslaved by it. But he ridiculed the implication that the workers' education movement was a conspiracy to take over the trade-union movement. In fact, the adult education movement inaugurated by Alfred at U.C.C. was to have a significant influence in many areas of Irish life. During the following thirty years a remarkable number of those who received diplomas after attending the courses achieved positions of leadership. These included not only national and branch secretaries of trade unions, executives of the largest co-operatives in the country, persons who held the highest offices in the Irish Countrywomen's Association, Irish Creamery Milk Suppliers' Association, Irish Farmers' Association, Macra na Feirme and Muintir na Tíre, but also executives in the construction industry and other major companies and T.Ds and senators, lord mayors and chairmen of county councils from all the political parties, except the Workers' Party. A further criticism was that 'there is an obvious risk that the schemes may be conducted on too clerical a basis. Protestants, for example, are not formally excluded; but it would be difficult for a Protestant to attend classes in which the first principle insisted upon was obedience to the Catholic Church's teaching on social and economic matters.' Alfred claimed that the classes were attended by persons of all religions and of none. Because of the religious composition of the population there was a preponderance of Catholics. However, he pointed out: 'We teach social philosophy not the theology of revelation; we deal with natural law and rights, the family, the State, and so on; the Constitution is our text-book. When the Church is mentioned, it is as a natural institution in a pluralistic community.' Finally, Alfred characterised much of the criticism as 'bigoted nonsense', but declared that it was worth answering as it was based on the assumption of 'neutrality propagated by the metropolitan intelligentsia'. In the event, it was entirely appropriate that he did answer it, as one of Alfred's abiding convictions was the truism that there was no such phenomenon as value-free education.[56]

At home Alfred was not slow to publicise the merits of the various adult education programmes, for which he had been responsible. The editorial in the *Standard* of 20 June 1952 quoted from his address to the annual congress of the Irish Vocational Association at Tullamore:

> We have given its due dignity to labour. We have helped the ordinary farmer to appreciate scientific principles. We have brought to the countryside the advantages hitherto confined to a few cities. We have strengthened our people against alien ideology. We have shown how religion can and should penetrate ordinary working life.

Alfred was disappointed that he was not invited to sit on the Commission on Higher Education 1960-67. He was requested by the chairman, Judge Cearbhall Ó Dálaigh, to make a submission to it, but declined to do so.[57] His absence and that of someone of his stature who would champion adult education in the university was clear in the disappointing conclusions on that subject reached by the Commission. It stated that to a large extent adult education was outside its terms of reference, accorded it a marginal status in its deliberations and recommended that it be provided by institutions and agencies other than universities. Had he been a member of the Commission, Alfred almost certainly would have written a characteristic minority report intensely critical of this attitude.

The deficiency of the Report of the Commission on Higher Education in regard to adult education was generally recognised. This prompted two further reports, the first, *Adult education in Ireland*, was published in 1973; the second, *Lifelone learning*, in 1984. In effect, these provide the guidelines along which adult education has been organised

56. *Times Educational Supplement* 20 July 1951; *Standard* 7 September 1951.

57. O'Rahilly Papers: letter, dated 15 November 1960, Ó Dálaigh to O'Rahilly.

throughout the country. Basic to them is the principle championed by Alfred, namely, that the university is crucial in the provision and recognition of adult education.[58]

Council of Education

In retrospect Alfred as an educationalist will be chiefly associated with the promotion of adult education. However, his influence on education in the country extended far beyond adult education. As noted elsewhere, he was consulted in 1920-21 by a Sinn Féin commission on secondary education with regard to mathematical studies and the incorporation of subjects in the curriculum which would contribute to an improvement in the country's agriculture. About that time also Mícheál Ó hAodha, minister for education from January to September 1922, consulted him on teacher training. In February 1922 Alfred was persuaded by Ó hAodha to act on the standing committee of the commission on secondary education and in April of the same year he was consulted on a number of occasions by Patrick Hogan, minister for agriculture, regarding agricultural education in U.C.C. His significant influence on the development of the N.U.I. and its constituent colleges at U.C.C. and U.C.D. has already been traced. His advice and support was sought by those who, in 1921-3, attempted to establish a National Academy of Ireland.[59] In addition, throughout his professional life he concerned himself with almost the whole range of education issues. Until the late 1940s he was a frequent and widely sought-after lecturer at gatherings of teachers. Apart from other topical subjects, invariably his principal contribution was to urge that teachers and others actively involved in education should have an influential part in its organisation. To this end, he proposed the establishment of a council of education on which the widest possible range of educational interests would be represented. This proposal arose from his commitment to the principles of *Rerum Novarum* which advocated the delegation by the central authority of responsibility and initiative to

58. M. W. Ó Murchú, 'The role of the universities and university-level institutions in continuing education', 31-6.

59. See J. A. Gaughan, *Alfred O'Rahilly I: Academic* and *Alfred O'Rahilly II: Public figure, passim.* For more on the National Academy of Ireland, see Appendix 7.

occupational groups and local bodies, with a corresponding diminution of State or bureaucratic control.

Alfred first publicly advocated a council of education in his draft constitution of 1922. Article 37 read:

> (1) In addition to territorial autonomy, legislation shall institute a measure of functional autonomy for the different branches of social service and economic life. In particular a council of education, a council of agriculture, a council of transport and a council of industry shall be established; and in each of these councils the relevant occupational groups shall be represented according to their social and economic importance. Legislation shall determine the advisory, supervisory and administrative capacity of such councils.
>
> (2) Drafts of important laws, involving social and economic laws, proposed by the executive council, shall be submitted to the council to which they appertain, for consideration and criticism, before they are introduced into the house of representatives. Bills may also be referred by the house of representatives to a council. The councils have the right of organising such bills themselves. Should the executive council disapprove of them, it must nevertheless introduce them into the house of representatives, with a statement of its own views.[60]

Alfred delivered the principal address at the annual congress of the Irish National Teachers' Organisation held in Easter week 1923. He spoke on 'Educational reform'. The most pressing educational reform, he declared, was the creation of a professional or functional council of education. He referred to the articles in his draft constitution of 1922 in which he advocated such a council. This council, he explained, would not be composed of nominees, politicians and pensioners, but would be elected by all those engaged in education. It would not be merely advisory, but would have administrative powers, such as those possessed by the old boards of education, and would have an important critical and initiatory function in relation to parliament.

The next reform, he advocated, was the securing of a professional status for national teachers. This would be acquired by

60. J. A. Gaughan, *Alfred O'Rahilly II: Public figure*, 462.

having a degree in education. He recalled the two schemes which had been proposed for the university training of teachers. According to the first scheme, after spending two years in one of the training colleges, teachers would undergo a university examination and spend a further two years in the university in order to obtain a degree. The second scheme, for which Alfred had canvassed at U.C.C. and among the national teachers of Cork city and county and of County Kerry, envisaged the training of every national teacher extending over three years concurrently in a training college and a university. He acknowledged that practical difficulties made it unlikely that either scheme would be implemented in the immediate future and suggested that in the meantime the most able teachers in training should be given an opportunity to pursue a university course.

Alfred also suggested that local education committees be established. These would supervise the cleaning, heating and equipment of school buildings; the provision of meals, clinics and books; the enforcement of school attendance; and the arrangement of programmes and scholarships. Such committees, he pointed out, would be of considerable assistance to hard-pressed school-managers.

In concluding, Alfred was particularly critical of the 'bookishness' of Irish education. As a result of this and snobbery, the best brains of the country were removed from productive economic work and transferred to the professions. He deplored the over-emphasis on literary training, as if the sole function of national schools was to feed the intermediate colleges. He pointed out that the vast majority of the pupils of primary schools would not proceed to second-level education. He argued that in a proper system of education most of them would go on to agricultural and technical institutes. In the primary school there should also be provision for the development of character, carefulness, patience, accuracy and conscientiousness. The object of the national schools was to form the character as well as to mould the minds of the future working men and women, and to help them to develop into good citizens and skilled workers for the glory of God and the honour of Ireland.

On 17 September 1932, Teachers' Day at the Cork Industrial Fair, Alfred lectured on 'The mission of the teacher'. That mission, he declared, was, in effect, to undo centuries of

Anglicisation. Ireland's defeat, he claimed, began in the latter half of the seventeenth century, when the English began a systematic nationwide war against Irish education. The priest, the schoolmaster, the Irish scholar, were singled out as the real enemies, after the soldiers had been massacred or shipped abroad. The process of Anglicisation was completed by the great famine and wholesale evictions.

It was not merely that the Irish language was almost obliterated; the war cut much deeper. Language was but a vehicle for ideas, the expression of a culture. They had lost their outlook on life, their political and social ideals. A mere revival of the language, unaccompanied by a restoration of ideals was useless. A nation would not be saved by a mere change of vocabulary. From the point of view of culture they were living on the credit of centuries-old Hiberno-Romanesque churches and illuminated manuscripts. Presently everything they thought or did was just a shoddy replica of England, sometimes spiced with Hollywood.

The 'de-Irishising' influences, which were once backed by penal laws and economic patronage, were now finding an unchecked entrance. English soldiers had been replaced by English capitalists; foreign laws by alien ideas. They called themselves the teachers of Ireland. They were not. They were merely the persons who helped young people to swot up fractions, names of rivers, dates of battles. For a brief period they controlled the bodies and the lips of the young but their minds and souls escaped them. The real educators were the movies, the press, the drama, the novel and pseudo-science.

To cope with this challenge he made a plea for less urbanisation and less centralisation in education. He reiterated a demand, which, he emphasised, he had already frequently expressed for a council of education. Such a council had also been demanded by the Labour Party and by the primary and secondary teachers. He denounced as tyrannical and undemocratic the current system, whereby a few anonymous civil servants in Dublin controlled and engineered practically the whole of educational policy. It was a scandalous anomaly that a government pledged to the referendum and to de-centralisation should retain a bureaucracy worse than England had. The only education which would save the country from moral, if not physical, extinction was one based on their own principles and adapted to their needs, and administered by working teachers adequately trained in philosophy and nationality. In this task the Irish teacher once again had to become a missionary.[61]

The annual conference of the Association of Secondary Teachers was held in U.C.C. in April 1933. The principal address was given by Alfred who dealt with 'The problems of education'. He was at his most provocative, stating that they were 'confronted with the utter failure of modern education'. The choice before the country, he warned, was the communism of Russia or guildism. He indicated that what he meant by the latter term in the context of education was the establishment of a council representative of all those involved in education, which, jointly with the central authority, would administer the educational system in such a way as to allow a fair measure of local autonomy and flexibility of practice.[62]

In an address to the national teachers of Cork city and county in the spring of 1934 Alfred urged the establishment of a guild of education which would include university as well as primary and secondary teachers. He described a council of education as an immediate priority. This would be chiefly composed of primary teachers and it should not be a mere advisory body. Any educational bill should be submitted to it for consideration and criticism before being introduced. The alternative was

61. I.N.T.O.: *Addresses at I.N.T.O. Congress, Easter 1923*, 'Educational reform' by Professor Alfred O'Rahilly; *Cork Examiner* 19 September 1932. For more on Alfred's attitude to the Irish language, see J. A. Gaughan, *Alfred O'Rahilly I: Academic*, 118-22, 137-8, 154-6. He was particularly critical of those who attempted to politicise the language revival movement. At the annual ardfheis of Conradh na Gaeilge in 1923 the general secretary, Proinnsias Ó Fathaigh (Frank Fahy, anti-treatyite T.D.), lamented the falling off in subscriptions to the organisation. This he attributed to a wave of Anglicisation which had swept over the country during the previous two years. The clear implication was that this was due to the acceptance of the Anglo-Irish treaty by the people. He also alleged a lack of commitment on the part of the National University of Ireland in the promotion of the Irish language. In an unsigned contribution to the *Cork Examiner* of 14 November 1923, Alfred replied sharply that there were many long-serving members of the Gaelic League who had endeavoured to keep the organisation clear of political controversies. They were not helped, he continued, by public allegations about so-called Anglicisation, attacks on the government or on the National University and, least of all, by League officials standing for parliament and then refusing to take their seats (*Cork Examiner, Irish Independent* 14 November 1923).

62. *Cork Examiner* 19 April 1933.

bureaucracy, 'the biggest danger and curse in the country at the moment'. He rejected what he described as the then widespread assumption that the State had a right to educate the people. The parents had the primary right and duty; the State had the right to supervise. He regretted the way in which the State was encroaching more and more in the field of education.

Alfred also commented on a topic then to the fore in the minds of national teachers, namely, their role in the attempt to revive the Irish language. He queried the educational merits of the manner in which the national school was being used to restore the language. In Wales, he pointed out, this was not attempted. Ignoring the essential differences between the situation in Wales and in Ireland, he continued there they relied on the home and the church. He suggested that the government should rather concentrate on ensuring that Irish remained the primary language of the Gaeltacht, which they should then try to extend. On another issue with which the executive of the I.N.T.O. was then concerned, he declared that it was no more than an elementary economic issue to see that every school that received State support had a proper quota of laymen and women and that they should be paid proper salaries.[63]

Alfred was invited to deliver the principal address at the annual congress of the I.N.T.O. at Killarney in mid-April 1936. Illness, however, prevented him from attending. Instead he sent a letter to Thomas J. O'Connell, the general secretary. Such was the importance attached to it that it was used as a veritable keynote address. After expressing regret at his inability to attend the congress, Alfred continued:

> The world-wide tendency to bureaucracy and totalitarianism is evident here at home, not least in the sphere of education. Your organisation, I take it, stands not only for the principle that those who serve the community should receive adequate remuneration and security; but also for the ideal of functional democracy: that is, that – subject to the ultimate sanction of the people – education should be managed by educationalists, by those who spend their lives in the schools, and not by doctrinaire commissars issuing administrative ukases from the metropolis.

63. O'Rahilly Papers: Scrapbook 1, press-cutting.

I hope that the teachers will persevere in their demand for the setting up of a council of education, and that meanwhile they will protest against the continued boycott of practical teachers by the bureaucratic devisers of schemes and programmes. I have lately come across examples of the working of the inspectorial system, which, in my opinion, is largely an instrument of pin-pricking and tyranny, entirely negative and perverse in its outlook, rightly denied the confidence of hard-working teachers.

State usurpation and control is steadily increasing, a phenomenon which many, ignoring papal encyclicals, regard as inevitable. It is in the control of education that such manifestation is most dangerous; witness the extreme instances of sovietism, fascism and nazism. It is amazing to me how obtuse to this subtly-increasing danger are Irish Catholics, even many clergy and religious who have to do with education.

Even the university authorities are beginning to sell their souls for a share of the commissars' fleshpots.

As a Catholic, as a parent, as an Irishman, as a teacher, I can look, under heaven, only to the I.N.T.O. as a magnificent professional corporation, as our only solid educational bulwark against the rising tide of bureaucratic despotism.

The tone of the letter caused something of a sensation and Alfred's comments were featured at length in the press coverage of the congress.[64]

The economic war with Britain threw the national finances into some disarray. The government passed the Temporary Economies Act, 1932, whereby the salaries of civil servants were reduced by 5%. Despite the opposition of the I.N.T.O., primary teachers were included in these reductions. The organisation mounted protest meetings on the issue throughout the country. Alfred was active to the same end at U.C.C., where the government sought to impose the same reduction of salary on his colleagues. By negotiation he succeeded in having the salary reduction modified.[65] He publicly indicated his support for the I.N.T.O.'s campaign and accepted an invitation from the executive to address a protest meeting in Cork on 21 November 1936.

64. *Cork Examiner* 16 April 1936.
65. J. A. Gaughan, *Alfred O'Rahilly I: Academic*, 117-18.

Educationalist

Alfred urged the teachers to become more militant. He warned them to resist being forced into the position of being regarded as civil servants. They were not civil servants and the people who should be protecting them at that time were the clerical managers of the country. But they found themselves to be nobody's child. 'You do not count politically and the politicians do not care a damn about you,' he declared. He pointed out that many of those interested in the Irish language were so because the Gaelic League had political influence. Likewise the politicians interested themselves in the language because of votes that could be influenced by the League. He suggested that teachers should do something political and become 'dangerously effective like the Gaelic League'. The current impasse between the government and the I.N.T.O. made the finest case possible for a council of education.[66]

Alfred was once again one of the guest speakers at the I.N.T.O. Congress held in U.C.C. at the end of March 1937. He congratulated the organisation on its interdenominational and all-Ireland character. He stressed the importance of education, describing it as 'the background of the future'. This was clear from the trends they could see in Germany, Russia, Spain and France. What was happening in those countries could become a reality in Ireland twenty years hence and the university in which they were assembled would have either a Catholic or a communist ethos. He emphasised the need for a partnership of all involved in education. This could best be achieved in a council of education. In the meantime, he urged that there should be some structure to express a unity of purpose and endeavour between primary and secondary teachers.[67]

Alfred published a critique of de Valera's draft constitution in the *Irish Independent*. He described article 15.3 as no more than a re-assertion of the mild hope or possibility which had been in the 1922 constitution: 'The Oireachtas may provide for the establishment or recognition of functional or vocational councils representing branches of the social and economic life of the people.' This, he declared, was mere 'pious claptrap'. Fianna Fáil no more than any other previous government had not the remotest intention of taking *Quadragesimo Anno* quite so literally. The I.N.T.O. and educationalists, like himself, had

66. *Cork Examiner* 23 November 1936.
67. *Cork Examiner* 31 March 1937.

for years been clamouring for a council of education. But the handful of bureaucrats who controlled education had been allowed to retain their stranglehold.[68]

The report of the Commission on Vocational Organisation was published in August 1944. De Valera and his colleagues who had been returned to power in the general election of the previous May were in no mood to be deprived of the spoils of office by the promotion of a national vocational assembly as a competing power centre. Consequently they ignored the report. This was resented by Alfred and most of those who had served on the commission. He considered that, as a gesture of its appreciation of the immense amount of time and effort given by the leading members of the commission to the production of its report, the government at the very least should have established a council of education. Thereafter his criticism in public and in private of the Fianna Fáil government on this issue became distinctly petulant.

Alfred was unable to accept an invitation to speak at the I.N.T.O. Congress in Cork in the second week of April 1947. Instead he addressed a letter to the Congress urging it to reiterate its demand for a council of education. Should the government still remain obdurate in the matter, he suggested the establishment of a Catholic council of education as had been done in the United States and France. Church and teachers, he maintained, should insist on their rights in view of growing State interference. If such a council were set up he hoped their Protestant fellow-citizens would set one up too. Although they used a different terminology from their colleagues in the I.N.T.O., members of the Association of Secondary Teachers were equally eager that a council of education be established. Their annual conference was in session during that same week in Dublin, where Alfred's letter was given as much prominence as at the I.N.T.O. Congress in Cork.[69]

On 21 January 1948 William Barry, president of the Educational Institute of Scotland, lectured on the 'Report on Scottish Primary Education' at U.C.C. In speaking to the lecture Alfred stressed the need in education for co-operation. He recalled the proposal in his draft constitution of 1922 that there should be a council of education to that end. Education, he gibed, was too

68. *Irish Independent* 14 May 1937.
69. *Cork Examiner, Irish Times* 9 April 1947; *Standard* 11 April 1947.

important to be left to a few people in a back office in Dublin. He urged all those who devoted their lives to education to come together and insist on having a council of education.[70]

In the general election of 4 February 1948 Clann na Poblachta won ten seats. The new party was strongly supported by members of the I.N.T.O. throughout the country. This was due to the alienation of national teachers from Fianna Fáil, as a result of their bitter, unsuccessful seven and a half months strike in 1946. On the hustings Clann na Poblachta promised to introduce substantial changes in the educational system, including the establishment of a council of education. A new government was formed on 18 February with the participation of Clann na Poblachta. The teachers' organisations were quick to remind the new government of the promises, particularly by representatives of Clann na Poblachta, with regard to a council of education.

It was generally known that influential members of the new administration, such as General Richard Mulcahy, the minister for education, were sympathetic to the idea. However, advocates of the council, including Alfred, were aware that there was little enthusiasm for it among those with responsibility for administering the educational system. Consequently those in favour of it continued to prompt the government on the issue. To this end, Alfred published an article in the *Standard* of 9 April 1948. At the outset he noted that advocates of a council of education were subject to a twofold criticism: (1) political bias against the Fianna Fáil government; and (2) a tendency to substitute the State for the Church in education. Quoting from his draft constitution of 1922, he illustrated his long-standing conviction of the merits of a council of education and his assumption that it would in no way infringe on the rights of parents or on religious education. He acknowledged the supervisory function of the State. But, he added, the practical issue was how this was to operate. Was it by the minister for education – who appeared to incorporate in himself the two boards of the British regime – plus a few civil servants plus a few unknown people with a pull? Or was it to be by the minister, guided and checked by a body of people engaged in educational administration and teaching, the kind of vocational body advocated by the Commission on Vocational Organisation?

70. *Cork Examiner* 22 January 1948.

Alfred concluded that, as the minister had stated during the previous week, it would be disastrous to attempt to set up immediately 'a full-blown vocational council of education'. The composition of such a council would require careful consideration and the various bodies concerned would have to be heard. In addition, its functions, and most particularly their limitations, would have to be specified. It was of the first importance to eliminate the idea that the council was to be an organ of the State with more powers than were then constitutionally possessed or tacitly claimed by the department of education. The council was to be an instrument of liberty not an aggravation of bureaucracy.

He warned that it was of crucial importance that the constitutional position of the government as regards education be clarified in a practical manner before setting up a council of education. He illustrated the need to do this by pointing to the widespread assumption that the national schools were State schools and national teachers were civil servants employed by the State. Hence he advised that there should be a preliminary phase, namely, the establishment of a small compact advisory council of independent educationalists, not 'representing' any particular bodies but standing on their own experience and achievement. The country was not yet ripe for a vocational organisation of education. Fears had to be allayed and the current equipoise maintained, so that such a body might have to operate for a considerable time. Meanwhile the members could act as assessors to the minister, give advice and criticism, secure investigations and reports, help in co-ordination, suggest improvements and developments. Such a body would in no sense be hostile to existing organisations, religious or lay. He emphasised that the establishment of the council of education, either informally or by law, made even more necessary the existence of Catholic educational organisations and ultimately the setting up of a general co-ordinating body such as the National Catholic Welfare Council of the U.S.A.

The tone of Alfred's article was much more moderate than any of his previous public statements on the advisability and importance of establishing a council of education. One reason, perhaps, for this was that the article was as much directed towards General Richard Mulcahy, the minister for education, as towards the public at large. A year earlier Mulcahy, as opposition spokesman for education, addressed the annual conference of the Association of Secondary Teachers and indicated his warm support for an advisory council of education.[71] The tone of the article may also have been influenced by the strong bond of affection and mutual respect which existed between Alfred and Mulcahy from the period of the war of independence.

In the event, Mulcahy set up the council of education in 1950. Considerable wariness on the part of vested interests ensured that its potential for initiating change was tightly circumscribed. It produced a report on the curriculum of the primary school in 1954 and on that of the secondary school in 1960. There was widespread disappointment on the publication of the latter in 1962 and the council was allowed to dissolve.

Champion of denominational education at primary and secondary level

Throughout 1942 and 1943 there was a wide-ranging public debate in England and Wales on education. Almost all the voices heard were either explicitly or implicitly opposed to denominational education. This prompted Alfred to publish three articles on 'Undenominationalism' in the *Standard*. In the first he answered the question posed in the sub-heading 'Are Catholics intolerant?' by drawing attention to papal pronouncements which clearly approved of denominational, publicly-supported education for Protestants and Jews as well as Catholics. In the second he emphasised the importance of respecting all religions. The third was neatly summed up in the sub-heading 'Against the growing power of the State the Church is your protector'. Later he published 'In defence of parents' in the *Standard* of 4 May 1943. He began with a reference to article 42 of the Constitution which he described as excellent in that 'it "acknowledges that the primary and natural educator of the child is the family", it "guarantees to respect the inalienable right and duty of parents" to educate, it recognises that, where requested, this education must be "religious", it admits the liberty of parents "to provide this education (a) in their homes or (b) in private schools or (c) in schools recognised or established by the State".' Alfred was at pains to point out that article

71. *Cork Examiner, Irish Times* 9 April 1947.

42 did not declare that the State shall provide free primary education but that it would provide *for* free primary education and referred to the duty of the State to 'endeavour to supplement and give reasonable aid to private and corporate educational initiative'.

Next Alfred quoted the *Memorandum on education after the war* issued by the British Trade Union Congress in 1942:

> (1) It is not disputed that the denominations concerned will be unable to carry out the building programme required.
>
> (2) On the other hand children in non-provided schools must not be denied the benefit of educational reforms which will be enjoyed by their contemporaries in the State-provided schools.
>
> (3) Therefore the State (through the Local Education Authorities) will have to accept responsibility for the education of the children in question.

Alfred translated these sentences 'into plain English, divesting them of all subterfuges' as follows:

> (1) There is an organised body of parents, chiefly, workers, who – while being forced to pay for the State schools – have had largely to support their own schools. With rising costs and higher standards enforced, these workers will be unable to bear the increased burden.
>
> (2) On the other hand, it would be grossly unfair to penalise the children of those Catholic trade unionists, to apply general taxation to improve the educational facilities open to the children attending State schools and to place an impossible burden on Catholic parents.
>
> (3) Therefore Catholic workers must be deprived of their parental rights; and their children, against the wishes of their poor parents and against their own, should be forced into the schools provided by the State.

Alfred agreed with the first two propositions and rejected the third. The proper conclusion, he contended, was that Catholic working-class parents should be helped proportionately to run and to improve their schools. Otherwise the State would be infringing on their natural rights.

Alfred declared that this was but one example of the way in which the British Trade Union Congress concealed its intolerance behind respectable jargon and mealy-mouthed illogic. He gave several other examples and decried the fact that it was the schools of Catholic workers which would be 'incorporated', whereas those attended by the children of wealthy Catholic parents would survive. His discussion of the subject he justified on the grounds of his sympathy with his fellow-Catholics, many of them Irish, in England and 'because every advance in bureaucratic tyranny over there is liable to influence our views'.[72]

In 'Freedom for all' in the *Standard* Alfred reviewed some other recent pronouncements in the U.K. on education, which he interpreted as part of a campaign to ensure the suppression of parental rights by the State bureaucracy. This, he argued, was nowhere more clear than in No. 10 of the twelve aims set out by the National Union of Teachers, in conjunction with the Trade Union Congress, the Co-operative Union and the Workers' Educational Association: 'A united system of administration to replace the dual control of schools'. This, Alfred declared, meant, in effect, that parents were to be ousted from all control of their schools and the State was to control the minds of the young. The issue was befogged by talk about denominations and churches. He quoted the *Memorandum* issued in 1942 by the T.U.C. and from Margaret Cole's *Education for democracy* (London 1942) and continued that to 'the slobbering of the T.U.C. and the cooing of Mrs Cole' he preferred the forthrightness of H. G. Wells: 'The modern State is bound to be the ultimate guardian of all children; and it must assist, replace or subordinate the parent as supporter, guardian or educator.'[73]

About this time Alfred was also preparing an article on 'Education and the Constitution'[74] for the *Educational Year Book 1943*, which was published in London at the beginning of 1944. In the meantime an English and Welsh Education Bill had come before the House of Commons. The Catholic bishops of England and Wales were intensely critical of it. Michael de la Bedoyere, editor of the *Catholic Herald*, requested Alfred to write 'in support of the stand *of his fellow-Catholics* in England and

72. *Standard* 5, 12, 19 February, 4 May 1943.
73. *Standard* 21 May 1943.
74. For his magisterial treatment of this subject, see Appendix 8.

Wales'.[75] Alfred did so in 'The invasion of the schoolmaster State' in the *Catholic Herald*, where he gladly availed of this wider stage to champion the case for denominational education.

He began: 'I will approach the question from the standpoint of article 42 of our Constitution in which "the State acknowledges that the primary and natural educator of the child is the family and guarantees to respect the inalienable right and duty of parents". While the State may insist on "a certain minimum education", it may not interfere with the "conscience and lawful preference" of parents, it may not compel attendance at State schools or at "any particular type" of school.' He showed that that assertion of the primacy of parental rights was not a mere abstract principle but had practical consequences by referring to a decision of the Supreme Court in 1942 with regard to the unconstitutionality of a section of a School Attendance Bill which had passed through the Dáil.

Alfred pointed out that article 42 did not mention the Catholic Church. In appealing to the article to secure denominational education for its adherents, the Church simply claimed the natural rights of an association of citizens who were parents. And, what Catholics claimed for themselves, they fully and cheerfully conceded in the case of Protestants, Jews and agnostics.

Alfred next turned his attention to the current discussion in England which he described as 'amazingly confused'. The *Memorandum* issued by the Trade Union Congress in 1942 stated: 'Denominational instruction of any kind should not be allowed in the State schools.' Denominational instruction, he explained, was education in accordance with the creed and the philosophy of certain organised bodies of parents; not, of course, one subject among many, but a fundamental view of life and a scale of values permeating all subjects; an education given in an environment, an extension of the home, approved by those parents; an education given by teachers who are author-

75. The fact that the editor of the English *Catholic Herald* requested Alfred on this and other occasions to write on educational matters was not the only indication that his reputation as an educationalist had spread beyond the shores of Ireland. In the *New York Times* of 1 September 1946 an article on the resumption of college activity throughout the U.S. included quotations from sixteen internationally-known educationalists and *literati*. Three of them were Irish: George Bernard Shaw, Oscar Wilde and Alfred. The quote from Alfred was: 'The test of education is the power to resist jargon.'

ised to act *in loco parentis*. An agreed syllabus was equally denominational; but being of diluted content it represented the views of a larger aggregate of parents who agreed 'in a process of boiling down'. And a purely secularist education was equally denominational. It represented the views of parents who took an agnostic or naturalistic view of life.

The ultimate reason for State schools, argued Alfred, was that the bulk of parents were too poor and too unorganised to pay directly for the education of their children. Therefore, the State intervened, not to supersede the parents, not to exercise a right to educate which it did not possess, but to restore distributive justice and to enable parents to exercise their natural rights. In effect, a State school was a school supported by the parents, not directly but *via* general taxation. The State collected the money and then disbursed it to the schools. There was no inherent reason why a tax-supported school should not be a parents' school run by an organisation or 'church', representing the parents. This was clear from the existence of State-funded denominational schools in Canada, Holland and Scotland.

Alfred maintained that the view of education which he had outlined represented the best in the tradition of liberalism. He quoted from the *Principles* of John Stuart Mill: 'A government is justified in requiring from all the people that they shall possess instruction in certain things, but not in prescribing to them how or from whom they shall obtain it.' He argued that to abandon his view of the limited supervisory power of the State and its function of facilitating parents without superseding them logically led to a totalitarian conception of the State. In England, he warned, there remained no generally accepted clear-cut philosophy which could halt the descent into a far greater tyranny than mere economic collectivism. In those circumstances the role of the Catholic Church was crucial. It stood for spiritual liberty, for pluralism and variety against the increasing menace of totalitarian monism. He recalled with regret that statements issued by the National Union of Teachers blandly assumed that parents did not count except as biological producers of the raw material of their industry, which, like other near-monopolies, must be a State enterprise. He acknowledged that the promoters of the English Education Bill were well-meaning, liberty-loving statesmen, aiming at a great improvement in the means of education. But they had fallen into a fundamental error in taking the view that the State was the primary educator. He concluded that he was proud of his own country which, with its overwhelming Catholic majority, had repudiated this basic principle of totalitarian ideology and had championed Protestant and Jewish as well as Catholic schools against the invasion of the schoolmaster State.[76]

Clash with Dr Simcox

The English Educational Bill became law in 1944. However, the Catholic authorities and publicists continued to voice opposition to it and urged that it be amended to ensure that parents' rights would be respected. Catholic apologists emphasised in their campaign that they were as eager to secure the parental rights of Protestants, Jews and agnostics as much as those of Catholics. In the course of the campaign Fr John V. Simcox, a priest and canon lawyer of the archdiocese of Westminster, publicly questioned the orthodoxy and the sincerity of their concern for the rights of non-Catholic parents. Despite cautions not to continue doing so, Simcox continued to express these views in the press and was eventually disciplined by his archbishop.

Thereafter Dr Simcox became a persistent critic of the Catholic Church in the secular press. He impugned the good faith of Cardinal Hinsley and other Catholic protagonists when, in the 1942-3 and subsequent campaign for private or voluntary schools, they upheld the rights of non-Catholic parents in this regard. Provocatively, he challenged Catholic bishops and editors of Catholic newspapers to tell him 'What the faith is?' He complained that Catholics would not tell him what Catholicism was. The Church, he asserted, was 'in danger of being turned into a home for half-wits, cowards and yes-men'. He exhorted Catholics to have 'the minimum courage to stand up for the Church against the plain idiocies of the churchmen'. In the secular press on a number of occasions he attacked the *Catholic Herald* on the grounds that it was the only Catholic newspaper likely to publish any of his letters and for having refused to do so out of cowardice, thereby proving that its pretensions to free speech were without foundation. In defence of his newspaper, Michael de la Bedoyere declared that if Simcox should state his

76. *Catholic Herald* 4 February 1944.

views in a single, complete statement he would endeavour to deal with them as a whole.[77]

Towards the end of 1946 Dr Simcox, in collaboration with two others, published a pamphlet *Is the Roman Catholic Church a secret society?* The editor of the *Catholic Herald* appealed to Alfred to reply to Simcox's views and criticisms of the Catholic Church. Alfred was reluctant to do so. Simcox was a member of a respected Cork family. His father, a prominent tea merchant of Patrick Street, was a close friend of Alfred. His sister was married to Joseph Brennan, governor of the Central Bank, at whom Alfred had directed a great deal of sharp public criticism in the early 1940s. To add a further irony, Alfred and Simcox had corresponded in 1940. At that time Simcox was reading the galleys of *Money* with a view to approving it for a *nihil obstat* of the archdiocese of Westminster. In a letter of 31 October 1940, Simcox expressed his admiration for the interesting monetary theories in the book and the massive amount of research marshalled therein.[78]

Eventually, after a further number of insistent appeals, Alfred contributed a comprehensive rebuttal of the views of Dr Simcox in the *Catholic Herald*. In the press Simcox had asked: 'From the Catholic point of view, does the argument for parental rights continue to hold even when the parents are in religious error and wish their children to be taught this error?' It was obvious that in his view the answer was in the negative. Alfred pointed out that the question was wrongly expressed. It should not be 'Have people a right to teach error?' but 'Have people a right to be permitted to teach error?' The answer to the first question was always No; the answer to the second was often Yes. Then he showed with copious illustration that this issue was not a specifically Catholic one.

Dr Simcox asserted that he suspected 'dishonest propaganda in the education campaign of 1942 and 1943'. 'Our pretence,' he stated, 'was that Catholicism was out for the right of all parents, non-Catholic as well as Catholic, to educate their children according to their conscience.' Using sources ranging from a statement by the English Catholic hierarchy on Low Sunday 1929 to the works of St Thomas Aquinas, Alfred illustrated that 'the doctrine of parental rights all round' was generally

77. *Catholic Herald* 24 January 1947.
78. O'Rahilly Papers: letter, dated 31 October 1940, Simcox to O'Rahilly.

accepted Catholic theory and practice for a very long time and had not first emerged in the recent campaign of English Catholics.

Simcox also asserted: 'I have never disputed the moral right of a Catholic State to allow non-Catholics to bring up their children in their faith. A Catholic might allow this on grounds of expediency and to avoid greater evils.' Alfred replied that the Catholic State had a duty to allow non-Catholics to bring up their children in their faith. He quoted Pope Pius XI to the effect that they were bound in distributive justice, not merely by charity or prudence, to help positively to this end. He instanced how this was done in his own country. This positive multidenominational attitude, as distinct from the so-called undenominationalism, was required on grounds of natural right, not just for ecclesiastical reasons. The fundamental reason for this attitude was that in a mixed State it was essential for the common good. He described as jejune, Simcox's enumeration of 'grounds of expediency and to avoid greater evils'. In a rhetorical conclusion he indicated that he regarded Simcox's polemics as no more than 'a mare's nest'.[79]

Prior Rights of Parents in Education

Alfred was invited once again by the editor of the *Catholic Herald* to uphold the Catholic position on parental rights in education at the beginning of 1950. The future of private as distinct from State schools was one of the most hotly debated issues in the run-up to the U.K. general election of 23 February. In the *Catholic Herald* of 20 January he summarised a booklet *National education* which Cardinal Edward Manning published

79. *Catholic Herald* 24 January 1947. In the *Catholic Herald* of 18 April 1947 Alfred published a short letter indicating that the editor had sent him a reply by Dr Simcox. This, it seems, mainly concerned the latter's 'rather personal and painful relations with his ecclesiastical superiors and others'. Alfred declared that he had replied to Simcox because the latter had complained that no Catholic 'would frankly and publicly answer his questions'. This he had attempted and Simcox had failed to state whether he differed from the analysis which he had set out or to show where he was wrong. He concluded that he was willing at any time to discuss educational principles but he was not prepared to obtrude on the question of the ecclesiastical position and behaviour of Dr Simcox. Towards the end of September 1947 Alfred sent a copy of his reply to Simcox to Archbishop Finbar Ryan, O.P., of Port of Spain in Trinidad, at the latter's request (O'Rahilly Papers: letter, dated September 1947, Ryan to O'Rahilly).

in 1889. The principles championed by the cardinal, he declared, should be the concern of others besides Catholics.

Manning, he pointed out, fully admitted the right of the State to supervise and to enforce education, but he strenuously denied the right of the State to oust parents. He emphasised the contrast from as early as 1883 between the Christian principles of educational liberty and the totalitarian view. Manning based his case for Catholic schools on the general principle of distributive justice which, Alfred explained, was just as applicable to Protestant, Jewish and secularist schools.[80]

To the question as to how he would organise these schools Manning replied (1) Let a school rate or tax be levied over the whole population as a part of the general taxation of the country; and (2) let all schools, with or without religious teaching, partake in the school rate. Manning realised that, owing to unequal distribution of the adherents of any one religious society, there would always be residual difficulties in certain areas. For such cases he made no practical claims. 'There are Catholics scattered in villages and in small towns by tens and by fives, or by single families here and there. We have too much common sense to demand of the majorities, be they Anglicans or Nonconformists, the breaking up not only of their schools but the sacrifice of their religious conscience and the change of legal status of their education to meet our objections . . . There must always be residual difficulties which cannot be met by legislation. They must be treated by common sense, justice and equity.'[81]

The I.N.T.O. organised a strike on 20 March 1946 for an increase in the salaries of its members and the settlement of a number of other grievances. This gave Alfred an opportunity to discuss in the Irish context the implications which followed from parental rights in education. In an article in the *Standard* he asked 'Are national teachers "public servants"?' He noted that it seemed to be generally assumed that the principals in the current dispute were the minister for education and the teachers whom the former called 'public servants'. Once again he had recourse to Article 42 of the Constitution, where, he pointed out, 'the State acknowledges that the primary and natural

80. Alfred returned to this theme in 'We claim same rights for other religious organisations' in the *Standard* of 24 July 1959.

81. *Catholic Herald* 20 January 1950.

educator of the child is the family and guarantees to respect the inalienable right and duty of parents to provide, according to their means, for the religious and moral, intellectual, physical and social education of their children'. The State may establish schools, but 'parents shall be free to provide this education in their homes or in private schools', subject to the children receiving 'a certain minimum education, moral, intellectual and social'. 'The State shall provide for free primary education', but not necessarily by State schools; it shall also 'give reasonable aid to private and corporate educational initiative'. From this, Alfred argued, it followed that the primary responsibility for educating their children devolved on parents. The role of the State arose by exception or supplement. Thus education was not part of the public services in the same sense as the police, the law-courts, the roads, the water-supply. Nor were teachers public servants in the sense in which those working in these services were.

Next Alfred surveyed *Rules and regulations of the commissioners of national education in Ireland*, issued in June 1890, and *Rules and regulations for national schools under the department of education* issued in August 1932. He argued that the latter seemed to be influenced by what he termed 'British secularism' almost as much as the former. In view of the position of parents vis-à-vis the State as portrayed in article 42 of the constitution, many of these rules were as unconstitutional in theory as they had been flouted in practice. Alfred argued that the attempts of the department of education to interfere with the working of family or national schools – even the claim to approve or disapprove of the books used – were invalid and should be resisted as an invasion of parental rights. To do so was all the more important because of the mentality of the department of education. That mentality, he suggested, could be gauged by the School Attendance Bill, 1942, a section of which read: 'A child shall not be deemed for the purposes of this Act to be receiving a suitable education in a manner other than by attending a national school, a suitable school or a recognised school, unless such education and the manner in which the child is receiving it have been certified under this section by the minister to be suitable.' This section had been found to be unconstitutional by the supreme court which declared that so long as parents supply 'a minimum standard of elementary education of general application' it was of the opinion that the manner in which it was given and received was a matter for the parents and not a matter in respect of which the State under the constitution was entitled to interfere. By virtue of that decision Alfred maintained the department of education was not entitled to make the grant of State-aid conditional upon the acceptance of the undenominational ideal, resulting in the submission to rules concerning religious worship and instruction, inscriptions and symbols, books, time-tables, etc. At the very least, he concluded, the public should not allow to pass unchallenged the statement that primary teachers were 'public servants'. That would be to betray the constitutional status of the schools.[82]

As the strike by national teachers continued into the summer, with no sign of a settlement, Alfred became increasingly critical of both sides. At the direction of their union, teachers in the Dublin metropolitan area had withdrawn their services. Their colleagues elsewhere in the country continued to work and sustained those on strike. The worst effects of the strike were felt by working-class parents and their children. At a conferring at U.C.C. on 16 July Alfred deplored this aspect of the strike which he described as not against the government but against the school-managers. He concluded: 'Surely some committee in this country – some collection of educationalists – could be found to propose some remedy for such a state of affairs. It is a scandal to our country, and I protest against the prolongation of a condition of things that permits 20,000 children in Dublin to be flung on the streets.'[83]

From the outset de Valera, it seems, was determined not to make any substantial concessions to the national teachers. Such was the influence he exercised over his cabinet and party that even Thomas Derrig, T.D., the minister for education and a former post-primary teacher, was not able to soften the stance of the government. The I.N.T.O. made a number of unsuccessful attempts to have the dispute mediated on. In the second week of October references to the dispute at the Fianna Fáil ardfheis indicated no change in the government's attitude.[84]

Alfred's combative instincts were aroused by the *non*

82. *Standard* 22 March 1946.
83. *Cork Examiner* 17 July 1946; *Standard* 19 July 1946.
84. T. J. O'Connell, *History of the Irish National Teachers' Organisation 1868-1968* (Dublin 1969) 218-22, 226, 229-30.

possumus attitude of the government. He prepared three articles on the strike. In the first, which appeared in the *Standard* of 18 October 1946, he sketched the past and current status of national schools and their managers and teachers. In the second, published on 25 October, he treated in detail the relationship between the national schools and the State, described most of the department of education's rules governing the national schools as outdated and asserted that, by virtue of the constitution, these schools were, in effect, family schools. He concluded by objecting vigorously to a threat by de Valera to lock out the teachers still at work in the national schools outside the metropolitan area.[85] In the third article, which was published on 1 November, he was intensely critical of de Valera's references to the strike in his presidential address to the ardfheis. He dismissed the Taoiseach's implication that national teachers were employees of the government like the police and the army. Then he replied to a number of other arguments put forward by de Valera, among them, that the I.N.T.O. was challenging the right of the government to govern and was damaging the common good. Not so, replied Alfred, in effect. All the teachers were asking for was independent arbitration or at least an investigation of their claims.

Alfred concluded that it had to be admitted that, with the growing complexity and interdependence of life, the right to strike or to lock-out was becoming an operation involving serious repercussions on the 'non-combatant' population. He quoted Benjamin J. Masse, S.J.:

> Moralists unanimously teach that certain conditions must be fulfilled before any strike can be considered legitimate, one of which is of the utmost importance right now. It is this: the good results which are expected from a strike must be proportioned to the evils which it causes. If, therefore, a strike brings evils, even though not intended, which are greater than any possible good the union hopes to achieve, the strike is immoral and the workers have an obligation to stay on the job, even if this involves a temporary injustice.

Alfred drew attention to the unintended and deplorable evil which the I.N.T.O. strike was inflicting on '40,000 innocent

85. *Standard* 18, 25 October 1946.

214

children'. On that basis he appealed for an end to it. He suggested that the teachers meet the managers and resume their high calling 'even if this involved a temporary injustice'. He expressed his conviction that this would redound to their credit and lead to a fair examination of their case.[86] Four days before the article was published Archbishop John Charles McQuaid had written in the same vein to Thomas J. O'Connell, general secretary of the I.N.T.O., and the strike ended on 31 October 1946.[87]

In 'Some thoughts on education' in the *Blackrock College Annual* for 1956 Alfred returned to the subject of the prior rights of parents *vis-à-vis* the State in regard to the education of their children and its corollary, namely, their resultant right to insist on denominational schools. In addition, by virtue of their prior rights he suggested that parents should be more insistent in having their suggestions heard, and, when practical, implemented with regard to the syllabus, text-books and examinations of the secondary-school programme. He implied that Patrick Pearse's condemnation of a certain type of education as a 'murder machine' could be applied to aspects of the current secondary-school system. The narrowness of the syllabus, the restricted range of text-books and the rigidly controlled and uniform examination procedures limited unduly the initiative and individual flair of teachers and the opportunity to accommodate to, and develop, a variety of abilities and capacities in students. He proposed a more pluralistic approach, with groups of colleges and schools, such as those in the charge of the Jesuits, Dominicans, Holy Ghost Fathers and Christian Brothers and the convent schools of various religious orders, developing their own *Ratio studiorum*. This would involve these colleges and schools testing their own pupils but with the aid of externs approved by the department of education. In this way the State, in the guise of the department, could insist on a general minimum standard. He advocated that oral as well as written examinations be held in language subjects and emphasised the need for more science teaching to be included in the secondary-school curriculum. While most educationalists then and since would agree that the freedom and extra room for initiative which he advocated for teachers was commendable, its provi-

86. *Standard* 1 November 1946.
87. T. J. O'Connell, *History of the Irish National Teachers' Organisation 1868-1968*, 230-1.

sion in the manner he suggested would have raised immense practical difficulties. In some quarters it would not have been regarded with much favour, as it would have involved an effective extension of clerical control in areas concerning the syllabus, text-books and examinations hitherto the responsibility of civil servants. However, some of the reforms he urged have been implemented. There has been a considerable broadening of the scope of the secondary-school syllabus and in the range of the text-books for the Intermediate and Leaving Certificate examinations. An oral examination has become an essential feature in testing students' proficiency in languages and there has been a considerable extension of the teaching of science subjects in secondary schools.

To counter what he termed 'Statism' or 'the schoolmaster State', Alfred urged greater unity among those engaged in education. This should begin by the forging of a strong bond between those responsible for the Catholic and Protestant schools. Such a bond should be easy to develop as the case for Catholic and Protestant schools was similarly based on the natural rights of the family, enshrined in the constitution. Next he advocated close co-operation between religious and lay teachers, both being *in loco parentis* and having a common liberty to defend against State encroachment. He regretted their current relationship, with no opportunity for joint discussion, no common meeting ground, no joint associations, no real appreciation of coincident interests. Above all, he urged that parents be made conscious of their rights and encouraged to take a positive and active interest in education. To this end, structures should be established to facilitate consultation between teachers and parents. He concluded that, if the teachers, including the religious authorities, and the parents were united, there would be no need to fear a take-over by the State of education, as had occurred in so many other countries.[88]

Denominational Education at Tertiary Level

Alfred was an upholder of denominational education not only at the primary and secondary level but also at the tertiary level. The *Sunday Independent* of 25 November 1951 carried an article critical of the N.U.I. and its constituent colleges. The

88. 'Some thoughts on education', *Blackrock College Annual 1956*, 58-61.

anonymous author declared that the N.U.I. was undenominational and yet he complained religion tended 'to weigh down
the scales' in appointments. In the *Standard* Alfred replied by
giving the 'Special Correspondent' a short lesson in 'the long
painful struggle whereby Irish Catholics secured to a large
extent a fair settlement of their claims to higher education':
'The Queen's Colleges were undenominational; we refused
them. Trinity College is profoundly undenominational; we
declined to accept it. But we did accept the N.U.I. – and now
we are coolly told that it too is "undenominational". What then
were we fighting for? And why were we satisfied with the
N.U.I.?' There was not one word, he declared, in the 1908 Act
or the N.U.I. charters which asserted that it was 'undenominational'. In any case such undenominationalism was not
psychologically or educationally possible except in a few
technical subjects. Other subjects, especially history, sociology
and philosophy, by their very nature required value
judgements.[89]

In a series of articles in *Studies* in the early 1960s[90] Alfred
returned to the theme of denominational education at university level. This he did at the request of Archbishop McQuaid. At
that time there was a lively public debate on the restrictions
imposed by the archbishop of Dublin, on behalf of the Irish hierarchy, on the attendance of Catholics at Trinity College. The
articles included a fine survey of the struggle of Irish Catholics
for education in general, and university education in particular.
The vigorous tenor of the articles leaves one in little doubt
about Alfred's strong support for the Irish bishops in their stand.
Privately, however, he indicated his fervent hope that the continuing impasse on that issue would be resolved. He also
expressed his regret that his intervention in this controversy
might be hurtful, especially to Provost Albert J. McConnell, for
whom for many years he had had the highest respect and considerable affection.[91]

---

89. *Standard* 7 December 1951.
90. 'The Irish university question', *Studies*, autumn 1961; 'The Irish university question', *Studies*, winter 1961; 'The Irish university question', *Studies*,
spring 1962; 'The Irish university question', *Studies*, summer 1962.
91. Interview with Rev. Dr Michael O'Carroll, C.S.Sp.

Alfred O'Rahilly III: Controversialist

The Classics

Alfred was a strong believer in the value of the classics in education. In 'The classics for Catholics' in the *Standard*,[92] over the pseudonym *Lector*, he took issue with Reverend Edward Leen, C.S.Sp., who in his *What is education?* (New York 1944) was intensely critical of the classical education system. Alfred rejected Leen's description of classical education as the result of a 'spurious classical tradition'. He pointed out that such education with its humanist emphasis was recommended by the Council of Trent, which was held towards the end of the period of the Renaissance movement. If ever excess of any kind was to be feared in the cultivation of the classics it was at that period. Moreover, the classics were central to the educational theory and practice of St Charles Borromeo and St Ignatius Loyola. The former founded seminaries which became prototypes of those established subsequently. And the latter's Society of Jesus with its *Ratio studiorum*, in which the study of the classics was central, had a seminal influence on all subsequent second-level Catholic education.

Alfred dismissed Leen's warning against the danger of having young minds 'nurtured on paganism presented in its most seductive form'. In addition, Leen had expressed his anxiety that young people would begin to admire the natural virtues and heroic deeds of the ancients. To offset this, he suggested that the writings of the Fathers be substituted for those of the *literati* of ancient Greece and Rome. He argued: 'The heroism and virtues portrayed in the pages of the Fathers are those which should be imitated and are different from those *simulacra*, which appear in the pages of the pagans which it is dangerous to admire.' Exhibiting an extensive knowledge of patristic literature, Alfred demonstrated that the Fathers themselves, as well as the moralists and anthologists of the middle ages and Dante, were eager students of the literature of the ancient world. He rejected Leen's assumption that, in the case of a young person's mind and heart which had been innoculated with the virus of the classics, recourse to the Fathers would act as an anti-toxin.

Alfred dismissed Leen's claim that he had 'the popes' at his back in his attitude to the texts of the classics. A letter from Pius

92. *Standard* 14 January 1944.

218

IX to the French bishops, quoted by Leen, was, declared Alfred, no more than a recommendation that the writings of the Fathers should be prescribed as part of the religious instruction to be given in seminaries. In urging his view, Leen appealed to a *Motu proprio* of Pius XI establishing a school of higher latinity at the Gregorian University. Alfred pointed out that, apart from the comment that 'many of the Fathers have written in a latinity which does not seem far inferior to that of the best heathen authors', the rest of the document was in unstinted praise of the classics and how to use them in the service of the Church. Alfred disagreed with Leen's contention that 'the cold, correct and perfectly controlled classical style' could not adequately express the 'tumultuous thought, the exultant enthusiasm and the spiritual intoxication' associated with the Christian message. Latin classical prose was the most perfect organ of expression ever contrived, superior even to the best prose of the Greeks and so an ideal vehicle for Christianity. To this effect he quoted Cardinal Sadoletus who wrote in the sixteenth century and Lactantius, one of the Latin Fathers of the Constantine period. In his polemic Leen frequently referred to Tertullian. Of him Alfred observed that, though a very learned man, his diction was wanting in grace and urbanity and was often exceedingly obscure. In his final sentence he turned the knife: 'I may add that Tertullian, in some of his attacks on the pagans, indulges in a scurrility that would have shocked any decent prose writer from Cicero to Tacitus.'

Advice to Students

During his forty years at U.C.C., Alfred had a remarkable rapport with the undergraduates. He was ever ready to address congresses and conferences of students. He was particularly supportive of the Catholic University Students' Union. When acting as host to the Union's annual congress at U.C.C. in the first week of July 1953 he personally provided most of the funding required for the events associated with the congress. He was also a staunch supporter of the Irish Association of Students, to which all Irish universities, including Queen's of Belfast, were affiliated and was the principal speaker at a number of its annual congresses. The last occasion on which he addressed the association was on 3 January 1951 when the

17. Garden party at U.C.C. during Catholic University Students' Congress, July 1953. *Left to right:* The papal nuncio, Archbishop Gerald Patrick O'Hara, Professor Denis Gwynn, the earl of Wicklow, Alfred

annual congress was held at U.C.C. As ever, his comments were both relevant and practical. He declared that students then worked harder than those of a previous generation. However, he regretted that they did not seem to work in a methodical manner nor to the best effect. For this he blamed the secondary schools which did no more than instil 'at hydraulic pressure a certain amount of information which was disgorged at subsequent examinations'. He emphasised the importance of social training, but by this, he pointed out, he meant mainly the interchange of ideas, not merely recreational activities. To be successful, he warned the students, they should concentrate on being legible, punctual and audible. He concluded that any university course worthy of the name should include the study of philosophy.[93]

On 3 May 1953 the community and students of Blackrock College hosted a reception for John Cardinal D'Alton who a short time previously had returned from Rome with the red hat. Alfred had been a contemporary of the new cardinal at the college and, with other distinguished *alumni*, attended the reception. He remained on in the college for a few days and, while there, at the request of Rev. Dr Michael O'Carroll, C.S.Sp., addressed the students.

After entertaining them with reminiscences of his years in college, Alfred offered some practical advice. At the outset he stressed the importance of good manners. Speaking very much as a teacher, he declared that while each student should have 'the three virtues of the big man', faith, hope and charity, he should also have 'the three virtues of the little man', punctuality, audibility and legibility. He stressed the necessity for developing a habit of accuracy and method. There followed advice on how best to take notes in class. He urged students to develop their powers of concentration and a commitment to thoroughness.

Alfred concluded on an apostolic note. Everyone had a vocation. He must work for God not a human master. It was the laity who made the Church. They had failed in France and Belgium. If the laity did not fulfil their responsibilities, Ireland would be like those countries forty years hence. He regretted that the schools appeared to be failing to produce lay social leaders, a failure the U.C.C. sociology course was attempting to remedy.

93. *Irish Times* 4 January 1951.

However, he was hopeful for the future when he regarded the Legion of Mary and the Foreign Mission movement, the only two achievements of the new Ireland which justified the horrors of the war of independence.[94]

After his ordination to the priesthood in December 1955 Alfred continued to reside in a flat in the Castle at Blackrock College until his death in August 1969. The senior boarders were housed in the Castle and he made himself available to them as one of their spiritual directors. He enjoyed meeting and talking to them, as well as the other students of the college. In the weeks before the Christmas and summer holidays he invariably visited the senior classes and presented them with sweets and chocolate. His kindness was reciprocated. Some of the students read to him when, in his last years, his eyesight failed. For all the students he became a familiar sight, especially in the afternoon as he walked in the grounds praying the Rosary. When he met students he generally chatted with them. One such exchange perhaps best summarises his overall philosophy of education. Frank Kelly, the actor, in the week before he sat for his Leaving Certificate examination, met Alfred in the college grounds. Alfred asked him what examination he was taking. Kelly said he was preparing to do his final. To which Alfred responded: 'I am too.'[95]

94. A report of his address was published as 'Dr O'Rahilly speaks to the students' in the *Blackrock College Annual* of 1953.
95. Interviews with Rev Dr Michael O'Carroll, C.S.Sp., and Frank Kelly.

18. Alfred addressing the students in Blackrock College on 5 May 1953

CHAMPION OF THE LOCAL COMMUNITY

For Alfred Ireland's most serious social problems were unemployment and emigration. He considered the encouragement of local initiative, the inculcation of a spirit of self-sufficiency and decentralisation crucial in any attempt to solve them. He was a strong supporter of organisations such as Bantracht na Tuatha (better known as the Irish Countrywomen's Association), Macra na Feirme and Muintir na Tíre which promoted the spirit of self-help in the local community. His association with Muintir na Tíre extended over more than twenty years.

Muintir na Tíre

Muintir na Tíre (the people of the countryside), a community development association, was founded by Fr John M. Hayes (1887-1957), a curate in Tipperary Town, in May 1931. Fr Hayes adopted the Belgische Boerenbond, the Belgian farmers' union, as a model. The aim of the new organisation was set out as follows: 'to unite the rural communities of Ireland on the Leo XIII principle that there must exist friendly relations between master and man; that it is a mistake to assume that class is hostile to class, that well-to-do and working men are intended by nature to live in mutual conflict. This new rural organisation . . . intends to unite in one body the rural workers of the country, not for the purpose of attacking any one section of the community, but to give the agricultural workers in Ireland their due and proper position in the life of the nation.' Much of the early success of the organisation was due to the energy and patent sincerity of Fr Hayes. Another valuable asset which he enjoyed was the interest and support of his colleagues in rural parishes throughout the country. This he ensured by addressing, at the invitation of the president, the senior students at St Patrick's College, Maynooth, each year. From the beginning Fr Hayes supervised the extension of the organisation by addressing groups of new members in what he described as 'fireside chats'. After a few years the organisation held an annual social week at Easter and a rural week each summer. The achievements of Muintir na Tíre in the 1930s, 1940s and 1950s were remarkable. To it must go much of the credit for facilitating the rapid extension of the rural electrification scheme, the establishment of local industries, the erection and extension of parish halls, the

19. Rural week 1948 at Knockbeg College, Carlow. *Left to right:* Canon John Hayes, Seán T. O'Kelly (president of Ireland), Most Rev. Thomas Keogh (bishop of Kildare and Leighlin), An tAthair Peadar Mac Suibhne (president of Knockbeg College)

completion of group water-schemes and sewerage schemes, the improvement of leisure facilities, the co-operative buying of plants and seeds, the purchase of agricultural machinery to be hired at a nominal charge, the drainage of land, the cleaning up of villages and the provision of free school meals in many rural schools. It also pioneered community information services.[1]

Before establishing Muintir na Tíre, Fr Hayes consulted a number of persons, among them Fr Edward Coyne, S.J., and Alfred.[2] Coyne was knowledgeable about Catholic Action and vocational organisations on the continent and it was probably due to his influence that Muintir na Tíre was modelled on the Belgische Boerenbond.[3] Alfred briefed Fr Hayes on the medieval guilds and their role in the society of that time. Significantly, from the outset parish and half-parish units of the organisation were known as guilds. Alfred had considerable affection for Fr Hayes who continued to consult him frequently. Alfred helped to draft appeals to the government for interest-free loans and financial aid for the organisation and lobbied de Valera to this end.[4]

Alfred followed the early development of Muintir na Tíre with interest. At his suggestion Fr Hayes was invited to speak to a paper on 'Religion and land in seventeenth-century Irish politics' at U.C.C. on 5 December 1932. The rising tension between the Irish Free State and British governments over a range of issues, the beginning of the economic war and the recent Eucharistic Congress clearly influenced the contributions. Fr Hayes attributed his presence to his association with 'the little movement which they had in the country to try to undo the work of Cromwell'. The impression the paper made on him was that the Irish people were like corn – the more they were rolled the more they grew. History repeated itself in

1. Stephen Rynne, *Father John Hayes, founder of Muintir na Tíre; people of the land.*

2. Interviews with Canon James P. Bastible and Con Murphy.

3. On 9 December 1933 Coyne read a paper on 'Social weeks in France' to members of the Academy of St Thomas and the workers' tutorial class at U.C.C. These events, he declared, had been in operation for the previous fourteen years. They were essentially Catholic and at the meetings businessmen, lawyers, doctors and other professional persons were given the opportunity to exchange ideas on subjects of importance to Catholics (*Cork Examiner* 11 December 1933).

4. O'Rahilly Papers: draft submissions to de Valera and the government prepared by Alfred on behalf of Muintir na Tíre.

curious ways. In 1666 England passed a law prohibiting the import of Irish cattle into England. There was immediate suffering in Ireland but then the people found foreign ports for their goods. One thing Ireland could not forget was the confiscation of her churches. In every parish they would find those old ruins – silent witnesses of the past. They were the most sacred things the nation possessed because they typified the constancy of the Irish people to their faith. The hope of the human race and of Ireland lay in 'the back to the land movement'.

Alfred was even more bitter than Fr Hayes. He asserted that the religious persecutions of the seventeenth century were carried on by people who professed the right of private interpretation. The real reason for that persecution was the desire for loot. They had got the loot and the descendants of the planters were still in Ireland. It was an extraordinary thing that the people who constituted 97% of the population had less than 40% of influence in the professions and 'everything that counted'. He did not agree that the Cromwellian aristocracy had disappeared. Those who had gone had taken the loot with them and there was, as a result, an impost on the land which the land could not bear. The problem of the land remained acute and required the application of social principles which appertained neither to capitalism nor communism.[5]

Popular lecturer at rural weeks and social weeks

Muintir na Tíre's first rural week was held at St Declan's College, Ardmore, Co. Waterford, in the summer of 1937. It was opened by de Valera, president of the executive council, and Alfred was among the attendance. In the following year Alfred was the principal speaker at the rural week which opened on 29 August at the same venue. Speaking on population and the land, he declared that the country's population was falling at about the rate of 17,000 a year and 40% of the native-born population was living outside the country. While Dublin had increased its population from 1926 to 1936 and in the same period the population of towns had increased by 10%, the rural population had fallen by 5%.

Alfred stated that the proportion of females to males in the Irish Free State then was 952 to 1,000. In England it was 1,088

5. *Cork Evening Echo* 6 December 1932.

227

to 1,000 and in the Irish towns it was 1,110 to 1,000. But in the Irish rural areas the figure was only 875 to 1,000, because more women than men emigrated from rural Ireland. The Irish marriage rate was the lowest in the world and the percentage of the unmarried was greater in the country than in towns. The potential adverse effect of this on the population structure was corrected by the uniquely high fertility rate of Irish marriages. A corollary of this was that Ireland was the only country in western Europe where the trend towards a falling population could be remedied by economic means.

The majority report of the Banking Commission, Alfred declared, had no measure to suggest which would help to check the decline in population. On the contrary it considered that farms should be enlarged, forgetting what was to happen to the displaced population. Such a policy was contrary to the trend of agricultural development in Europe, where, apart from England and Russia, a mixed family farm of thirty to forty acres was typical. However, the situation in which the Irish farmer found himself was unenviable. An investigation in the Golden Vale in 1933-34 revealed that the average income on farms up to seventy acres was only £40 per year per unit of non-hired labour. In other words, the farmer was worse off than the agricultural labourer.

The level of agricultural production, continued Alfred, was at a very low ebb, being only about £3 per acre. This was mainly caused by a price system which was unfair to the agricultural producer. Farmers could produce abundant food for the people but they had not the money to buy it. The heart of the problem was a lack of purchasing power. In the present depressed climate the financial pundits advocated even more belt tightening and a restriction of credit. This was at total variance with the response of Catholic social philosophy. Only the implementation of this philosophy, he declared vaguely, would revive the country's agriculture. He concluded by calling for a crusade to that end.[6]

In March 1939 Alfred helped to convene a meeting to form a committee of distinguished Cork citizens to organise a Muintir na Tíre weekend at Rochestown College, near Cork city, that Easter. In his address Alfred said he was glad to be among

6. *Cork Examiner, Irish Independent* 5 September 1938; *Catholic Herald* 9 September 1938.

persons whose aim was to benefit the beet grower, the farmer in general, the farm labourer and every man and woman on the land. Hitherto, he concluded, there had been too much theory and too little action.[7]

As part of Muintir na Tíre's social week held in Tipperary in mid-March 1940 Alfred lectured on the shroud of Turin. He said he did so because he believed that any forward movement in the country should be based on a religious revival. This should be their front against the paganism and brutality of the modern world. He had no belief in so-called practical schemes which were not based on spiritualist philosophy and religion. We want, he said, 'more of the spirit engendered by organisations like Muintir na Tíre and the Legion of Mary – a greater appreciation of our brotherhood in Christ'. It was reported in the press that such was the interest in Alfred's lecture that over three hundred persons could not be accommodated in the hall and had to follow the lecture on a loudspeaker erected outside.[8]

Alfred was again the main attraction at Muintir na Tíre's rural week at Virginia, County Cavan, in August 1940 when he spoke on 'Muintir na Tíre and the soul of Ireland'. Muintir na Tíre, he said, was trying to go back to the middle ages when the guilds were both religious and social. There were thousands of parish guilds in England as long ago as the thirteenth century. They failed for various reasons, but mainly because religion declined. When the gospel of money and greed came in such things died out. Centralisation was another cause of their failure when the unit of society became nationwide. In Muintir na Tíre they were trying to revive the old system and regain local responsibility. People were then voting in a political way and had no responsibility over their own trades or vocations. After risking their lives for freedom they had failed to produce a system of their own. They should get rid of central bureaucracy and get back some of the spirit they had in the Volunteer days of the 1918-21 period.

Alfred continued that there was a tremendous lot they could do in a parish in the doing of which they did not need a civil service. There was no need either to provide an elaborate constitution for Muintir na Tíre, as the type of organisation that suited one parish might not suit another. The main thing was for

7. *Cork Examiner* 13 March 1939.
8. *Cork Examiner, Irish Independent* 18 March 1940.

people to get together. As much work as possible that could be done locally should be done locally. Referring to a new local government bill, he said that, if a parish did not establish a council and run its own affairs, the county council would fill the vacuum. The parish council would be voluntary but it would have to be given the necessary power to fulfil its functions. He instanced some of these as looking after the maintenance of schools, the owning and running of parish halls, maintaining local roads and providing work for local labour. Why, he asked, should the local unemployed not be given work draining the farmers' land, with the farmer paying the difference between the 'dole' and the men's wages? They were paying a subsidy in the form of a tariff to nearly every firm in the country, so why should they not pay a subsidy to the farmer?

Agriculture, Alfred declared, was more than a vocation or a trade; it was a way of life. He urged the establishment of a central council for agriculture elected by diocesan guilds, directly or indirectly through the parish councils. The small towns were dependent on the prosperity of the farmers and were an integral part of rural Ireland. They should be represented on the council. It was essential to try to bring functional democracy back to Ireland. They in Muintir na Tíre were not anti-parliamentarian, but the local people could do things that parliament could not do. They did not want experts on a council representing rural Ireland. Experts had been bossing them for too long. What was required was a voluntary advisory federation, representing all the units in agricultural industry. That was the goal for Muintir na Tíre to strive for. They wanted extra powers, but neither bureaucracy nor red-tape.

Concluding, Alfred said he felt strongly that unless they built on a religious foundation, unless there was a new spiritual revival, their work would not be successful. The brother or sister philosophy of the middle ages was one that they should emulate and then they would save their own souls and the soul of Ireland. They had Christ's own words for it: 'What you do for the least of my brothers and sisters you do for me.'[9]

9. *Anglo-Celt* 17 August 1940. Alfred's address struck a deep chord in the audience and was received with great enthusiasm. Bishop Patrick Lyons of Kilmore was effusive in his vote of thanks, concluding: 'May God spare Alfred O'Rahilly of the mighty brain, eloquent tongue and eager personality. Almighty God has given many sons to Ireland who have served her well, but I question

Still in the after-glow of his triumphant participation in rural week, Alfred published an article 'What the parish can do' in the *Standard*. He described a recent debate in the Seanad on the local government bill (1940) as largely academic. Then he set forth views which, he declared, he had learnt from men prominently associated with Muintir na Tíre. The general idea underlying the establishment of a parish council was to enable the inhabitants of a rural area to apply their religious and social principles in a practical way, to become accustomed to co-operation and joint action, to get rid of selfish individualism and to soften differences with the realisation of common interests. He acknowledged that in the local government bill (1940) such bodies were rightly called 'local councils', as modern Catholic parishes were not usually units of civic administration.

Alfred listed the functions of a local or parish council under three headings. (1) The council could effect improvements as regards good feeling and arbitrating in disputes and understanding the difficulties of various classes and ventilating their grievances. It could also concern itself with the care of local monuments and graveyards, the upkeep of the local schools, apply for the assistance of agricultural instructors, improve by-roads, acquire ground for the unemployed to till, etc. He suggested that those interested should apply to Muintir na Tíre for a list of things parish councils had already done. (2) There were functions which could be exercised by delegation from the local authority, whether the county council or the county manager. In this regard, he quoted section 70 of the local government bill

---

if any one of her sons in the last hundred years has done such practical and courageous work as Professor O'Rahilly for the land he loves' (ibid.). In raising the issue of the local unemployed being given temporary work by farmers Alfred was really questioning the requirement that an unemployed person engaging in any type of work must lose his dole or unemployment benefit: this rule meant that the worker 'benefiting' from the State scheme could not take a day's work, say from a farmer or a haulier, without risking the loss of his unemployment money – and prosecution for fraud as well! It was, of course, known that contraventions of this particular rule were taking place, but it took forty-five years more before the ban was officially eased and beneficaries under certain schemes were allowed supplement their income from casual work. Bishop Lyons and the other members of the Irish hierarchy, with the exception of Archbishop John C. McQuaid, were enthusiastic supporters of Muintir na Tíre. Archbishop McQuaid's lack of enthusiasm for it, it seems, was due to its interdenominational character (R. Burke Savage, S.J., 'The Church in Dublin: 1940-1965', *Studies* 54 (1965) 324-5).

which provided for a county council erecting a parish hall and then delegating its management to a local council. (3) There were functions which could be delegated from the central authority. The nature and extent of these would have to await the development of parish councils. In this regard he made a plea for something to be done urgently about the waste and degradation involved in the dole. Some joint effort by the central authority and parish councils could be devised whereby the local unemployed would be given a chance to do useful work for the parish.

On the status of parish councils Alfred commended section 69 of the local government bill which decreed that they would be voluntary rather than statutory bodies. He declared that from their considerable experience the leaders of Muintir na Tíre were emphatically of the view that the parish council should be a voluntary body. The consequences were that the initiative to have a parish council or not would be left with the locality, no method of election to it would be prescribed and the approved council would not be a legal entity nor even be incorporated. Not the least merit of this arrangement was to take the parish council out of the sphere of interest and influence of local party politics. In the establishment of parish councils, he urged the county council to enlist the help of Muintir na Tíre.

Next Alfred proceeded to describe Muintir na Tíre as a voluntary federation of voluntary parish councils, whose function was to be the soul of the new movement. The movement was especially new in that it arose spontaneously around the inspiring energy of Fr Hayes. It had no links with any political party. In Muintir na Tíre councils would find help in starting, advice in functioning and criticism in slackness. It would help to keep the spiritual and social ideal alive and would guard against the evils of selfishness and bureaucracy.

Despite his opposition to centralisation, Alfred proposed the establishment of a National Rural Council. The ultimate constituents electing such a council would be the parish councils. These would have members who were both agriculturalists and non-agriculturalists, such as shopkeepers, teachers, doctors, priests, etc. In effect, membership was open to those who resided and worked in rural Ireland. The task of the National Rural Council would be to represent rural life as a whole and to subordinate individual interests to the general good of the rural community. Harking back to the vocational councils which he proposed in his draft constitution of 1922, he declared that the National Rural Council should have the right to discuss, for example, drainage and rural housing; to have every bill dealing with agriculture or rural life submitted to it before being presented to the Dáil and to advise and criticise the ministry of agriculture. Implicit in its brief should be the duty and the right to consult recognised specialist bodies, such as the Beet Growers' Association, when particular matters arose for discussion or decision. It should have the power to appoint outside experts to advise it or to make reports. Most important of all, it should be a body representing the countryside as a whole, with its roots in local rural life, inspired by a new sense of vocation and by an ideal of practical applied religion, of which Muintir na Tíre was the pioneer exponent.[10]

There was considerable discussion in the autumn of 1940 as to how Muintir na Tíre parish councils and emergency committees should co-ordinate their activities in dealing with the hardship caused by the war. Muintir na Tíre organised a public meeting in the Mansion House, Dublin, on 22 November 1940 to clarify the issue and Alfred was invited to preside. At the meeting, which was described in the press as having been useful, Fr Hayes spoke as did representatives of other organisations.[11]

Alfred delivered the final lecture at Muintir na Tíre's social week in Tipperary in early April 1941. He suggested that what the country needed was a lay religious order to bring religion into daily tasks. In Muintir na Tíre they had a body which could do this. They had a magnificent country, with food potential for twice their population. They had concrete, scrap, wool. It would be the object of Muintir na Tíre to provide food and fuel and to build houses for the people throughout rural Ireland.

The question would be asked where was the money to come from to finance this work. There was £90 million of 'dead money' in the country, declared Alfred. Money was but a human

10. *Standard* 13 September 1940. These ideas were reflected later in the report of the Commission on Vocational Organisation (1943), of which both Alfred and Fr Hayes were members. For more on the Commission on Vocational Organisation (1939-43), see J. A. Gaughan, *Alfred O'Rahilly II: Public figure*, 328, 332, 338, 340, 405.

11. O'Rahilly Papers: Scrapbook 2, press-cuttings.

institution and an instrument for carrying out the physical processes of production. He continued rather vaguely that, if they were sincere about implementing Catholic philosophy, the financial problem would be solved. In any case, if the government did not provide money for the production of food and fuel, then Muintir na Tíre guilds would appeal to the people for help with the initial finance to this end.[12]

In the *Standard* Alfred described his visit to Tipperary which he suggested could be renamed Hayesville, the town where Fr Hayes resided and propagated the ideas embodied in Muintir na Tíre. He listed the activities of the local Muintir na Tíre guild: the erection of a lime kiln and a handball alley; the provision of 150 tons of turf, most of which had been supplied to workers and the poor at as little as half the current price; the encouragement of persons to tend a plot and grow potatoes and vegetables; the provision of potatoes at a much reduced price for the old and the poor. The most important achievement, he reported, was the spirit of co-operation and brotherhood which initiating and carrying out these projects engendered among farmers, agricultural labourers, town workers and members of the professions. He urged the government to avail of such local initiative, organisation and patriotism to ensure the provision of adequate supplies of food and fuel for the coming year in town and country. It was high time, he declared, that the government cut through its red tape and adopted a scheme of giving interest-free loans to Muintir na Tíre to be used by local guilds for this purpose.[13]

Alfred continued to have an active interest in Muintir na Tíre throughout the 1940s. Rural week was held at U.C.C. in the last week of July 1943 and he presided at the concluding session at which Fr Hayes paid him a remarkable tribute. Muintir na Tíre, he said, had Professor O'Rahilly with them all the time since their beginning. They all knew that he was the greatest mind in Europe and he wished to thank him most sincerely for all he had done for them. He was a man of whom they were all proud, and of whom Ireland could well be proud.[14]

Alfred availed of every opportunity to promote Muintir na Tíre. In the *Standard* he described a visit to Ballybunion which

12. *Irish Independent* 7 April 1941; *Cork Examiner* 8 April 1941.
13. *Standard* 11 April 1941.
14. *Cork Examiner* 2 August 1943.

he had not seen since his boyhood. He suggested that more could be done to develop the amenities of the resort. In this regard he asked if the residents had heard of Muintir na Tíre and its record for mobilising local communities.[15]

On 31 March 1945 Alfred broadcast the sixth in a series of eight talks on 'Social principles' from Radio Éireann. It concerned, he said, an important part of the philosophy which inspired Muintir na Tíre. At the outset he dealt with national self-sufficiency and the relationship between rural and urban populations. He stressed the importance of agriculture in the life of the nation, not alone as a means of supporting life, but as a mode of life in itself. Then he quoted the cases of the islands of Lewis and Hawaii, of how the sturdy independence of people could be lost 'by the peaceful penetration of commercial travellers'. Next he used a lengthy but apt quotation from St Thomas Aquinas on the importance of self-sufficiency among communities. A nation which had not the minimum of self-sufficiency could not control its own social policy, while national self-sufficiency led to the creation of an environment in which other ideals could be pursued. He did not object to participation in world markets but rather to such a dependence on foreign trade that national values were subordinate to it. His quarrel was not with internationalism but with a cosmopolitanism so huge that it could not be controlled.[16]

Alfred was once again one of the principal speakers at rural week in Mungret College, Limerick, in mid-August 1949. He spoke after James Dillon, minister for agriculture, who had sounded a hopeful note on efforts being made to deal with increasing emigration. Alfred was not as reassuring. 'If we lose the countryside – and I am not as optimistic as the minister is about emigration – then the outlook is black for our nation,' he said. Rural Ireland was vital for the survival of the country. They were faced with the unpleasant fact that the metropolis was growing bigger and bigger, while the countryside was facing a rapid decline in population. They should try to keep their country life Christian, vigorous and free of class warfare. If rural Ireland became infected with class warfare, and with a reluctance to accept the values embodied in the principles of Muintir na Tíre, there was no hope for the Church or the country. They

15. *Standard* 1 October 1943.
16. *Cork Examiner* 1 April 1945.

should not delude themselves that they could remain immune from world forces. Dark days were coming when they would all be put to the test.

Referring to a debate then in progress within Muintir na Tíre, Alfred emphasised that the organisation stood for 'the primacy of the people on the spot'. He declared that he did not like the prospect of one controlled organisation taking the place of the separate parish guilds, united to others only by their common ideal, but working out by local discussion and observation their own problems. They did not wish to supply the octopus of the centralised government with more local tentacles. In that connection he was glad to hear the minister for agriculture assert that there would be no interference with the affairs of Muintir na Tíre, that as minister he would help, would co-operate, but would not rule. He believed in fostering the practical side of rural life but that was not all that was required. They were faced with the responsibility of keeping their rural population but had also to fight for the minds of their young people. In this regard education was all-important and was the responsibility of parents as well as clergy and teachers.[17]

Alfred addressed a Muintir na Tíre gathering for the last time on 24 February 1952. The occasion was a conference of the Cork County guilds at U.C.C. He followed Fr Hayes who had spoken on the theme that as Christians they had more to do than merely condemn moral wrongs. They had an obligation to assume responsibility for the solution of the problems that affected the essential living conditions of people. The remedy for emigration, poverty and discontent required understanding that they were all brothers in Christ.

In his contribution Alfred described the work done by the U.C.C. adult education departments in general, and the courses which had been initiated at rural centres during the previous few years, in particular. He declared that those attending the

17. *Standard* 19, 26 August 1949. By that time Alfred had developed almost an obsession with regard to the shortcomings of civil servants. And he made no effort to moderate or hide it. In *Ireland's new foundations* (Dundalk 1943) Arnold Marsh pointed out that 'a big proportion of the best brains in the country' was to be found in the public service. But the talents of such able persons were not being properly used. In his review of the one hundred-page booklet in the *Standard* of 6 August 1943 Alfred, somewhat unfairly, commented on this remark by merely cautioning against 'bureaucracy' and 'the growing menace of totalitarianism'.

courses were fired with a spiritual motivation. The people of the countryside should realise that it is to themselves they must look in the work of improving their lot. To this end, they had three great rural movements, Bantracht na Tuatha (Irish Countrywomen's Association), Macra na Feirme and Muintir na Tíre. He suggested that the three should come together and establish their head office in Cork, where all the facilities of U.C.C. would be at their disposal. The importance of their work for the country required a common front.[18] Alfred's suggestion was well received and subsequently with the assistance of Con Murphy, who had organised the adult education courses at rural centres, he attempted to initiate negotiations between the various organisations with a view to their joining in a federation. A meeting was held but was adjourned *sine die*. The failure of the initiative, it seems, was largely due to Fr Hayes. He was an individualist and his lukewarm support for the initiative quickly vanished when he realised the implications of having Muintir na Tíre join in a federation with other organisations.[19] In the light of Alfred's insistent advice against the development of a centralised structure in Muintir na Tíre, it seems fair to conclude that his enthusiasm for such a federation was also easily dissipated.

Macra na Feirme

Besides his long and close association with Muintir na Tíre, Alfred was also supportive of Macra na Feirme, which was founded in September 1944 by a small committee, composed of rural science teachers, agricultural advisers and young farmers. It was a voluntary organisation for young people of the rural community, irrespective of party political allegiance or religious belief, to enable them to work for their mutual benefit through an educational, cultural and social programme. The control and leadership of the organisation was reserved to persons belonging to the rural community. Its head office was located in the Town Hall, Athy, County Kildare, until 1959 and thereafter in Dublin. Macra na Feirme's first annual convention was held in U.C.C. at the end of October 1951.[20]

18. *Cork Examiner* 25 February 1952.
19. Interview with Con Murphy.
20. Brochure issued by national headquarters of Macra na Feirme.

20. Delegation from Macra na Feirme to meeting at U.C.C. to discuss under Alfred's chairmanship a proposed federation of Bantracht na Tuatha (I.C.A.) Macra na Feirme and Muintir na Tíre. Left to right: James Cusack, Thomas Fitzgeren, Alfred, Harry Meredith, John Mooney.

Alfred had been instrumental in having the convention at U.C.C. and, in welcoming the delegates, said that he and his colleagues wanted to show that the college founded a hundred years before by an alien government belonged to the 'Murphys' of the country. In their adult education movement they had moved out into the country and had 123 farmers attending their six centres and twenty participants in their course for women. All were taught economics and how to be better farmers and leaders. 'The countryside is in your hands,' said Alfred, and 'our job is to help make you leaders.' He told them that in the following Easter they hoped to bring together 200 men and women of the countryside for a week's intensive course to enable them to be efficient secretaries and leaders of rural organisations. U.C.C. was at their disposal. He urged them to make full use of it especially to acquire a knowledge of economics. Agricultural statistics and questions of production were the most important questions in the country. He commended the organisation's intention to establish a credit union movement. Agricultural credit should not be run by individuals; it should be run on a co-operative basis or by the community itself. He concluded by offering U.C.C. to Macra na Feirme as a kind of centre. This proved to be useful, as the college at that time had the largest collection of film-strips in the country and Macra na Feirme, along with Muintir na Tíre and the Irish Countrywomen's Association made good use of them in their local branches.[21]

Alfred's offer was also taken up to the extent that Macra na Feirme for some years held its annual dinner in the college. At the first of these, in mid-July 1952, the toast of Macra na Feirme was proposed by Alfred, described as an honorary member. He availed of the opportunity to advertise the U.C.C. extra-mural course in rural and economic science. Such a forum, he urged, was essential to discuss the problems facing young farmers, not least of which was that the farming community seemed to be intent on committing social suicide. He illustrated this by revealing that the average age of male farmers was 55, of which 30% were over 65. Of the 17% women farmers, the average age was 62, threequarters of them being widows. Of the male farm workers and their relatives, 60% were unmarried.[22]

21. *Cork Examiner* 29 October 1951. See also M. W. Ó Murchú, 'The role of the universities and university-level institutions in continuing education', 55.
22. *Cork Examiner* 14 July 1952.

21. Macra na Feirme annual dinner at U.C.C., July 1952. *Left to right:* Alfred, Patrick McGrath (lord mayor of Cork), Thomas Walsh (minister for agriculture)

Irish Countrywoman's Association

Alfred was very appreciative of the valuable contributions which the Irish Countrywomen's Association (I.C.A.), founded in April 1935, made to local communities. He was occasionally requested to address guilds and generally obliged. These talks tended to be topical and exhortatory as when he addressed the I.C.A. Summer School at Crosshaven, County Cork, in July 1950.[23] On 1 July 1951 he was more specific and self-serving when addressing the County Tipperary Federation of the Irish Countrywomen's Association at Kilsheelan, near Clonmel. He referred to the courses in adult education provided by U.C.C. to help 'the three great rural organisations, Muintir na Tíre, Macra na Feirme and the I.C.A.' to make the fullest possible contribution to the betterment of the people. Courses of these kind were vital to ensure that women were trained to deal with the social issues facing them. He stressed the vital necessity that members of the I.C.A. should never lose sight of the main aim of their association, which was to inspire them to develop their initiative, so that each and every member and centre would take a full part in the work of the association and assume full social responsibility.[24]

Adult education at rural centres

Alfred's close association with Muintir na Tíre and strong support for Macra na Feirme and the I.C.A. proved invaluable when Con Murphy, of U.C.C.'s adult education department, set about establishing courses at rural centres. By April 1951 courses for farmers and farm workers were in progress at Dungarvan, Macroom and Newcastle West and further courses were begun later that year at Charleville, Clonakilty and Hospital. On 17 October 1951 a course for a diploma in social and home science for women was inaugurated at Coachford.[25]

23. *Irish Independent* 13 July 1950.
24. *Cork Examiner* 2 July 1951.
25. Interview with Con Murphy. For more on the rural courses, see C. Murphy, 'Adult education: the new rural courses', *Cork University Record*, Christmas 1950; 'Adult education in U.C.C.', *Cork University Record*, summer 1951; and A. O'Rahilly, 'Course for rural executives', *Cork University Record*, summer 1952.

Introducing the course at Coachford, Alfred declared that the women of the rural community were among the forgotten classes of the country and that it was time that they were equipped to take part in the life of the nation. He said that the course was the first of its kind and that he was sure that this pioneering movement would spread to other parts of the country. The two-year course would include sociology, national and social developments, food and nutrition, rural crafts and home crafts, home hygiene and the care of children. The sociology would help women to find solutions to problems in housing, mother and child schemes, education and many other matters. There were two major problems facing the country. The first was the low level of the country's production relative to other countries, the second was emigration which was largely due to girls leaving the countryside for a life in Britain. It was the women of the countryside who would solve this second problem. The reasons for it were not purely economic. The fostering of ideals and a sense of values and an appreciation of what their own country had to offer would contribute to a solution of the problem. However, it had to be acknowledged that there was an absence of amenities in the countryside and a life of unnecessary drudgery and oftentimes incompetence about food and diet, household management and the training of children. But, with electric light and power and better continuing education facilities, there was no reason why life in the country should be drearier and less attractive than in the city.[26]

Con Murphy, in his work as organiser of courses at rural centres, was also helped by the fact that Alfred availed of every opportunity to meet as many of the key people of the countryside as possible. He frequently visited the centres where classes had been established. These were not his only visits to country areas. He spent the second week of July 1951 on what he described in the *Standard* as 'a hurried journey through the countryside'. This included a meal with twenty-five farmers who were attending the U.C.C. adult education course at Newcastle West, a visit to the Agricultural College conducted by the Salesian Fathers at Pallaskenry, a conference with teachers at Kilfinane relative to the inauguration of a course at nearby

26. *Cork Examiner* 18 October 1951; *Irish Independent* 19 October 1951.

22. Group at inauguration of course for farmers and farm workers at Clonakilty on 11 December 1951. *Front row, left to right:* D. Leo White, Liam O'Brien, unidentified, Con Murphy, Alfred

Hospital, a visit to Kilfinane Agricultural Show and a few days stay with Fr Hayes, then parish priest of Bansha.[27]

Alfred's links with the rural organisations and their leaders were also responsible for the extraordinary support given to the one week courses at U.C.C. in April 1951 and 1952 for training the secretaries of rural organisations. At the first of these Alfred disclosed that the course had to be limited to a hundred, although twice that number had applied to take it. He declared that they were the first men and women of rural Ireland to attend the College for help and advice on improving country life by their own efforts and organisations. He hoped that the State would allow them to do so and not impose unnecessary restrictions on their initiative. In a closing address to those attending the second course Alfred listed the problems facing rural Ireland as follows: emigration, depopulation, marriage rate and marriage age. This last, he stated, was a complex problem involving in its solution questions of land tenure, agricultural rating, cooperative credit, rural amenities and small industries. He warned of the need for increased and more efficient production. With growing exchange difficulties and increasing taxation, this was becoming urgent. He promised that U.C.C. would publish studies of these various problems and so help the people of the countryside to deal with them.[28]

Supporter of Summer School at Clongowes Wood College

Apart from his support for the main rural organisations, Alfred was ever ready to help others who concerned themselves with the betterment of society in general and the local community in particular. Typical was his support of Fr Fergal McGrath, S.J., who from 1935 onwards organised a Social Order

27. *Standard* 13 July 1951. While staying with Fr Hayes, Alfred, it seems, had a meeting with Rev. Professor (later bishop) Cornelius Lucey and Fr (later archbishop) Thomas Morris. The future archbishop vividly recalled the meeting, as Alfred smoked incessantly in spite of Lucey's discomfiture who was notorious for his dislike of the habit.

28. *Cork Examiner* 4 April 1951; 7 April 1952. These studies were subsequently published by U.C.C. For more on these one-week courses, see C. Murphy, 'Adult education in U.C.C.', *Cork University Record*, summer 1951, 15; 'Training for youth leadership', *Cork University Record*, Christmas 1951, 24-7; and A. O'Rahilly, 'Course for rural executives', *Cork University Record*, summer 1952, 7, 9.

Summer School in Catholic Sociology at Clongowes Wood College each mid-July. Alfred's paper on 'The future of industry in Ireland' was generally regarded as the highlight of the 1938 session of the Summer School.[29] Besides contributing to sessions, Alfred helped Fr McGrath to persuade persons prominent in academic and public life to take part in the Summer School. Even when Alfred was not present at the Clongowes Wood Summer School,[30] his ideas dominated the proceedings. In the report in the *Catholic Herald* of the 1937 session it was stated that one of the highlights was the reception given to the ideal of corporations or of guilds. Questions were asked why the detailed plan for a guild, drawn up and published six years earlier by Alfred, after meeting with so much approval from both sides of industry had not been put into operation. The reporter caught the mood of those present: '"If Professor O'Rahilly were here he would tell us!" – said someone, and the hall rocked with laughter at the thought of the frankness with which that militant labour champion would state his case. This type of exchange recurred again and again.'[31]

In January 1941, after a great increase in unemployment because of the war, Alfred was instrumental in establishing in

29. *Irish Independent* 19 July 1938. The report on the Summer School in the *Standard* of 22 July 1938 captured the iconoclastic tone of Alfred's lecture with a listing of 'the sparks from Professor O'Rahilly's anvil' as follows: 'living on Catholic Action is like bombinating in vacuo'; 'get rid of secrecy in business'; 'an honest financier is a man who gets knowledge to which he is not entitled'; 'nationalisation is a blessed word like Mesopotamia that covers a multitude of ignorance'; 'my labour friends do not like the word corporatism, let us call it conciliarism'; 'a small metropolitan gang, that is the State'; 'we protect Oliver Cromwell and Co. of Dublin against Oliver Cromwell and Co. of Birkenhead'; 'economics are essentially nationalist'; 'we should get some Mormon principles [in reference to the fact that by means of barter the Mormons put 83,000 unemployed into employment]'; 'we are the most Protestant-Catholic country in the world: most of our religion consists in skin-saving'; 'does it require bloodshed to wake us up, as it woke Spain up, to turn us into the crusaders we ought to be?' Alfred left his hearers in no doubt as to the spirit behind his lecture. He recalled a conversation between W. T. Stead and Cardinal Manning: 'W. T. Stead: "It was the working-man brought me to Christ." Cardinal Manning: "It was Christ who brought me to the working-man."' He concluded by quoting St John: 'If any man says he loves God, and loves not his neighbour, he is a liar and the truth is not in him.' Few, it seems, were unduly surprised by Alfred's performance which had been keenly anticipated (see *Irish Press* 13 July 1938).

30. Interview with Fr Fergal McGrath, S.J.

31. *Catholic Herald* 23 July 1937.

Cork a club for the unemployed, similar to the Mount Street Club in Dublin. The Mount Street Club, which was founded in 1934, assisted unemployed men to help themselves by providing them with accommodation, tools, raw-materials, seeds and opportunities to work on allotments in a farm run by the club. With Mgr Patrick Sexton, dean of Cork, he organised a number of meetings, at which some of Cork's wealthy and public-spirited citizens were persuaded to back the project.[32]

Irish Credit Union Movement

From the 1970s onwards the Irish Credit Union movement has shown what can be achieved by the local community when it exercises initiative and believes in itself. Alfred did not survive to witness its extraordinary success, but he followed with interest the efforts to establish it throughout the country. Much of the emphasis on the merit of ongoing adult education, the importance of a co-operative spirit and voluntary service in the local community and the need for people to have control over their money supply which underlies the Credit Union Movement is to be found in Alfred's extensive lecturing and writing on these subjects for some thirty-five years. Nora Herlihy, Seán Forde and Séamus Mac Eoin, who are generally regarded as the pioneers of the movement,[33] have generously acknowledged their debt to Alfred's lifelong campaign for a more effective and just use of the country's resources. Forde and Mac Eoin recalled that they began their search for a credit system which would be a viable alternative to capitalism and communism after attending the first extra-mural course in social and economic science at U.C.D. in 1948-50. Mac Eoin, in his comment, noted that the course 'was based on the work of Professor Alfred O'Rahilly, president of U.C.C.'[34]

By general consent Nora Herlihy is given most credit for ensuring the ultimate success of the Irish Credit Union Movement. In the 1950s she was a tireless propagandist to that end. In preparing a lecture at the end of September 1957, she decided

32. *Irish Press* 21 January 1941; O'Rahilly Papers: Scrapbook 2, press-cutting, dated 21 January 1941.
33. For more on Herlihy, Forde and Mac Eoin, see A. T. Culloty, *Nora Herlihy: Irish Credit Union Pioneer* (Dublin 1990).
34. Ibid., 36-7.

to quote at some length from Alfred's *Money*. She wrote to him requesting permission to do so. In a reply of 2 October, he graciously granted this and continued: 'My ambition was to get just one credit union started in connection with my adult education classes. But alas! I had to retire before my work was finished.'

To a comment by Miss Herlihy that there was a need for a booklet on legislation about credit, he agreed, but, ignoring a hint that he might prepare one, added: 'You refer to the Friendly Societies Acts 1896 and 1908. I do not know the details of these. How do they compare with regulations in the U.S.A. and Canada?' He concluded by endorsing her enthusiasm for the Credit Union Movement, observing that 'a local credit union would have enormous effect in bringing the rural people together in a practical way'.[35] In retrospect the letter could be construed as one champion of the local community handing on the torch to another.

35. Herlihy Papers: letter, dated 2 October 1957, O'Rahilly to Herlihy.

EPILOGUE

This first part of Volume III traces Alfred's career as a controversialist in his role as a social reformer during a period of some forty years. During that time his commitment to social justice and his conviction how that could best be achieved remained unchanged. For him the social teaching of the papal encyclicals was the only viable alternative to the extremes of capitalism, fascism and Marxism.

Alfred was not content merely to disseminate as widely as possible a knowledge of the social teaching which he considered could be the leaven of a just society. He attempted to persuade the influential Society of St Vincent de Paul to become actively involved in its implementation. Later he sought more successfully to have it implemented as an arbitrator in industrial disputes over some thirty years. As a delegate to the International Labour Conferences in Geneva in 1924, 1925 and 1932, his remarkable contributions in support of progressive labour legislation were inspired by the same motive.

His obvious sincerity in the pursuit of social justice enabled him to have an extraordinary influence over many workers and their leaders. This he used to ensure that Irish Labour was represented by a party led by social democrats. To this end he led a sharp anti-communist crusade from 1944 to 1952.

Alfred's commitment to Catholic social theory made him a powerful and insistent advocate of denominational education at primary, secondary and tertiary level. The right to denominational education, guaranteed equally for those of all religions and of none, was for him genuine pluralism. His commitment to Catholic social theory also prompted him to be indefatigable in his support of Muintir na Tíre, Macra na Feirme and Bantracht na Tuatha which he regarded as essential champions of the local community.

Historians describe the attempt to organise the institutions of the State in accordance with Catholic social principles as integralism. Alfred was one of the most important figures in this movement. He would have been proud to have been regarded as such.

EDITORIAL BY ALFRED O'RAHILLY IN *STANDARD* OF 7 MARCH 1940

LABOUR COURT AND STRIKES

The removal of the ceiling on wages left us in a dangerous position, for it added a new factor making for inflation. Many people hold that the control should not have been removed so soon, but that the allowable rise might have been increased. But in view of the failure to curb profits, such a continuation of control over wages would have been very unpopular. The government, with the strong approval of the trade unions, set up a Labour Court. This at least provided an orderly method of procedure, it furnished an impartial tribunal for appraising demands and for discouraging discrepancies in advances which sections in a privileged position might enforce without consideration for the general interests.

The functions of the Labour Court have already been explained in *The Standard*. For our present purpose it will suffice to quote section 68 of the Industrial Relations Act (1946):

> The court, having investigated a trade dispute, shall make a recommendation setting forth its opinion on the merits of the dispute and the terms on which, in the public interest and with a view to promoting industrial peace, it should be settled, due regard being had to the fairness of the said terms to parties concerned and the prospects of the said terms being acceptable to them.

It is, therefore, provided that, where a trade dispute exists or threatens, the court may investigate and make a recommendation thereon. This recommendation is not necessarily binding. It should, of course, be treated with respect; it should as a rule be accepted at least for a trial period. But the court is not to be endowed with infallibility or finality. It is a human institution, liable to miscalculation as to 'the prospects of its terms being acceptable'. In actual fact, as far as we know, its recommendations have been accepted in all but a few instances. We are glad that this is so; and it is a tribute to the fairness of the court.

But what is to be done in the few exceptional cases? Let us hope that the recommendations will be reconsidered either by the court itself or by some other agreed intermediary. There is no call to impute to the court's findings a greater value than is given to them in the Act.

The real difficulty is the exercise of the right to strike in the case of industries which are national or municipal monopolies. It is this aspect, and not its unofficial character, which made the beet-sugar strike so deplorable. Undoubtedly labour has not yet acquired a full sense of responsibility. But we must give the workers time to learn. It would, we think, be premature to advocate compulsory arbitration in such cases, though it may come to that if there are further strikes in monopoly industries by workers whose use of their privileged position causes widespread hardship. But let us first see how far labour is willing to learn not to abuse its rights. The right to withdraw services is a valuable right; it would be very drastic for us to imitate communism by even a partial suppression of it.

We need an educational campaign to impress on the workers the principle that not every exercise of the right to strike is morally justifiable. There must be some balance between the injustice under which the particular workers assert they are labouring and the suffering which a strike would inflict on the general mass of the citizens, particularly on the workers themselves. How could a handful of workers, in order to enforce a rise of a few shillings a week on wages which are not flagrantly inadequate, be morally entitled to take action which will deprive thousands of the poor and the sick of, say, bread or gas? They may have a genuine grievance – but have they the right to declare war on the community, deliberately to inflict great suffering in order to extort a remedy by sheer force? In such circumstances they may be morally bound to continue under the grievance at least for a time, to defer action, to seek some other remedy such as propaganda or arbitration.

In saying this we are merely expressing the accepted view of Catholic sociologists, which, unfortunately, seems to be ignored by some sections of labour. Is it not high time that responsible labour leaders should express this view clearly to the rank and file? A trade union should accept and exercise greater responsibility and authority. It should not automatically accept the majority vote of a small and shortsighted local section bent on asserting at all costs its own particular demand. Labour should educate and discipline itself. If it fails to do so, we are afraid that the hard-pressed consuming public may easily become hostile and may be induced to take restrictive measures against those small sections of workers who happen to have power to inflict grave injury on the community. Were the employers in such cases to declare lock-outs, the reaction of the public and especially of labour would be vehement and vociferous. We have no right to have two different measures of social justice. Both sides must learn their obligations to the community.

ALFRED O'RAHILLY'S RESPONSE TO THE ANNUAL REPORT
OF THE DIRECTOR OF THE INTERNATIONAL LABOUR
ORGANISATION, 1932[1]

Mr O'Rahilly (*government delegate, Irish Free State*) – Mr
President, I am here not merely as representing a small and
perhaps materially unimportant nation. I am here as a member
of a great international entity, a parliament of man unique in the
world's history.

[When I last ascended this platform in 1925 I said that a
medley of individual national apologies did not make an international conference, they merely made a multi-national
meeting. Now my remark may seem abstract, but it has very
practical consequences. There are now two corporate institutions, two new non-territorial, international bodies – the International Labour Organisation and the League of Nations each
with an individuality of its own, something distinct from the
mere total of the individualities of the component members:
they are international, not multi-national, bodies, and whatever
lawyers, who are the slaves of an out-of-date terminology, may
think, this organisation is an international person with all the
rights and responsibilities such a person possesses. Therefore
this organisation can formulate an opinion, and that opinion
may not necessarily be the same as the opinion of the League,
because of the technical composition and the functional representation which are uniquely characteristic of this assembly.
And this holds good, even if you regard the League and ourselves as a two-storey organisation, of which this is the lower
house and the League the senate.] We are here associated with
employers and industrialists and, what from the merely
numerical and from the human point of view is more decisive,
with the representatives of the workers of the world. We have
a task today which is our own, which we cannot shirk, and
which is the task of no other assembly in the world.

[Now in past conferences our most important work lay in
drafting recommendations and conventions; but the centre of
gravity today has completely shifted. The outstanding item on

1. This is the full text as recorded by the I.L.O. Secretariate (Department of
Labour, microfilm of record of Sixteenth Session of International Labour Con-
ference 12-30 April 1932, 441-4). The passages in brackets were omitted in the
Irish Press report of 27 April 1932.

our programme, I hold, is the director's report.] What is the use of discussing the employment of children when their fathers are workless? Why discuss dockers when shipping is idle? Why ask for the abolition of fee-charging employment agencies, when the grim spectre of unemployment is desolating the world? Today these things are comparatively trivial, and to lay undue emphasis on them would be mere elegant trifling. [The other day we had here a futile discussion to end discussions, and with the consciousness of the gravity of the issue before us I shouted 'Abstention'. I refused to interevene.] The real issue, I said, is the director's report. [It may be viewed merely as a masterly summary of the present economic crisis, and in this sense I have myself induced my own university to adopt it as a text-book for our students; but in another sense] we may well call Mr Albert Thomas *le petit roi qui pleure.* When he sees the state of the world in which the ideals and methods of this organisation are supposed to be carried out, he, the head of this little kingdom, weeps. But it is our duty to shout, to use this assembly as a megaphone, not merely to startle the city of Calvin and Jean-Jacques [Rousseau], but to reach the ears of governments, and to awaken hope in the hearts of millions.

[There is, I feel, a perfectly appalling situation of apathy and listlessness even among many of us who have come to Geneva at what is really one of the dramatic moments of social history.] We seem to have been affected with the canker of quiet helplessness. We are faced with the stupendous complication of a world fatality; we say with an indifference born of despair *Morituri te salutamus.* The soporific droning of a listless assembly seems to me to be like that of a meeting of the chamber of commerce of Pompeii just before they were engulfed by the lava. As often happens, the sideshow of an entertainment is better and more vigorous. [Two evenings ago I was present at the meeting of the resolutions committee and I was struck with the different atmosphere. The atmosphere was electric there, because we were discussing the Jouhaux-Mertens-Schürch resolution. We were not discussing an abstract economic survey or thesis, but action; and that is the issue before us at this assembly.

To a certain extent I am responsible for the present form of the double discussion procedure and, I say, let us apply that method to the director's report.]

Last year speaker after speaker stood up debating, expounding, deploring, analysing; and at the conclusion the Japanese delegate, Mr Yoshisaka, asked: 'What should we do now, after so many days of warm debate? The conference might disperse without having taken any action on this vitally important question.' He proposed a resolution to consider 'what effect might be given to the proposals for the continuance and development of the action of the Office to remedy unemployment and its consequences.' The resolution was unanimously adopted – which means that it had no particular significance [as regards action].

[Gentlemen, the first reading is over. We are not an annual debating society; we are not sent here to discuss economics and to indulge in academic futilities.] We are at the parting of the ways. Either we are to give a resounding call to action or else we have to brand ourselves as impotent and ineffective speechmakers. It may be our last chance; it is certainly our greatest. Are we going to rise to the second reading? Are we capable of formulating any definite practical conclusions? [Are we going to publish to our constituents, to the world, a great and solemn convention, a vindication of our duties and responsibilities as the real and only parliament of man? Or are we going to take a mean refuge in interminable discourses, debates and analyses?] The world asks for bread; are we going to give it a stone?

[That, I repeat, is the issue before us at this conference. This organisation was founded in 1919, on the assumption that the pre-war rhythm was to continue; that, apart from the mysterious phenomena of trade cycles, the world was going to move spirally towards greater and greater prosperity. Economics was left beyond our competence, as something with which we had no concern, as something which was fixed and stable in a fluctuating world.

We were simply to prescribe calisthenics for a healthy patient, and now we find that the patient is dying.] We have no time even for a surgeon. There is no use in telling a man with a broken leg that we intend to continue our study of surgery; there is no use in adopting a convention for the provision of crutches! The time-factor is vital. We require a bone-setter; we have to act.

Millions, who have not studied our constitution and who do not understand its limitations, assume that we are going to do something. They are asking what is to be our action. They are not interested in our studies and researches and statistics; they are not even interested in our conventions. Here, those of us who know our constitutional limitations tell us that we cannot act; that any action of immediate effect must be in the economic, financial and political fields, which are closed to us. I agree, but if we ourselves cannot act we can at least give a call to action. After all, we are the only body through which millions of workers can speak; we are the only organisation which can expose their plight and voice their demands to those bodies for whom action is possible; and the primary body concerned is our fellow organisation, the League.

When the League was in difficulties concerning the economic settlement of the coal industry, it did not hesitate to ask this organisation to take action within the field of the regulation of labour conditions; and when the work of this organisation is hampered by economic and financial conditions it is not only our right but our duty to turn to the League and demand action from it. We know that the ratification of the eight hours convention and the miners convention has been prevented largely by the reparations problem. Even great countries have hesitated to ratify the forced labour convention, lest by sheer economic pressure they should be compelled to adopt the appalling remedy of labour conscription in lieu of starvation.

It is surely monstrous to argue that we here should be confined to fixing the niceties of employment when the real problem is that employment is ceasing to exist. Unless we are going to allow this organisation to sink into ineptitude, we must demand instant action by the League – action, I say, not mere studies and statistics. We must ask the League to summon international conferences on the economic problem, on the financial and monetary problem, and on the problem of international public works, and we must urge that these should be conferences of plenipotentiaries, and not advisory conferences whose advice will be transmitted from sub-committee to committee, from committee to conference, from conference to council, until nothing whatever is done.

I am not advocating universal free trade; I am simply assuming that, in the interlocked world now existing, problems like tarriffs are essentially problems for international adjustment, co-operation and conference, no longer to be set up haphazard by this country or that, but to be internationally co-ordinated. As for a monetary conference, there is nothing revolutionary in that; there is nothing even unorthodox in it in terms of economics. It was asked for ten years ago at Genoa, and we ask that there should be a settled devalorised gold standard, with new and stable parities, so that international credits can be arranged and international public works initiated.

We are not doing anything extraordinary even in asking the League to intervene in what is commonly called the Lausanne Conference. Article 24 of the covenant states that 'all commissions for the regulation of matters of international interest hereafter constituted shall be placed under the direction of the League'. These matters are surely not of purely local interest. They are international. Directly or indirectly they affect all nations, great and small, and the settlement of the problem of debts and reparations is fundamental for the solving of our present economic crisis. It concerns not merely three or four big powers, but the whole community of nations, which the League alone is competent to represent, and which it has an international obligation to undertake in virtue of that article.

I have referred at some length to the problem of immediate action, but I feel it my duty to make one or two brief remarks to record my own view that there is no ultimate solution in such action. We must certainly be interested in doing, but at the same time we must think. We must readjust. We must be prepared when the present crisis is thus remedied to begin to readjust our fundamental principles.

In the first place, with reference to the planned economy mentioned by the director, this applies not merely to international relations. It is the right and duty of each country, and particularly of the small country which I happen to represent, to plan its own internal economy. I must congratulate Mr Albert Thomas on his conversion to the medieval principle of regulation, as opposed to the modern *laissez faire*, to the principle of regulative guilds and fixed prices, and the adjustment of agriculture and industry. We cannot emerge from the present chaos until we aim at the coincidence of economic and political units and reduce international trade to its proper function as supplementary, as the interchange of superfluities and exotics.

I must make a passing reference to the problem of machinery and mass production which has been referred to by some speakers. It is a curious illustration of our weakness and confusion on fundamental principles that on the other side of the partition in this hall in which we are meeting there are graphs and illustrations published by the International Management Institute – subsidised, I understand, by this office – which tell people how to produce more unemployment by putting in new machinery. It seems to me that somewhere there is a scandalous confusion. We are aiding and abetting unemployment on one side of the partition and discussing how to get rid of it on the other side. More machines mean less employment, less wages, less demand for machine products: the vicious circle of the modern world.

In 1794 Malthus startled the world by saying that the world was outrunning its food supplies. That has been believed even to this day; but what a mockery when we have hungry men confronted with bursting granaries and ill-clad workers in the presence of mountainous bales of cotton! What is wrong with the world is that it has outrun its job supply, and in spite of our vaunted progress the greatest manufacture of the world today is the manufacture of unemployment.

Mr Jouhaux spoke two days ago of keeping the machines and shortening hours of work, but he is too modern, too up-to-date, to state the problem in all its bluntness – the control of machinery. We have in Geneva at present a conference for the reduction and limitation of armaments. I hope that one day we shall have a conference for the reduction and limitation of machinery. Men or machines? Mr Lambert-Ribot spoke of reducing labour costs, unconscious of the vicious circle to which I have referred, and unconscious that what he suggested was a negation of the fundamental principle of this organisation, that labour is not a commodity. What must come first is men and women of flesh and blood – what is usually called labour. Machines must be adjusted to men, not men to machines. Christ put the financiers out of the temple long ago, but the modern financiers have decided to put Christ out of the temple and to put up a notice 'No admittance except on business'.

I have confined myself to these few general remarks, because there are various minor points in the report with which I am not in agreement, but I think that what I have said is sufficient. I agree in this call for action. We call this the *Bureau international du Travail* – *mais, mon Dien; c'est le travail qui manque!* We are becoming an international bureau of nothing, of zero. The sands are running out. We do not know if there will be an International Labour Conference next year. The death of a single aged statesman of eighty-four may produce a world catastrophe for all we know. We are here in a position of immense responsibility. We are here to voice the mute inglorious millions who are suffering. We have to be our brothers' keepers and not mock suffering humanity by discussing minutiae of an employment which does not exist. Let not the discussion this year fizzle out in high-sounding platitudes. Let us give this call to action which it is our duty to give. Gentlemen, place your ears to the ground and listen to the heavy tramp of a hundred million of the hungry and unemployed.

ARTICLE BY ALFRED O'RAHILLY ON THE OATH OF ALLEGIANCE IN THE *JOURNAL DE GENÈVE* OF 20 MAY 1932[1]

La voix de l'Irlande

Ceux qui résident hors d'Irlande ne peuvent que difficilement comprendre le point de vue irlandais. Qu'il me soit donc permis de présenter quelques brèves observations à l'intention des lecteurs du *Journal de Genève*.

La question du serment d'allégeance est pour les Irlandais une question à la fois brûlante et d'une portée pratique considérable. M. de Valera se trouve en présence de deux partis extrémistes. D'une part, il y a le parti qui désire utiliser le serment d'allégeance envers la Couronne britannique comme une marque de soumission politique et imposer à la majorité du peuple irlandais des sentiments qu'il lui est impossible d'éprouver. D'autre part, il existe le parti des ultra-républicains qui se refusent à reconnaître la validité du Parlement et l'autorité de l'armée. En face de l'opposition de ce dernier parti, M. Cosgrave a dû constater qu'il lui était impossible de gouverner sans s'arroger un pouvoir absolu de dictateur et sans organiser un système coercitif de police secrète. M. de Valera souhaite restaurer un gouvernement démocratique et faire prévaloir la volonté de la majorité. Il ne peut obtenir ce résultat qu'en rendant l'accès au Parlement absolument libre de toute contrainte et en obligeant ainsi les républicains extrémistes à se faire élire en se présentant au suffrage du peuple. Ainsi, tandis que la question du serment d'allégeance a un caractère très réel pour les Irlandais, elle n'a pas d'importance pour la Grande-Bretagne. En droit anglais, le serment politique – qui a été complètement aboli en France – est prescrit simplement par une loi qui pourrait être rapportée d'un jour à l'autre; ce serment n'impose d'ailleurs pas d'obligation pouvant donner lieu à une action judiciaire. De plus, le British Commonwealth of Nations – que par erreur on dénomme fréquemment 'Empire britannique' – a atteint maintenant un stade de développement auquel il est admis que les membres qui le constituent sont des Etats souverains au point de vue du droit interne, mais unis entre eux par certains liens

1. Although Alfred had a competent knowledge of French, he wrote the article in English and it was translated by a man, named Davoren, who was a friend of Seán Lester.

d'association externe. Cette situation ressemble quelque peu à celle des Communes lombardes du moyen âge qui faisaient partie du Saint Empire romain.

Mais, c'est avant tout pour des raisons d'ordre moral que les Irlandais revendiquent une souveraineté interne complète. (Ils n'ont jamais reconnu et ne reconnaîtront jamais la légitimité d'une ingérence anglaise dans les affaires d'Irlande.) Il ne faudrait cependant pas en déduire qu'ils se proposent de vider ou de répudier le traité qu'ils ont conclu en 1921 avec la Grande-Bretagne. L'auteur de ces lignes a rempli les fonctions de conseiller juridique auprès de la délégation irlandaise qui a négocié ce traité et a fait partie de la commission qui a élaboré la Constitution de l'Etat Libre d'Irlande. Sans vouloir entrer dans le détail d'une argumentation juridique, il tient à exprimer sa conviction que le serment d'allégeance – qui d'ailleurs est à peine un serment puisqu'il omet délibérément le nom de Dieu – n'est pas prescrit obligatoirement par le traité. La formule du serment a été insérée dans le traité simplement pour empêcher que l'on prescrive un serment républicain de la nature de celui qui était usuel à l'époque où le traité a été signé. Au surplus, le traité lui-même reconnait que l'Etat Libre d'Irlande bénéficiera de tous les avantages constitutionnels qui seraient éventuellement obtenus par les Dominions. Or, en octobre dernier, le Parlement britannique a adopté le 'Statute of Westminster', qui est en réalité une loi de renonciation par laquelle la Grande-Bretagne a abandonné tout droit de contrôle sur la législation des Dominions. La suppression du serment d'allégeance étant purement une question d'ordre intérieur, il appartient au peuple irlandais lui-même de la régler et toute intervention de la Grande-Bretagne serait contraire au Statut de Westminster.

Il n'est peut-être pas inutile de rappeler qu'en 1924, le gouvernement de M. Cosgrave a fait enregistrer le traité anglo-irlandais au secrétariat de la Société des Nations. Le gouvernement britannique a d'ailleurs protesté contre cet enregistrement. La Grande-Bretagne conteste le caractère international du traité qu'elle considère comme une loi promulguée unilatéralement par le Parlement britannique. L'Irlande n'a jamais admis la validé de cette thèse. D'ailleurs, si la Grande-Bretagne prétend que le traité anglo-irlandais n'est pas un acte international, mais un acte du Parlement britannique, elle ne saurait accuser l'Irlande de violer un véritable traité. Le 'Statute of Westminster' déclare expressément qu'aucune loi édictée par un Dominion ne doit être considérée 'comme dépourvue de valeur et inapplicable par le seul fait qu'elle est contraire à une loi de Grande-Bretagne'. Si, par conséquent, le traité est simplement une loi de Grand-Bretagne l'Irlande est maintenant fondée à la modifier ou même à la rapporter.

Comme on peut donc le constater, l'action de l'Irlande concernant la suppression du serment d'allégeance peut s'appuyer sur une argumentation juridique très convaincante. Par justice envers l'Irlande, l'opinion étrangère devrait comprendre que l'action du gouvernement irlandais n'est dictée par aucun esprit d'hostilité à l'égard de la Grande-Bretagne et que l'Irlande n'a nullement l'intention de répudier ses obligations internationales; elle se borne à prendre des mesures qui sont absolument indispensables pour assurer le fonctionnement normal d'un gouvernement démocratique. Que personne d'ailleurs ne s'imagine que les Irlandais attachent une importance excessive à cette question. Sa solution constituera simplement un premier pas vers la stabilité politique. Dès que cette question aura été réglée, les efforts du gouvernement de l'Etat libre tendront à résoudre les problèmes beaucoup plus importants de la réforme économique et sociale. Il est essentiel pour l'Irlande d'accroître sa production nationale, de combattre une spécialisation excessive visant exclusivement à l'exportation, d'enrayer l'invasion de trusts étrangers et d'encourager les petites industries disséminées à travers le pays. C'est sur ces questions-là que l'attention de l'Irelande est actuellement concentrée et c'est, en vue de la réalisation de ce programme politique, que le président de Valera a été appelé au pouvoir.

Alfred O'Rahilly

ALFRED O'RAHILLY'S TRIBUTE TO ALBERT THOMAS, DIRECTOR OF THE INTERNATIONAL LABOUR OFFICE IN *IRISH PRESS* OF 14 MAY 1932

The poignantly unexpected death of the director of the International Labour Office calls for more than a perfunctory notice. He was in the prime of his life and vigour. It is hard for those of us who heard him speak only ten days ago that this man with such amazing vitality and torrential eloquence has so suddenly and quietly passed away. He died as he would have wished, in harness; he had just directed and, indeed, dominated the sixteenth session of the Labour Conference, which was his religion and his life-work. To him more than to any other man is due the marvellous success of this unique organisation for social justice throughout the world.

All Irishmen who have gone to Geneva will remember him with affection and respect, for Albert Thomas was a true friend of this country. This was due, not only to his genuine love of freedom, but also to his close association with that distinguished Irishman, E. J. Phelan, on whose unrivalled judgment and juristic abilities he so greatly relied. On my three visits to Geneva I myself experienced the greatest kindness and encouragement from Albert Thomas. On my arrival this year he at once sent for me to express his pleasure that I had come and to ask for my co-operation at what he felt to be the most critical meeting of the Labour Conference. He at once suggested that I should try to become chairman of the 408 committee. When someone afterwards pointed out that the president of the conference was a Canadian and that an Englishman and an Indian were to be chairmen of two other committees, and that there were forty-four countries outside the British Commonwealth of Nations, he laughingly replied, 'Oh, Ireland is a Republic!' Which shows how confident he was that the representatives of this country would be quite independent and would make their own contribution.

Views on Machinery

He was very pleased with my speech on his report, and in his reply referred three times to what I said. To my surprise I found on my return to Dublin that some people were under the impression that I had attacked the director. They misunderstood my reference to *le petit roi qui pleure* – a joke which M. Thomas himself enjoyed very much. This was the title of a popular play in Geneva. I compared the director to 'the little weeping monarch', for he was the head of an international non-territorial state, and in his report he wept at the awful unemployment crisis which was threatening the ideal and the work of the Labour Office. I did indeed hint that M. Thomas had unconsciously reverted to Catholic medieval principles, and I said that I held a different view as regards machinery and mass-production. But, to my amazement, he told me privately afterwards that our views were not so different, even as regards the problem of machine production.

On Friday, 29 April, I dined privately with him in his own home, where I met his mother, Madame Thomas, whom I already knew, and one of his daughters. Though he seemed a little tired, I had no suspicion that he was suffering from diabetes. He was worried about the desperate world depression, which seemed likely to wreck all efforts at social amelioration. He was most anxious about my resolution which was to be voted on next morning, and went to the telephone to speak to Dr Beneš (of Czechoslovakia) about it. He felt that the Labour Office could not continue its work unless the League took immediate vigorous action concerning reparations, monetary stabilisation, and public works – the Labour Office having no authority to deal with economic or financial questions. During the evening he asked me a lot about the Irish question, in which he was very interested. As we were talking in French, I once pronounced the name of (Jim) Thomas in the same way in which (Albert) Thomas is pronounced, and he smilingly protested against any relationship! He told me he was going to write to President de Valera to thank him for the work done by the Irish delegation, and he expressed the hope that in the near future he would visit Ireland.

Not Anti-Clerical

Thomas was the disciple and friend of Jaurès, and he showed me the book which had caused his death; the picture of Jaurès in a German helmet which was on the cover had incited the fanatic to murder him. But though a radical-socialist, Thomas was by no means anti-religious or anti-clerical. He was broadly tolerant and wished to unit all social agencies in a common fight against injustice. Under his wise leadership the earlier asperities of the 'Amsterdam' workers' representatives have become softened. I could notice the change for the better that took place during my seven years' absence from Geneva. The Christian trade unionists no longer have to fight for recognition, no one shudders when a papal encyclical is quoted – Albert Thomas has done so himself! – and a French Jesuit is on the staff of the Labour Office. Much of this spirit of friendly co-operation was due to the inspiration and example of this truly great man, whose religion was as wide as humanity. As one who appreciated and admired his great qualities, as the most recent head of a delegation to which he showed marked friendliness, I have taken the liberty of writing this brief tribute to his memory.

RADIO TALK BY ALFRED O'RAHILLY
ON ECONOMIC LIBERTY[1]

What *Quadragesimo Anno* calls 'the idols of liberalism and the errors of the economic individualist school' have had their day. The choice is between functional pluralism and what the same encyclical calls 'economic dictatorship'. The latter will begin under the guise of 'security': this word being understood not in the active sense of allowing people to look after themselves individually or as in groups, but in the passive sense of being made secure. When men are left in a desperate plight, they may clamour for this solution without realising its implications and the cost in liberty which must be paid. They may even realise it but regard it as the lesser of two evils, just as a tramp may break a window to get into jail for the winter. There he will have full security – food and shelter – plus compulsory labour. He will, however, get out for the summer. But if the workers once adopt collectivist security, they may never get out again; and, as contemporary history testifies, their children can easily be trained by the State to like this servitude.

This, of course, is not the way in which the case against liberty will be put. Says Stephen Leacock, humorist as well as economist: 'Give me the houses and the gardens, the yachts, the motor-cars and the champagne, and I do not care who owns the gravel-crusher and the steam-plough.' This would be too ambitious for a wage-earner. So let us represent him as saying: Give me a house, bread, clothes and I do not care who is the landlord, the baker and the textile manufacturer. But suppose the State controls all these functions and lays down the conditions under which the worker gets his rations. To quote a recent book by John Strachey: 'The problem would be automatically solved if the ownership of the means of production were restored to the people – but that is socialism'. Would it console an incarcerated man to be told that the prison was owned by the people? Would it make men freer to replace a multitude of employers by one Big Boss, the State? This juggling with the word People, first in the distributive sense and then in the collective, is the great fallacy that has overrun the world since the French Revolution. This unctuous pseudo-democracy is

1. Broadcast from Radio Éireann on 25 March 1945. The typescript is in the Written Archive of Radio Telefís Éireann.

primarily an ideological device adopted by those intellectuals who wish to replace the capitalists as the dominant class. Neither class has any desire to decentralise economic power or to democratise private property. In my last talk I quoted Pius XI as denouncing the 'immense power and despotic economic domination' of a few capitalists and financiers so that no one can breathe against their will'. So let me now cite Pius XII, in his radio address of 1 September 1944, denouncing 'the dictatorship of a political group which will, as the ruling class, dispose of the means of production and at the same time of the daily bread and hence of the will to work of individuals'. These two denunciations remove all ambiguity or sycophancy from the Catholic defence of private property.

Both the capitalists and the communists are animated by a profound distrust in ordinary men and women. Many years ago G. K. Chesterton wrote as follows: 'The socialist system, in a more special sense than any other, is founded not on optimism but on original sin. It proposes that the State, as the conscience of the community, should possess all primary forms of property; and that obviously on the ground that men cannot be trusted to own or barter or combine or compete without injury to themselves. Curiously enough, exactly the same attitude is expressed by Big Business. I will quote from the report issued by Suburban and Provincial Stores Ltd. in October 1941: 'Much nonsense about the displacement of little business is talked by ignorant and thoughtless people and by politicians of a certain type . . . Many a man and woman, who as an independent trader would be dishonest or extortionate or a petty tyrant, is a far better citizen in a position in which he or she is under less severe economic pressure or not free to give way to bad tendencies in his or her own character.'

This argument for chain-stores is identical with the concealed argument for the Chain-State: namely, anti-libertarian pessimism. It is better for men not to be free lest they give way to their bad tendencies. To remove temptation, deprive men of responsibility and control. Place them under an anonymous company with no soul to save or to spoil. The argument would not in the least be changed by telling us that the chain-stores are owned by the people, by a multitude of shareholders. For we know that behind these nominal owners the real power is exercised by a handful of directors and managers. Similarly the proper name for communism is the Managerial State. That the ordinary workers would be better-behaved and better-disciplined under a small clique of managers, keepers, commissars: that is the argument against private property. Significantly enough, it also perfectly expresses a sentence to penal servitude.

Do men still want economic liberty? Are they prepared to assume personal responsibility? Or will they sacrifice human values to the lure of physical efficiency and to the bait of servile security? That is the great issue of the world today.

ALFRED O'RAHILLY'S SPEECH TO THE FIFTH ANNUAL MEETING OF THE CONGRESS OF IRISH UNIONS IN 1949[1]

I am grateful for the invitation to be present. I take it to be a testimonial to my association with the workers of Ireland. My job is like that of a kind of mental transport worker, a skilled trade, to transport not merely information but ideals into the minds of my fellow Irishmen. It is a job which concerns you, particularly, and I talk about it all the more confidently here, because I know your ideals and mine are the same. I know you are interested in material things. You have got to be. We have bodies as well as souls. Nobody would endorse more fully than myself that we want more distributive justice. Trade unionists are concerned with big issues in the world. The trade unionists of every country and the workers are the majority. They have the votes and they have the organisation. The fate of Ireland depends not on the professional classes but on the workers. It is yours to make within the next generation or to allow it to be unmade.

We are not going to be left here in isolation. There are hostile forces at work and we have got to get ready for them. You have the men and they have the ideals.

It is not enough to say, as some British trade unions say, that they are going to put the communists out of their unions. You cannot work that way because, today, communism is crypto-communism. If you put the communist out one door in the clothes of Stalin, he will come back dressed as Wolfe Tone through the back door. You have a positive job to do. You have to train your own men to appreciate your ideals and to stand for them. We want leaders and we have been neglecting that job. We train them in technical schools and give them apprenticeships. That is not enough. We want them as human beings, as brothers in Christ with a spiritual destination and on whom the destinies of the world depend. We have to train them, not alone to be first-class trade unionists, but to be able to stand up to anybody, and not to be ashamed of the ideals for which they stand. We have no apology to make to communists or anybody else. We have a great social gospel here. We have got to learn it, apply it and live it. We proved it can be done in our diploma course in social science. It is up to you to see it applied every-

1. C.I.U., 1949 *Report*, 31-2.

where in Ireland. We are producing leaders, men who understand their job, who appreciate the ideals and the sacrifices of our forefathers, men who could have bettered themselves, but who gave up their lives. We are not going to take that bribe in this country.

You have these big issues and that is why we ask for your co-operation. I have opened the gate of my college to the people of Ireland. It is your college, now, not as it was founded one hundred years ago, and now the workers walk in, not by charity, but by right as students of the college. We hope that our experimental weekend conference will develop into a proper summer course where the workers can come to discuss their big problems.

I want to keep the ideal in your minds. We are not trying to dogmatise or dictate to labour. We are showing them where their rights and duties lie. We have a positive policy to show them. We must have the leaders ready to meet communism, men who are not going to be gullible, men who are not going to stand for this disguised totalitarianism. There is grand raw material in the country both religious and intellectual. The workers are a fine body of men and women. They have not had a chance. Now, we are endeavouring to give them every chance. Regard me as part of your movement, back me, and try to extend these courses so that the capital city of Dublin will take the lead in this matter. That is my appeal to you. We are trying to provide a positive remedy for the ideals you are anxious to see in this country and for which my generation risked their lives. Show that you are determined to carry out the ideals for which men in the past gave their lives, so that this country might be free, not merely from Britain, but free to carry out the ideals in which you and I believe.

ALFRED O'RAHILLY, THE NATIONAL ACADEMY OF IRELAND AND THE ROYAL IRISH ACADEMY

In the period from 1916 to 1921 the council of the Royal Irish Academy showed itself to be determined to make no concession to the emerging new Ireland. This prompted a number of academics, most of them from University College, Dublin, some of whom were members of the R.I.A., to establish a National Academy of Ireland. This, it was hoped, would, in effect, in due course, replace or absorb the R.I.A. At a preliminary meeting on 3 June 1921, under the chairmanship of Professor Hugh Ryan of U.C.D., a National Academy Drafting Committee was set up. The eleven members of the committee were: Professor Arthur W. Conway (registrar, U.C.D.), chairman, Professor Eoin Mac Néill (U.C.D.), Reverend Dr Michael Cronin (U.C.D.), James Creed Meredith (U.C.D.), Reverend Professor Patrick Browne (St Patrick's College, Maynooth), Professor Robert Mitchell Henry (Q.U.B.), Professor Thomas P. Dillon (U.C.G.), Professor Hugh Ryan (U.C.D.), Reverend Professor Patrick Boylan (U.C.D.), Professor Matthew J. Conran (U.C.C.), and Reverend Professor Timothy Corcoran, S.J. (U.C.D.), the committee's most enthusiastic member and its secretary.

The committee began work early in July and decided to proceed on the main organising principles of the Institute of France and its five constituent academies. The sections were to be: Irish; letters, philosophy and history; mathematics and physics; biological science and fine arts. A dozen meetings were held and the task was completed on 25 February 1922. Alfred and his brother, Thomas Francis, were listed as foundation members, the former under letters, philosophy and history, the latter under Irish.

In the meantime two incidents occurred which must have confirmed the organisers of the new Academy in their purpose. In October 1921 George N. Count Plunkett, in his capacity as Dáil Éireann's minister of fine arts, invited the council of the R.I.A. to nominate two members to an advisory committee which he was setting up. The council declined to do so. A month later Plunkett organised a Dante sexcentenary celebration at the Mansion House, Dublin, for 6 December. The opening address was to be given by Alfred.[1] The council of the R.I.A.,

1. For more on this, see J. A. Gaughan, *Alfred O'Rahilly II: Public figure*, 129-31.

when offered as many tickets as they required, showed their continuing disdain for Dáil Éireann and Sinn Féin by indicating that they would not be represented at the event.

On the completion of their work the National Academy Drafting Committee issued a comprehensive statement to the press. This was carried in full in the *Freeman's Journal* and the *Irish Times* of 28 February 1922. It indicated that the project of establishing a new academy had been discussed informally for two years before being initiated at the meeting which established the Drafting Comittee. The statement continued that the proposed academy would be fitted by its exacting standards for membership and by its general organisation to promote and secure public recognition for all progressive work in the liberal sciences and arts which were cultivated and studied in the country. It was also envisaged that the new academy should secure for the Irish language and its literature and history a primacy of influence and inspiration at home and for all Irish work and research an extended measure of appreciation among the learned academies of Europe and the U.S. The members of the Drafting Committee were listed and considerable detail was provided on the constitution, electoral boards, autonomous sections and procedures of the proposed academy.

On 20 March 1922 Fr Corcoran sent a copy of the proposed constitution to the listed foundation members with an invitation to accept foundation-membership. Alfred replied to the invitation and an appeal for advice by seeking further information. On 7 April Corcoran informed him that the Drafting Committee had no power whatever once the foundation meeting had proceeded to business. Further, he stated that everything was equally open to alteration at and by the foundation meeting. To Alfred's query: 'Are the members committed to any definite policy regarding the Royal Irish Academy, Royal Dublin Society, etc.?' Corcoran replied: 'In no way whatever.' He continued: 'Three individual members of the Drafting Committee, invited recently to act as co-opted members with nine previously chosen members of a "Reforms Committee" of the R.I.A., consulted the Drafting Committee. (These were Drs Conway, Boylan, Ryan and Professor J. J. Nolan joined in.) The Drafting Committee advised them to decline, and they did so, on the stated grounds that the scope of the reforms indicated was entirely too restricted. The R.I.A. Committee replied that it would not go outside the royal charter of 1786. The four concerned and our Drafting Committee held that this would involve a low or no standard of membership, two sections only and election of all members by members at large. As these were vital points to Drs Conway, Ryan and all of us, they sent identical replies to the invitations and there the situation stands.'

Of the first 120 persons invited to accept foundation-membership, 92 accepted. Notwithstanding Corcoran's informative reply to his queries, Alfred declined to become a member of the new academy. His brother, T. F. O'Rahilly, also declined the invitation.

The foundation meeting of the National Academy of Ireland was held on 19 May 1922. The constitution prepared by the Drafting Committee was adopted and the list of foundation members, then 126, was approved. Apart from the difficulties inherent in establishing a rival academy and the chaos, uncertainty and disillusionment arising from the civil war of 1922-3, the organisers failed to win widespread support for the National Academy. The reaction of George W. Russell (AE) was fairly typical of that of literateurs, scholars and academics not associated with the National University of Ireland. He informed W. B. Yeats, another invited foundation member, in a letter dated 30 March 1922, that his secretary, Susan Mitchell, had described it as 'a kind of Catholic Young Men's Association'. Nor did Yeats, who, like Russell, declined to become a foundation-member, show much enthusiasm for it either.

After its first annual general meeting on 15 November 1923 the National Academy of Ireland ceased to exist. This followed the resignation of Professors Boylan, Conway, Nolan and Ryan, all of whom were also members of the R.I.A. However, the episode convinced the council and members of the R.I.A. that they had to come to terms with the new political situation in Ireland. Much was also achieved to this end by Professor J. J. Nolan.[2] He had been one of the joint-secretaries of the National Academy of Ireland. In March 1923 he was elected secretary of the R.I.A. and was subsequently to become one of its most highly regarded and active members, serving as secretary to 1949 and as president from 1949 until his death in 1952.

2. For more on J. J. Nolan, see P. J. McLaughlin, 'Professor J. J. Nolan', *Studies* 41 (1952) 317-22.

Appendix 7

Alfred was elected to membership of the R.I.A. in 1940. Two years later, at the request of Professor J. J. Nolan, he submitted two papers on special relativity to be read to a meeting of that body and later published in the *Proceedings of the Royal Irish Academy*. The papers were entitled 'Fresnel's formula' and 'The Sagnac effect'. However, the referees appointed, at Alfred's request, to assess the value of the papers advised against their publication. In letters, dated 18 December 1942 and 1 February 1943, to Professor Nolan, Alfred did not accept the decision of the referees in good grace and he resigned in protest from the Academy at the end of February 1943.[3]

3. 'A National Academy or Institute for Ireland', *New Ireland* 11 March 1922; R. J. Finneran, G. M. Harper, W. M. Murphy (eds.), *Letters to W. B. Yeats* II, 407-9: J. Meenan, *George O'Brien, a biographical memoir* (Dublin 1980) 151; T. Ó Raifeartaigh (ed.), *The Royal Irish Academy, a bicentennial history 1785-1985* (Dublin 1985) 80-85; *Royal Irish Academy, Dublin. List of council and officers, members, honorary members and Cunningham medalists* (Dublin 1932-63); Royal Irish Academy: Correspondence of the Publication Committee, Alfred O'Rahilly file; University College, Dublin, Archives department, Papers of Timothy Corcoran, S.J., LA 20/4-8; Papers of Alfred O'Rahilly, letter, dated 7 April 1922, Fr Timothy Corcoran, S.J., to O'Rahilly; and information from Rev Professor James McConnell.

EDUCATION AND THE CONSTITUTION[1]

Constitutional Provisions

The constitutional status of education – I am thinking chiefly of primary and secondary – in the Republic of Ireland is radically different from the position in Great Britain (and Northern Ireland). This is not merely due to the fact that we have a written Constitution which the supreme court can interpret to invalidate legislation. The difference arises much more from the principles and norms embodied in the Constitution, which preclude the operation in Ireland of measures similar to the British Education Acts. The action of the State is severly limited, and local education authorities, except the committees for vocational education, do not exist.

The provisions of the Constitution concerning education differ so profoundly from the ideas current, at least in governmental circles under the former régime, that even in Ireland their implications are not yet fully realised.

The time may come when certain regulations of the department of education, which are really a hangover from the British days, will be challenged; but so far the supreme court has been invoked only once concerning an education bill. Moreover, there exists as regards education considerable misunderstanding concerning the status of the Catholic Church, to which the great majority of the people belong.

Finally, we in Ireland – and our voice has recently been heard in Strasbourg – hold that our constitutional principles guarantee parents against State encroachments and educational control. It may therefore be of general interest to consider in broad outline what are the principles which we profess.

For reference purposes the short article of the Constitution on education will first be quoted in full:

---

1. This article, written by Alfred when President of University College, Cork, appeared first in the *Educational Year Book 1951* (London 1951), was printed in 1952 as a Cork University Press pamphlet with the title 'The constitutional position of education in the Republic of Ireland' and was reproduced in *Hibernia* of July-September 1956.

Appendix 8

The Constitution of Ireland (1937)
Article 42: Education

(1) The State acknowledges that the primary and natural educator of the child is the family, and guarantees to respect the inalienable right and duty of parents to provide, according to their means, for the religious and moral, intellectual; physical and social education of their children.

(2) Parents shall be free to provide this education in their homes or in private schools or in schools recognised or established by the State.

(3) (a) The State shall not oblige parents in violation of their conscience and lawful preference to send their children to schools established by the State or to any particular type of school designated by the State.

(b) The State shall, however, as guardian of the common good, require in view of actual conditions that the children receive a certain minimum education, moral, intellectual, and social.

(4) The State shall provide for free primary education, and shall endeavour to supplement and give reasonable aid to private and corporate educational initiative and when the public good requires it, provide other educational facilities or institutions with due regard, however, for the rights of parents, especially in the matter of religious and moral formation.

(5) In exceptional cases, where the parents for physical or moral reasons fail in their duty towards their children, the State, as guardian of the common good, by appropriate means shall endeavour to supply the place of the parents, but always with due regard for the natural and imprescriptible rights of the child.

The Church

Perhaps, at least to outsiders, the most significant and surprising aspect of this article is that it does not contain so much as a casual mention of the Church, which, as such, is not conceded any constitutional right in education.

The only institution (except itself) in which the State acknowledges the right of education is the family. The only exception recognised is the case of the moral or physical disability of the parents. Then, and only then, may the State endeavour to supply the place of the parents, that is, by carrying out the duties which they are unable to perform. Constitutionally, *vis-à-vis* our mixed State, the Catholic Church is recognised only in so far as it represents the families.

It is true that there is another article (44), which has often been misquoted, and recently – I venture to think – quoted irrelevantly even by our own supreme court: 'The State recognises the special position' of the Catholic Church 'as the guardian of the Faith expressed by the great majority of the citizens.' But this is merely the statement of a statistical fact which involves certain social amenities and respect. The article goes on to say that 'the State also recognises' Episcopalians, Methodists, Quakers, Jews, etc., and guarantees freedom of conscience and religious profession and practice. Beyond making a ceremonial obeisance, the Constitution introduces no legal discrimination between the various religious organisations.

The same Article (44) continues: 'The State guarantees not to endow any religion. The State shall not impose any disabilities or make any discrimination on the ground of religious professions, belief or status.'

It follows that, as regards formative education, no Church, *qua* Church, has any constitutional status, and also, in so far as the Catholic Church, as an organisation for implementing parental rights, has a constitutional status in education, every other religious denomination has an equal status.

Looked at from the inside, as regards ourselves who admit its supernatural authority, the Catholic Church is much more than a natural association of parents.

But as regards the Constitution of this State, we have, though numerically preponderant, the same status as the Church of Ireland or the Jews. Each of these bodies is recognised educationally only as it represents the parents who agree to send their children to the respective schools.

This pluralistic outlook does not mean that the State is indifferent to religion; on the contrary, religion is regarded as an essential constituent of education. It is nowadays increasingly recognised that there is a minimal social creed necessary for the continued survival of any community. But beyond this the Irish State makes no religious demand on its citizens, it guarantees the religious conscience immunity from all coercive pressures

276

exerted by any agency of government. It does not deny or even doubt religious authority; it simply refuses itself to act as such; it holds that its ends will be best effected by ensuring the legal equality of all religious associations.

The Family

In Ireland education stands apart, morally and constitutionally, from the services which it is the duty of the public authorities to provide.

The 'primary and natural' provider of the service is the family, acting singly or in association. It is the 'inalienable right and duty' of parents to provide education, which consequently is not a public service in the same sense as are police, law courts, roads.

Our primary schools (which we call 'national schools') are not owned by the State or by the municipal authorities. They are an example of 'private and corporate educational initiative', which the State is bound 'to supplement' and to which it should 'give reasonable aid'. The national teachers are not public servants. Legally they are employed by the managers, even though for convenience the State as the manager's agent may directly transmit salaries to them. Neither have the teachers any intrinsic rights apart from having a professional status; they are *in loco parentis*.

In this country secondary schools are private, State-aided institutions, which provide excellent, relatively cheap education in accordance with the cultural and academic wishes of the parents. (Incidentally we have here no such class distinctions as used to be involved between 'public' and board schools.) But what are our primary or national schools? They are not public schools run by the State or by local authorities; constitutionally they are not Church schools. Their status is really that of parental or family schools.

Are they 'denominational'? They are *de facto*, in accordance with the wishes of parents of all creeds. But not *de jure*; the Constitution imposes no such obligation. If a sufficient number of parents in any locality wishes to establish an interdenominational or an undenominational school, there is nothing to prevent them, and they have a valid claim to the financial help of the State. It is purely a practical problem to give scope as far as possible to the denominational wishes of parents.

Though the State helps in transportation, it is not always reasible for parents of a scattered religious minority to have a school of their choice; moreover, a few Protestant parents deliberately send their children to Catholic schools. Of the national schools 460 (or 9.2%), though under Catholic management, have one or more non-Catholic pupils enrolled; only 90 (1.8%) are under non-Catholic management but have Catholic pupils. These are inevitable border-line cases. Presumably section 4 of Article 44 of the Constitution was designed to meet this contingency:

> Legislation providing State aid for schools shall not discriminate between schools under the management of different religious denominations, nor be such as to affect prejudicially the right of any child to attend a school receiving public money without attending religious instruction at that school.

Only here, in the article on religion, is there a reference to religious schools, and even here the Catholic Church is simply one of a number of legally equal religious denominations. The vague term 'the right of any child' presumably guarantees the parents against the child's compulsory attendance at formal religious instruction. There is no imposition of a 'mixed' school.

There is, of course, nothing revolutionary in the educational principles of our Constitution. The assertion of the inalienable rights of parents – vindicated for the Jews in the middle ages – and the rights of parents in distributive justice to obtain proportional aid for the schools of their choice will be found embodied, eight years before our Constitution was enacted, in a papal encyclical: *The Christian Education of Youth*, issued in 1929 by Pius XI. The same practice has been brought into operation in such places as Holland and Quebec. The same claim has been made in Great Britain by Cardinal Manning and in many subsequent episcopal pronouncements; it is contained in the French Catholic claim of *repartition proportionelle scolaire*.

The interesting aspect of the position in Ireland is that this equitable solution has been voluntarily included in the Constitution by an overwhelming Catholic majority.

Appendix 8

The State

The State has the right to see that the family schools carry out their task properly with qualified teachers and under suitable conditions. Ever since the old régime, our department, while tacitly dropping certain usurpations, has continued exerting a certain control over syllabuses and textbooks, which is of extremely doubtful validity. In 1942 the government secured the passing of a School Attendance Bill which contained the following clause:

> A child shall not be deemed for the purpose of this Act to be receiving a suitable education in a manner other than by attending a national school, a suitable school or a recognised school, unless such education and the manner in which such child is receiving it have been certified under this section by the minister to be suitable.

This bill – which was rumoured to be aimed at certain private schools and at the sending of children to be educated in England – raised a storm of protest. It was brought before the supreme court, which decided that the claim was unconstitutional. It was admitted that 'a certain minimum education' could be defined by parliament, but 'without contravening any of the other provisions of the Constitution' and provided it was 'a minimum standard of elementary education of general application'. The court then declared:

> So long as parents supply this general standard of education, we are of opinion that the manner in which it is being given and received is entirely a matter for the parents and is not a matter in respect of which the State under the Constitution is entitled to interfere (*Irish Law Reports*, 1943, pp. 334-47).

After this rebuff, no further attempt has been made to define the minimal standard of elementary education. The State does in fact exert a certain amount of pressure concerning 'the manner' of education in State-aided schools, from which it would probably be ousted if the issue were again raised.

According to the Constitution, 'the State shall provide for free primary education'. The version in the Irish language removes any ambiguity: 'The State must arrange that primary education is available gratuitously.' This does not imply that the State, directly or through local bodies, must itself undertake primary education, but only that it must make such education available gratuitously, e.g., by subsidising parental enterprise. All parents, of course, need not avail themselves of this; they can themselves educate their children at home, employ tutors, or use fee-paying schools. If the State were to establish schools, these would merely be at the disposal of parents who might choose to avail themselves of them.

Assuming, then, that it is not part of the normal function of the State to teach, let us ask why State aid should be necessary for schools. The ultimate reason is that the bulk of parents do not receive what Catholic sociologists call a living wage. They are too poor and too unorganised to pay, directly and completely, for the education of their children, as the majority of them cannot provide for sickness or old age.

And so the State has to intervene, not to exercise a right to educate which it does not possess, but by a measure of distributive justice to enable parents to exercise their duties and rights. In thus giving financial assistance the State is not providing a public service; it is acting as an organisational intermediary in redistributing income so as to help parents with insufficient means to exercise their inalienable right and duty.

In this country there is a constitutional barrier preventing the State from taking advantage of the poverty of working-class parents to force on them some form of ideology which they do not want.

Thus it is apparent that in Ireland we take a definite stand on the great issue which confronts the world today. This is not primarily an economic question of the control of material goods, it concerns not private property but private souls. The fundamental issue is: Who is to control and to mould the minds of the young? The struggle is not between the Church and State, it is between the Church-State and the family. For when the State starts to be schoolmaster, it ceases to be neutral and liberal, it begins to inculate a creed and to suppress all cultural rivalry and diversity, it becomes a monopolistic Church backed by physical force and overwhelming economic pressure.

We in Ireland – Catholic, Protestant or Jew – are determined to resist any State-imposed ideology.

SOURCES

1. SOURCES IN GENERAL

Writings of Alfred O'Rahilly and sources as listed in J. A. Gaughan, *Alfred O'Rahilly I: Academic* (Dublin 1986) and *Alfred O'Rahilly II: Public figure* (Dublin 1989).

2. PRIMARY SOURCES CITED

(a) Manuscripts

Dublin, Archdiocesan Archives, Dublin 9
　　Alfred O'Rahilly file.
Dublin, Dublin Institute of Adult Education, 1-3 Mountjoy Square
　　Souvenir brochure of official opening and blessing by Archbishop Dermot Ryan of the Dublin Institute of Adult Education, December 1980.
Dublin, Irish Jesuit Archives, 35-36 Lower Leeson Street
　　Papers of Fr Edward Coyne, S.J.
　　　　Letter, dated 27 September 1948, Fr Edward Coyne to O'Rahilly.
　　　　Letter, dated 7 October 1948, Fr Edward Coyne to O'Rahilly.
　　　　Letter, dated 12 October 1948, O'Rahilly to Fr Edward Coyne.
　　　　Letter, dated 12 October 1948, O'Rahilly to Michael Tierney.
　　　　Letter, dated 20 October 1948, O'Rahilly to Fr Edward Coyne.
　　　　Letter, dated 10 November 1948, Fr Edward Coyne to O'Rahilly.
　　　　Copy of note, dated 13 November 1948, O'Rahilly to Peadar O'Curry.
　　　　Letter, dated 15 November 1948, Fr Edward Coyne to O'Rahilly.
　　　　Cope of note, dated 15 November 1948, O'Rahilly to Peadar O'Curry.
　　　　Letter, dated 16 November 1948, O'Rahilly to Fr Edward Coyne.
　　　　Letter, dated 30 November 1948, O'Rahilly to Fr Edward Coyne.

Note, dated 24 January 1948, Jesuit provincial to O'Rahilly.

Letter, dated 25 January 1949, O'Rahilly to Fr Edward Coyne.

Letter, dated 26 February 1949, O'Rahilly to Fr Edward Coyne.

Dublin, Irish League of Credit Unions, Castleside Drive, Dublin 14

Papers of Nora Herlihy

Letter, dated 2 October 1957, O'Rahilly to Nora Herlihy.

Dublin, Macra na Feirme, National Headquarters, Irish Farm Centre, Bluebell, Dublin 12

Brochure issued by Macra na Feirme.

Dublin, National Library of Ireland

Papers of Thomas Johnson, MS 17267:

Irish Labour Party Committee of Inquiry: Report of the Committee prepared for the Administrative Council and the Parliamentary Labour Party.

Papers of William O'Brien, MS 13960:

Letter, dated 7 January 1943, Patrick J. O'Brien to William O'Brien.

Letter, dated 12 February 1944, Patrick J. O'Brien to O'Rahilly.

Note, not dated, O'Rahilly to Patrick J. O'Brien.

Letter, dated 14 February 1944, O'Rahilly to Patrick J. O'Brien.

Letter, dated 16 February 1944, Patrick J. O'Brien to William O'Brien.

Letter, dated 21 February 1944, Patrick J. O'Brien to William O'Brien.

Letter, dated 23 February 1944, Patrick J. O'Brien to William O'Brien.

Dublin, State Paper Office, National Archives, Four Courts, Dublin 7

Department of the Taoiseach, S 6812: Representation of the Irish Free State at International Labour Conference.

Dublin, University College, Archives Department

Papers of Bridget Stafford (P 63).

Papers of Michael Tierney (LA 30).

Letter, dated 24 September 1951, O'Rahilly to Tierney.

Sources

Dublin, Fr Brian Connolly, P.P., St Jude's Presbytery, Rossmore Road, Willington Lane
Typescript containing 'Memoirs of Joseph Connolly'.
Dublin, County, Fr Michael F. McCarthy, C.S.Sp., Blackrock College
Papers of Alfred O'Rahilly
I Scrapbooks No. I, II, V: press-cuttings.
International Labour Conference 1924: report to President Cosgrave.
International Labour Conference 1925: report to minister of industry and commerce, dated 25 June 1925.
Draft submissions to Eamon de Valera and the government prepared by Alfred O'Rahilly on behalf of Muintir na Tíre.
II Letters and telegrams:
Letter, dated 19 February 1920, Miss Anita McCarthy to O'Rahilly.
Notification, dated 15 November 1920, Cork City Council to O'Rahilly.
Letter, dated 17 January 1922, Risteárd mac Coitir to O'Rahilly.
Letter, dated 13 November 1922, Patrick Higgins to O'Rahilly.
Letter, dated 2 July 1924, Seán Lester to O'Rahilly.
Letter, dated 18 August 1924, E. J. Phelan to O'Rahilly.
Letter, dated 12 February 1925, E. J. Phelan to O'Rahilly.
Letter, dated 25 March 1925, Gordon Campbell to O'Rahilly.
Letter, dated 27 March 1925, R. C. Ferguson to O'Rahilly.
Letter, dated 2 April 1925, R. C. Ferguson to O'Rahilly.
Letter, dated 17 April 1925, E. J. Phelan to O'Rahilly.
Letter, dated 24 March 1932, E. J. Phelan to O'Rahilly.
Letter, dated 5 April 1932, Frank Gallagher to O'Rahilly.
Telegram, dated 7 April 1932, 'Industry and Commerce' to O'Rahilly.
Letter, dated 20 May 1932, Seán Lester to O'Rahilly.
Letter, dated 7 July 1932, E. J. Phelan to O'Rahilly.
Letter, dated 20 July 1932, Michael MacWhite to O'Rahilly.
Letter, dated 6 September 1932, Eamon de Valera to O'Rahilly.
Letter, dated 9 September 1932, E. J. Phelan to O'Rahilly.

Letter, dated 27 September 1932, E. J. Phelen to O'Rahilly.

Letter, dated 28 September 1932, E. J. Phelan to O'Rahilly.

Letter, dated 5 October 1932, E. J. Phelan to O'Rahilly.

Letter, dated 19 October 1932, E. J. Phelan to O'Rahilly.

Letter, dated April 1933, E. J. Phelan to O'Rahilly.

Letter, dated 1 May 1933, E. J. Phelan to O'Rahilly.

Telegram, dated 14 June 1933, Frank Gallagher to O'Rahilly.

Copy of letter, dated 14 June 1933, O'Rahilly to Frank Gallagher.

Letter, dated 17 June 1933, E. J. Phelan to O'Rahilly.

Letter, dated 31 October 1940, Fr John V. Simcox to O'Rahilly.

Letter, dated September 1947, Archbishop Finbar Ryan, O.P., to O'Rahilly.

Letter, dated 15 November 1960, Cearbhall Ó Dálaigh to O'Rahilly.

Letter, dated 20 December 1961, E. J. Phelan to O'Rahilly.

Letter, dated 7 September 1983, Gerald Y. Goldberg to Fr J. Anthony Gaughan.

Dublin, County, Mgr G. Thomas Fehily, P.P., 4 Eblana Avenue, Dún Laoghaire

Papers of G. Thomas Fehily

Letter, dated 19 January 1963, Seán Lemass to Fr G. Thomas Fehily.

Kerry, County, Dr Ita Cremin, 'Tuosist', Coast Road, Killarney

Typescript containing 'Memoirs of Cornelius Cremin'.

(b) Newspapers

Anglo-Celt 17 August 1940.

Catholic Herald 23 July 1937; 9 September 1938; 4 February 1944; 24 January, 18 April 1947; 10 September 1948; 11, 18 March 1949; 20 January 1950; 13 July 1951.

Cork Evening Echo 30 July, 6 December 1932; 26 January 1934; 8 February, 13, 20 June 1936; 9 December 1938; 9, 26 April 1947; 24 June 1948.

Cork Examiner 11, 13, 14 November 1922; 13, 14, 22 November 1923; 2, 11, 18 June, 15 October 1925; 22 January 1926; 11 August 1930; 8 April, 26, 30 July, 17 August, 19 September 1932; 19 April, 5 June, 11 December 1933; 26 January,

22 August 1934; 3, 11, 13 May 1935; 27 January, 10 February, 16 April, 20, 30 June, 23 November 1936; 1 February, 31 March 1937; 5 September, 8 December 1938; 13 March 1939; 18 March 1940; 8 April 1941; 28, 31 October, 6 November 1942; 28, 30, 31 January, 1, 5 February, 2 August 1943; 26 August 1944; 1 April 1945, 17 July, 15 October, 7 December 1946; 21, 25 February, 9, 10, 12, 19, 23, 24, 26, 29 April, 8 July 1947; 22 January, 24 June, 17, 18, 19, 20 August, 29, 30 September, 1, 6 October, 10, 17, 23 November 1948; 21, 22 February, 7 March, 24 May 1949; 10, 17, 18 July, 13, 20 November 1950; 4 April, 2 July, 18, 29 October 1951; 25 February, 7 April, 14 July 1952.

Evening Press 24 June 1955.

Freeman's Journal 28 February 1922.

Hibernia July-September 1956.

Irish Independent 13 October, 14 November 1923; 25 June 1924; 1, 2, 16 June 1925; 16 April 1932; 14 May 1937; 19 July, 5 September 1938; 18 March 1940; 7 April 1941; 1 February 1943; 13 July, 11, 13 November 1950; 19 October 1951.

Irish Press 14, 16, 26, 27 April, 2, 9, 14, 27 May, 20 July, 3, 20 September 1932; 6, 16, 20, 24, 28 June, 20, 23, 25 September 1933; 13 July 1938; 21 January 1941.

Irish Times 28 February 1922; 6 August, 15 September 1945; 9 April 1947; 4 January 1951; 24 August 1991.

Journal de Genève 20 May 1932.

Limerick Leader 10 November 1948.

Nationalist and Leinster Times, The 28 May 1949.

Standard 3 July 1936; 7 March, 13 September, 20 December 1940; 11 April 1941; 5, 12, 19 February, 4, 21 May, 11 June, 6 August, 1 October 1943; 14, 28 January, 4, 18 February, 10 March, 21, 28 July, 29 September, 13 October, 3 November, 15 December 1944; 14 September 1945; 22 March, 19 July, 18, 25 October, 1 November 1946; 7, 21 March, 11 April 1947; 26 March, 2, 9 April, 14, 21 May, 16 July, 20, 27 August, 17 September, 1 October, 19 November 1948; 27 May, 15 July, 19, 26 August 1949; 14 July 1950; 13 July, 10 August, 7, 28 September, 7 December 1951; 13, 20 June, 31 October 1952; 4 May, 22 June 1956; 24 July 1959; 26 April 1963.

Times Educational Supplement (London) 20 July 1951.

Times Pictorial 15 November 1947.

Unity 19 October 1944.

(c) Official Publications

Congress of Irish Unions: 1948, 1949 *report*.

Dáil Éireann: *Díospóireachtaí parlaiminte, tuairisc oifigiúil: Parliamentary debates, official report*, vol 11, cols 689-708, 30 April 1925.

Department of Labour: microfilm of *Record of Sixteenth Session of International Labour Conference, 12-30 April 1932*, 441-4.

Irish Labour Party: 1932, 1943, 1944 *report*.

Irish National Teachers' Organisation: *Addresses at I.N.T.O. Congress, Easter 1923*.

Report of the Commission on itinerancy, Dublin 1963.

University College, Cork: *Official Gazette*, March 1916.

(d) Persons

Bastible, Canon James P., St Patrick's Presbytery, Cork.

Fehily, Mgr G. Thomas, 4 Eblana Avenue, Dún Laoghaire, County Dublin.

Gageby, Douglas, 'Riverside Barn', Riversdale Avenue, Dublin 6.

Kavanagh, Bishop James, 181 Swords Road, Dublin 9.

Kelly, Frank, 12 Stradbrook Lawn, Blackrock, County Dublin.

Kent, S.J., Fr Edmond, St Vincent's Nursing Home, Herbert Avenue, Dublin 4.

McConnell, Rev. Professor James, 11 Avondale Park, Killiney, County Dublin.

McElligott, Thomas J., 'Byron House', Strand Road, Sutton, Dublin 13.

McGrath, S.J., Fr Fergal, 35-36 Lower Leeson Street, Dublin 2.

McGrath, Walter, 5 Ferncliff, Bellevue Park, Cork.

MacPartlin, Miss, Maureen, 7 Kincora Road, Dublin 7.

Morris, Archbishop Thomas, Archbishop's House, Thurles, County Tipperary.

Murphy, Cornelius, 8 Sycamore Crescent, Mount Merrion, County Dublin.

O'Carroll, Tadhg, 'Tinode', Roebuck Road, Dublin 14.

O'Flaherty, Professor Kathleen, 'Ard na Gréine', Coolgarten Park, Cork.

Walsh, P.P., Very Reverend Christopher, Parochial House, Monkstown, County Cork.

Sources

(e) Radio Telefís Éireann Written Archive

Broadcast by Alfred O'Rahilly on 25 March 1945.

(3) SECONDARY SOURCES CITED

(a) Unpublished theses

Byrne, Declan, 'Placing the Catholic Worker's College 1951 to 1958 in its societal context'. Thesis for Bachelor of Arts degree in industrial relations, National College of Industrial Relations, March 1989.

McKevitt, James B., 'The split in the Irish Labour Party and the general election of 1944'. Thesis presented, as part requirement, for M.A. degree at University College, Dublin, September 1984.

Ó Murchú, M. W., 'The role of the universities and university-level institutions in continuing education'. A dissertation submitted for the degree of Ph.D. to the department of education, University College, Dublin, National University of Ireland, 1986.

(b) Books, collections , pamphlets and articles

Bewley, Victor (ed.), *Travelling people* (Dublin 1974).

Blackrock College Annual 1953.

Burke Savage, S.J., Roland, 'The Church in Dublin 1940-1965', *Studies* 54 (1965).

Butler, Harold, *The lost peace* (London 1941).

Clarke, R. Dardis and Roberts, Ruaidhrí, *The story of the people's college* (Dublin 1986.

Collectanea Hibernica: Sources for Irish History 26 (1984) 155.

Coughlan, Anthony, 'C. Desmond Greaves, 1913-1988: an obituary essay', *Saothar* 14, 1989.

Culloty, A. T., *Nora Herlihy: Irish Credit Union Pioneer* (Dublin 1990).

Cunningham, Patrick, 'Labour Doings', *Irish Rosary*, Jan.-Feb. 1944.

Faughnan, S., 'The Jesuits and the drafting of the Irish constitution', *Irish Historical Studies* XXVI (1988-9).

Gaughan, J. A., *Thomas Johnson (1872-1963): first leader of the Labour Party in Dáil Éireann* (Dublin 1980).
—— *Alfred O'Rahilly I: Academic* (Dublin 1986).
—— *Alfred O'Rahilly II: Public figure* (Dublin 1989).
Hillery, Brian and Lynch, Patrick, *Ireland in the International Labour Organisation* (Dublin 1969).
Hogan, James, *Could Ireland become communist?* (Cork 1935).
Ireland, John, 'The founder of the Olympic Games', *The Bell*, July 1945.
Keating, S.J., Joseph, 'Ireland in transition', *Month*, October 1923.
Larkin, O.F.M.Cap., W. P., *Marxian socialism* (Cork 1917).
Lucey, Rev. Professor Cornelius, 'Strikes and compulsory arbitration', *Studies*, June 1936.
McCarthy, Charles, *Trade unions in Ireland 1894-1960* (Dublin 1977).
McSweeney, O.P., A. M., 'A study of poverty in Cork city', *Studies*, March 1915.
—— *Poverty in Cork* (Cork 1917).
Martindale, C. C., *Charles Dominic Plater, S.J.* (London 1922).
Meadows, Denis, *Obedient men* (London 1955).
Milotte, Mike, *Communism in modern Ireland: The pursuit of the Workers' Republic since 1916* (Dublin 1984).
Moynihan, Maurice, *Speeches and statements by Eamon de Valera 1917-73* (Dublin 1980).
Murphy, C. K., *The spirit of the Society of St Vincent de Paul* (Dublin 1940).
—— *Thoughts on the lay apostolate of charity* (Cork 1941).
—— *Humble of heart: origins of the spirituality of the Society of St Vincent de Paul. In commemoration of Frederick Ozanam (1853-1953)* (Cork 1953).
—— *The lay apostolate and other essays. Foreword by Most Reverend Finbar Ryan, O.P.* (Cork 1959).
Murphy, Cornelius, 'Adult education: the new rural courses', *Cork University Record*, Christmas 1950.
—— 'Adult education in U.C.C.', *Cork University Record*, summer 1951.
—— 'Training for youth leadership', *Cork University Record*, Christmas 1951.
Norton, William, *Cemeteries of liberty: communist and fascist dictatorships* (Dublin 1937).

Sources

O'Connell, T. J., *History of Irish National Teachers' Organisation 1868-1968* (Dublin 1969).

O'Flaherty, Kathleen, 'Dr O'Rahilly and U.C.C. – An appreciation', *Cork University Record*, summer 1955.

O'Rahilly, Alfred [B.K.S.], 'The social views of Christ', *Studies*, March 1914.

—— [A. J. Rahilly], 'The abuses of the poor law', *New Ireland* 19 June 1915.

—— [A. J. Rahilly], 'Education and citizenship', *Catholic Truth Annual* 1916.

—— [A. J. Rahilly], *A guide to books for social students and workers* (Cork 1916).

—— [A. J. Rahilly], 'The university and the worker', *New Ireland* 12 February 1916.

—— [A. J. Rahilly], 'The education of the Irish worker', *Highway*, April 1916.

—— [A. J. Rahilly], 'Social study in Cork', *Catholic Social Guild Bulletin*, April 1916.

—— [A. J. Rahilly], 'Social study in Cork', *Catholic Times* 1916.

—— [A. J. Rahilly], 'Co-operation in Cork', *New Ireland* 9 September 1916.

—— [A. J. Rahilly], 'Education in Ireland', *Workers' Year Book* 1917.

—— [A. J. Rahilly], 'The social problem in Cork', *Studies*, June 1917.

—— [A. J. Rahilly], 'The Catholic Social League', *Irish Monthly*, July 1917.

—— [A. J. Rahilly], 'The education of the Irish worker', *New Ireland* 13 October 1917.

—— [A. J. Rahilly], 'Ozanam's ideal of social work I', *Irish Monthly*, April 1918.

—— [A. J. Rahilly], 'Ozanam's ideal of social work II', *Irish Monthly*, May 1918.

—— [A. J. Rahilly], 'Ozanam's ideal of social work III', *Irish Monthly*, June 1918.

—— [A. J. Rahilly], 'Socialism and co-operation', *Irish Commonwealth*, March 1919.

—— [A. J. Rahilly], 'Socialism and co-operation', *Irish Commonwealth*, April 1919.

—— *Christ, the brother of the worker* (Dublin 1936).

—— 'Education and the Constitution', *Educational Year Book 1951* (London 1951).

—— *The constitutional postion of education in the Republic of Ireland* (Cork 1952).

—— 'Course for rural executives', *Cork University Record*, summer 1952.

—— 'Some thoughts on education', *Blackrock College Annual* 1956.

—— 'The Irish university question', *Studies*, autumn 1961.

—— 'The Irish university question', *Studies*, winter 1961.

—— 'The Irish university question', *Studies*, spring 1962.

—— 'The Irish university question', *Studies*, summer 1962.

O'Sullivan, Denis (ed.), *Social commitment and adult education: essays in honour of Alfred O'Rahilly, an Irish adult educator* (Cork 1989).

O'Sullivan, John, 'Fr O'Sullivan's notebook', *Link-Up* (Bulletin for the Dublin diocese) November 1991.

Phelan, E. J., 'The International Labour Organisation: its ideals and results', *Studies*, December 1925.

—— 'Ireland and the International Labour Organisation I', *Studies*, March 1926.

—— 'Ireland and the International Labour Organisation II', *Studies*, September 1926.

—— 'Industrial and social aspects of the economic crisis', *Problems of peace* (Seventh series – lectures delivered at the Geneva Institute of International Relations, August 1932, published by Allen and Unwin, London 1933).

—— *Yes and Albert Thomas* (London 1936).

—— 'Some reminiscences of the International Labour Organisation', *Studies*, autumn 1954.

Ryan, Liam, 'Urban poverty', *One million poor* (ed. S. Kennedy, Dublin 1981).

Thompson, W. H., *War and the food of the Dublin labourer* (Dublin 1916).

Tierney, Michael, *Report of the president, University College (Dublin 1958-59* (Dublin 1959).

Van der Slice, Austin, *International labour diplomacy and peace 1914-1919* (Philadelphia 1941).

See also sources cited in footnote 2, page 272, and footnote 3, page 273.

INDEX

Index

293

Index

296

Index

Index

Index

301

Index

Index